▶弁護士専門研修講座

国際法務をめぐる交渉・文書作成術

Ability to research, analyze, and write professionally in common law practice

東京弁護士会
弁護士研修センター運営委員会／編

ぎょうせい

はしがき

　価値観の複雑・多様化に伴い，現代社会はあらゆる分野において複雑・多様化が進み，紛争解決に対してもより高度な知識や能力を要するものが多くなっています。弁護士に対してもより高い専門性が求められ，複雑化した案件に対し適切に対応できる実践的能力が求められています。弁護士が日々研鑽を重ね，市民の法的ニーズに応じた能力を身につけることが必要なことは言うまでもありません。

　東京弁護士会では，弁護士研修センターを設置し，弁護士の日常業務の研鑽に加え，専門分野の研修にも力を注いできました。特に平成18年度後期からは，特定の分野に関する専門的知識や実務的知識の習得を目的とする専門講座を開設し，研修の質を高めて参りました。本書は，平成29年度前期に行われた「国際法務」専門講座の講義を収録したものです。

　本講座は，契約，外国法・外国法取引に関する経験的知識の体得を目的として企画され，基礎知識から応用まで網羅的かつコンパクトに講義したものです。多くの弁護士にとって，示唆に富み，弁護士業務を行ううえで役立つものと確信しております。

　本講座を受講されなかった方におかれましても，是非本書をお読みいただき，国際法務における交渉・法務文書作成に関する理解を深めていただき，日々の業務遂行にお役立ていただければ幸いです。

　平成31年1月

東京弁護士会

会長　　安井　規雄

講師紹介

Marc Lassman

Adjunct Professor at Beasley School of Law, Temple University, Japan Campus. A licensed American attorney in Colorado with more than seven years of domestic legal experience, and a LLM in International Law from the University of Nottingham in England. He has more than a decade of comparative legal experience in common law and civil law jurisdictions, having directed multi-million dollar internationally funded projects strengthening the laws and legal institutions of numerous countries in Eastern Europe, the former Soviet Union, and the Middle East.

マーク・ラスマン

テンプル大学ジャパンキャンパス・ロースクール特任教授。米国内で7年以上の経験を持つ米国コロラド州弁護士。英国ノッティンガム大学でも国際法法学修士号を取得している。英米法，大陸法の両方を理解している法務者として数百万ドル規模の国際的な法律や法務プロジェクトに携わり，東欧，元ソビエト連邦，中東など多くの国で活躍。

[Organizer]
Tina Saunders

Director and Associate Professor of Instruction in Law at Temple University, Japan. She received her J.D. from the University of Maryland School Of Law, and is licensed to practice in Maryland. Following law school, she was a law clerk for the Maryland Court of Appeals, the highest court in Maryland. While in private practice at Venable LLP, Ms. Saunders focused on complex commercial and pharmaceutical/medical device civil litigation, primarily representing clients as national counsel in class action and multi-district litigation. She is experienced in handling litigation in state and federal courts throughout the U.S. She has taught Civil Procedure and Torts at TUJ.

ティナ・サンデス

テンプル大学ロースクールディレクター，上級准教授。メリーランド大学で法務博士を取得し，メリーランド州の弁護士資格を取得。メリーランド州の高等裁判所にて法務書記官として勤務。Venable LLPで弁護士として活動し，ビジネスと医療に関わる複雑な民事訴訟に関わる。法律顧問として管轄区を越えて顧客の代表として活動し，州および連邦裁判所での訴訟を手がける。テンプル大学ロースクールでは民事訴訟と不法行為を担当。

CONTENTS

はしがき
講師紹介

Lecture 1

弁護士業務における英米法の基礎知識
並びに法務調査及び分析技法
Fundamentals of Common Law Research and Analysis

第1部 米国の法律制度と訴訟プロセス ····················· 3
　——American Legal System and Litigation Process

1. 英米法と大陸法の比較 ································ 3
   Common Law vs. Civil Law

2. 米国における裁判所制度 ···························· 7
   Structure of the U.S. Court System

3. 米国における裁判所制度の基礎〜3階層構造 ··············· 8
   Basic U.S. Court System Structure –Three Tier System

4. 米国における裁判所制度の基礎〜連邦裁判所と州裁判所 ········· 9
   U.S. Court Structure-Federal Courts and State Courts

5. 連邦裁判所と州裁判所の管轄権 ························ 11
   Federal vs. State Court Jurisdiction

6. 米国における訴訟のプロセス ·························· 15
   U.S. Litigation Process

第2部 米国法の源 ······································· 22
　——Sources of U.S. Law

1. 一次的法源と二次的法源 ······························ 22
   Primary vs. Secondary Sources

2. 米国法における4つの一次的法源 ······················· 24
   Four Main Primary Sources of U.S. Law

3. 米国憲法 ·· 24
   Constitutional Law

4. 裁判所による3種の法創造 ····························· 25
   Court Decisions : Common Law

1

5. 制定法 ……………………………………………… 26
   Statutory Law
6. 行政規則 …………………………………………… 27
   Administrative Regulations

第3部　英米法のリサーチにおける戦略 …………………… 28
——Strategies for Common Law Research

1. 戦略を実行する〜5つのステップ ………………………… 28
   Implementing a Strategy –Five Steps
2. ステップ1：事実の収集と分析 …………………………… 29
   Step 1: Collect and Analyze the Facts
3. ステップ2：法律問題の選別と用語の選定 ……………… 33
   Step 2: Identify Legal Issues and Search Terms
4. ステップ3：管轄の確認 …………………………………… 35
   Step 3: Verify Jurisdiction
5. ステップ4：法を調べる …………………………………… 36
   Step 4: Finding the Law
6. ステップ5：法の読み込みと通用性の確認 ……………… 38
   Step 5: Read and Update the Law

第4部　英米法における法律問題の分析 …………………… 40
——Analyzing Legal Questions in the Common Law

1. 自分の事案に適用することができる法的論拠を確定する ………… 40
   Determine the Legal Authority Applicable to Your Case
2. 制定法の分析手法 ………………………………………… 41
   Strategies for Statutory Analysis
3. 判例の分析手法 …………………………………………… 42
   Strategies for Case Law Analysis
4. 自分の事案の事実関係に法的論拠を提供する－IRAC方式 ………… 42
   Apply the Legal Authority to the Facts of Your Case–The IRAC Formula
5. IRACのI：問題点の同定作業 …………………………… 44
   IRAC: Issue Spotting

6. IRACのR：何が法か？ 45
    IRAC: Rule –What is the Law?

7. IRACのA：分析－弁護士の腕の見せどころ 46
    IRAC: Analysis-The Art of Lawyering

8. IRACのC：結論－意見を伝える 47
    IRAC: Conclusion- Give an Opinion

9. IRAC－参考例 48
    IRAC- Example

10. 事案のセオリーを考える 51
    Theory of the Case

11. 事案のセオリーを考える参考例 51
    Example Theory of the Case

第5部　英米法の法務文書における引用形式の基礎 52
——Basics of Common Law Legal Writing Citation Forms

1. 引用とはどういうことか？ 53
    What is a citation?

2. 引用－3つの基本パーツ 54
    Citations-Three Basic Parts

3. 判例の引用 55
    Case Law Citations

4. 法学雑誌の引用（二次文献） 58
    Law Review Article Citations (Secondary Sources)

5. 法的引用の参考例 59
    Example of Legal Citations

Lecture 2

弁護士業務における英文リーガルライティングの基礎と応用
Principles of Legal Writing for Lawyers in Common Law Practice

第1部　法務文書の種類 63
　　——Types of Legal Writing

1. 弁護士の役割に応じたリーガルライティングの類型 ・・・・・・・・・・・・・・・ 63
   The Types of Legal Writing Depends on the Lawyer's Role

第2部　実務での法務文書の形式 ・・・・・・・・・・・・・・・・・・・・・・・・・・・・ 64
   ——Predictive and Persuasive Writing Styles in Law Practice

1. 弁護士業務におけるわかりやすく説得的な文書作成スタイル ・・・・・・・ 65
   Predictive and Persuasive Writing Styles in Law Practice

2. 弁護士業務におけるわかりやすく説得的な法務文書の類型 ・・・・・・・・・ 66
   Predictive and Persuasive Legal Writing Types in Law Practice

第3部　法務文書作成のプロセス ・・・・・・・・・・・・・・・・・・・・・・・・・・・・ 67
   ——The Legal Writing Process

1. 法務文書の作成プロセス ・・・・・・・・・・・・・・・・・・・・・・・・・・・・・・・・・・ 68
   The Legal Writing Process

2. 作成前の分析：最初に検討すべき要点 ・・・・・・・・・・・・・・・・・・・・・・・・ 69
   Pre-writing Analysis: Important Initial Considerations

3. リーガルライティングの基礎 ・・・・・・・・・・・・・・・・・・・・・・・・・・・・・・ 74
   Legal Writing Fundamentals

4. リーガルライティングの構造 ・・・・・・・・・・・・・・・・・・・・・・・・・・・・・・ 82
   Legal Writing Structure

5. IRAC方式 ・・・ 83
   IRAC Format

6. IRAC方式による参考例 ・・・・・・・・・・・・・・・・・・・・・・・・・・・・・・・・・・ 84
   Legal Writing Example: IRAC in Action

第4部　法と判例の解釈と分析 ・・・・・・・・・・・・・・・・・・・・・・・・・・・・・・ 87
   ——Statutory and Case Law Interpretation and Analysis

1. 事業取引に関する制定法と判例の分析 ・・・・・・・・・・・・・・・・・・・・・・・・ 87
   Statutory and Case Law Analysis in Business Transactions

2. 制定法－典型的な構成 ・・・・・・・・・・・・・・・・・・・・・・・・・・・・・・・・・・・・ 90
   Statutes — Typical Structure

3. 制定法を分析するためのツール ・・・・・・・・・・・・・・・・・・・・・・・・・・・・・ 91
   Tools for Analyzing a Statute

4. 制定法を解釈する際の基礎的ルール ·············· 93
   Basic Rules for Statutory Interpretation
5. 判例の解釈と分析―事案の読み方―着目すべき事項 ········ 97
   Case Law Interpretation and Analysis

第5部　ケースブリーフの作成 ················· 104
　　　――Practices for Common Law Case Brief Writing

1. ケースブリーフの基礎 ······················· 104
   Case Brief Basics

2. ケースブリーフの書式と内容 ················· 106
   Case Brief Format and Contents

3. ケースブリーフの例 ······················· 107
   Sample Case Brief

Lecture 3

依頼者に対して提示する文書の作成において求められるライティングコミュニケーションスキルの基礎と応用
Professional Lawyering Skills for Written Communications with Clients

第1部　英語で初回法律相談を実施する際の実践的スキル ······· 113
　　　――Practical Skills for Initial Client Interviews in English

1. 到達点と目的 ···························· 113
   Goals & Purposes

2. 事情聴取のプロセス ······················ 115
   Interview Process

第2部　委任契約書の作成と依頼者との最初の文書でのやり取り ·· 125
　　　――Drafting Engagement Letters and Initial Written Communications to the Client

1. 委任契約書とは何か？ ···················· 125
   What is an Engagement Letter?

2. 委任契約書はどうして重要なのか？ ············· 127
   Why is an Engagement Letter Important?

3. 委任契約書の要点 ･･･ 128
   Essentials of an Engagement Letter
4. 委任契約書・リテイナー条項の例 ･･････････････････････････ 136
   Sample Engagement Letter/Retainer Agreement
5. 依頼者とのその他の文書によるやり取り－情報や資料を求める文書‥ 140
   Other Written Communications to Clients: Letter Requesting Information or Documents
6. 依頼者とのその他の文書によるやり取り－業務終了にあたって提供する文書 ･･･ 142
   Other Written Communications to Clients: Closing Letter

第3部　依頼者に向けた意見書や事案評価書の書き方 ･･･････････ 143
　　　　—Writing Opinion Letters and Case Assessments for the Client

1. 意見書・事案評価書とは何か？ ････････････････････････････ 143
   What is an Opinion Letter or Case Assessment?
2. 意見書・事案評価書の例 ･･････････････････････････････････ 144
   Opinion Letter/Case Assessment: Sample Template
3. 意見書・事案評価書における留意点 ････････････････････････ 147
   Opinion Letter/Case Assessment: Points to Remember
4. 意見書の参考例 ･･ 149
   Sample Opinion Letter
5. 依頼者に対する業務報告書の参考例 ････････････････････････ 153
   Sample Progress Report to Client

Lecture 4

依頼者を除く内部関係者に対して提示する文書の作成において求められるライティングコミュニケーションスキル
Practical Writing for Legal Office and Case Status Memoranda

第1部　弁護士業務におけるメモランダムの作成 ････････････････ 159
　　　　—Drafting Legal Memoranda in Law Practice

1. メモとは何か？ 159
   What is a Memo?
2. メモを作成する目的は何か？ 160
   Purpose of a Memo
3. メモランダムの書式 161
   Memorandum Format
4. メモランダムの重要ポイント 163
   Essential Parts of a Memorandum

第2部　企業内弁護士がやり取りをする文書の作成 178
　　　——Drafting In-house Attorney Communications

1. 企業内弁護士の立場で行う典型的な文書作成 178
   Typical Drafting for In-house Attorneys
2. 文書作成のためのヒント 179
   Tips for Drafting
3. やり取りの例 184
   Examples of Communications

第3部　進捗報告のためのメモランダムの作成準備 197
　　　——Preparing Case Status Memoranda

1. 進捗報告のためのメモとはどんなものか？ 197
   What is a Case Status Memo?
2. 参考例 198
   Sample Format
3. 検　討 205
   Sample Language Review

Lecture 5

国際法務における交渉及びこれに伴う契約文書作成の基礎と応用
Negotiating and Contracting Drafting in International Law Practice

第1部　国際法務における契約交渉を行う弁護士のための専門スキル ……………………………………………… 215
　　　—Professional Lawyering Skills for Negotiating Contracts in International Settings

1. 交渉に成功するためのヒント ……………………………… 216
   Tips for Successful Negotiations

2. 典型的な契約条項に関する交渉のためのヒント ………… 223
   Tips for Negotiating Typical Contract Provisions

第2部　レターオブインテント（LOIs）作成の法律実務 ……… 229
　　　—Legal Practices for Drafting Letters of Intent

1. レターオブインテント（LOIs）の戦略的な利用 ………… 229
   Strategic Uses of Letters of Intent (LOIs)

2. レターオブインテント作成上の留意点 …………………… 230
   Letter of Intent — Drafting Considerations

3. 検討：レターオブインテント作成上の主な考慮事由 …… 235
   Review — Main Considerations for Letters of Intent

第3部　契約文書の作成プロセス，分析，検討 ………………… 236
　　　—The Writing Process for Contract Drafting, Analysis and Review

1. 契約文書にも使えるライティングの基本 ………………… 237
   General Writing Principles Applicable to Contract Drafting

2. 国際取引における契約書の作成スタイル ………………… 239
   Contract Drafting Styles in International Context

3. 契約書を作成する際のヒント ……………………………… 240
   Language of Contracts — Drafting Tips

4. 標準的な英文契約書の条項 ････････････････････････････ 245
   Standard English Language Contract Provisions

第4部　秘密保持契約に関する交渉と契約書作成 ･･･････････ 256
　　　　—Negotiating and Drafting Non-Disclosure Agreements

1. 秘密保持契約書はどのように用いられるか ･･････････････ 256
   When to Use an NDA

2. 秘密保持契約における留意事項 ････････････････････････ 257
   Key Elements of NDAs

3. 典型的な秘密保持契約書の条項 ････････････････････････ 258
   Typical NDA Provisions

4. 検　討 ･･･ 262
   NDA Provisions

Lecture 6

米国民事裁判手続の基礎と裁判前の法務文書作成の留意点
Practical Legal Writing for U.S. Civil Litigation in th Pre-Trial Phase

第1部　米国の民事裁判手続に関わる弁護士のための訴訟前の戦略 ･･ 281
　　　　—Pre-Trials Strategies for Lawyers Handling U.S. Civil Litigation Cases

1. アメリカ司法システムにおけるディスカバリー制度 ･････････ 282
   Discovery in the U.S. Legal System

2. 相手方弁護士からの要望への対処法 ････････････････････ 289
   Receiving and Responding to Requests from Opposing Counsel

3. ディスカバリー制度を利用する場合の企業内弁護士の役割 ･･････ 293
   In-house Counsel during Discovery

第2部　文書によるやり取りと秘匿特権付き情報 ･･････････････ 304
　　　　—Preparing Written Communications for Attorney/ Client and Privileged Information

1. 米国法における代理人と依頼者との秘匿特権 ･･････････････ 305
   Attorney/Client Privilege under U.S. Law

2. 企業内弁護士と秘匿特権 ･･････････････････････････････････ 306
   In-house Counsel — Protecting Attorney/Client Privilege

第3部　米国民事裁判手続における秘密情報保持の法律実務 ････ 312
—Law Practices for Confidential Information in U.S. Civil Litigation Cases

1. 秘密情報を守る方法－ディスカバリーへの応答と秘匿特権リスト（プリビレッジ・ログ）･･････････････････････････････ 313
   Methods for Protecting Confidential Information - Discovery Reponses - Privilege Logs
2. 秘匿特権対象リスト（プリビレッジ・ログ）—どの時点で何をリスト化するのか ･･･ 314
   Privilege Logs — When and What to Log
3. 企業内弁護士と秘匿特権－英文メールの参考例 ･･･････････ 316
   In-house Counsel Protecting Attorney/Client Privilege—Sample E-mails
4. 秘密情報を守る方法－秘密保持命令 ･･････････････････････ 318
   Methods for Protecting Confidential Information - Protective Orders

第4部　和解契約をめぐる交渉と文書作成 ･･････････････････ 319
—Negotiating and Drafting Settlement Agreements

1. 和解契約── 一般的な留意事項 ･････････････････････････ 320
   Settlement Agreements - General Considerations
2. 和解交渉──あらゆる不測の事態を想定して交渉する ･･････ 321
   Settlement Negotiations - Negotiate all Contingencies into Final Agreement
3. 和解契約書 ── 一般的な規定 ･･･････････････････････････ 324
   Settlement Agreements —Common Provisions

あとがき

Lecture 1

弁護士業務における英米法の基礎知識並びに法務調査及び分析技法

◆

Fundamentals of Common Law Research and Analysis

専門講座シリーズの前提となる事項を確認する目的で，英米法の基礎知識について概説するとともに，法務調査やその結果に関する分析技法について，弁護士業務に関連づけて説明します。

First, let me thank everyone for coming. Let me officially welcome you to the "Legal Writing and Professional Lawyering Skills in Common Law Practice," lecture series that is a cooperation between the Tokyo Bar Association and Temple Law School, Japan Campus.

My name is Marc Lassman and I will be the lecturer for this lecture series, and I look forward to being with you throughout the series.

In general, I believe that this course was created with the understanding that legal practice with non-Japanese clients has been changing in Japan. More and more lawyers are finding themselves dealing directly with foreign clients, or they are finding themselves dealing with cases that have lawyers from the U.S. and other common law countries involved.

I hope the lecture series will be very useful for people to improve their skills with regard to Common Law practice.

While you are dealing with clients or lawyers from common law countries, specifically America, it is important to understand the differences in the systems such as what their different obligations are, what your obligations are or how the systems are different and then how to practice in a common law system. This is the goal of this lecture series.

The first lecture will be about the U.S. court system in general, how it is structured, the litigation system, how to research in the common law and then how to create legal arguments in the common law. The second lecture will focus on general principles related to legal writings, case interpretations, statute interpretations and analysis, and then also writing case briefs and memoranda.

The remaining lectures numbers three through six will focus on specific topics and situations that you will handle during your practice. For instance, we will talk about client communications, engagement letters when you take on clients, opinion letters for clients, how to write a memorandum, case file management, negotiating contracts and letters of intent and handling confidential information.

Our goal is to make this series as practical and useful as possible for you with many examples.

> **Lecture One:**
> **Fundamentals of Common Law Research and Analysis**
>
> Agenda:
> - American Legal System and Litigation Process
> - Sources of U.S. Law
> - Strategies for Common Law Research
> - Analyzing Legal Questions in the Common Law
> - Basic Common Law Legal Writing Citation Forms
>
> Marc Lassman
> Adjunct Professor of Law
> Temple University School of Law, Japan Campus
> April 14, 2017
> 18:00 – 20:00

In this first lecture we will talk about the American legal system and litigation process, sources of law in the U.S., strategies for common law research, analyzing legal questions in the common law, and basic common law legal writing citation forms.

第1部 米国の法律制度と訴訟プロセス
——American Legal System and Litigation Process

1. 英米法と大陸法の比較
Common Law vs. Civil Law

As you know, the U.S. is a common law system. Traditionally, countries have either common law systems or civil law systems. What we are looking at here on the top left in slide 1 is the basic principle of a common law system. Japan has had influences from the U.S. in its legal system as well as from European countries.

Common Law vs. Civil Law

Common Law System	Civil Law Systems
❖ Generally uncodified: no comprehensive, unified compilation of legal rules and statutes.	❖ Generally codified: written constitution and specific codes that define basic rights and duties, substantive laws, and procedures.
❖ Based on precedent: judicial decisions already made in similar cases. These precedents are binding.	❖ Legislative enactments are binding. Judges are less crucial in shaping law.
❖ Judges have a significant role in shaping American law. Precedents applied to each new case are determined by the presiding judge.	❖ Judge's role: establish the facts and apply provisions of the code. Judge actively participates in seeking evidence and questioning witnesses.
❖ Generally everything is permitted that is not expressly prohibited by law.	❖ Courts tend to be organized specifically to the subject matter of the codes. Usually have separate constitutional court, administrative court and civil court systems.
❖ Adversarial system: Juries of ordinary people are commonly used to decide the facts of the case. Parties produce trial evidence and judges are solely impartial referees.	❖ A civil law system is generally more prescriptive than a common law system.

In general, a common law system is uncodified which means there is no comprehensive, unified compilation of legal rules and statutes. In common law systems, as well as the U.S., there are statutes and constitutions, but there is no single, comprehensive list of laws. That is where we differ from civil law systems. On the other hand, civil law systems are codified. There are written constitutions and they have specific codes that define your basic rights and duties, substantive laws and procedures. One of the main differences when you deal with American law is you do not go to one place to look for the law. You have to go to several different sources to find out the law.

The common law system is based on precedent. What "precedent" means is that these are judicial decisions, which have already been made in similar cases. What is unique about the common law system is that these judicial decisions are binding on courts. In essence, judicial decisions become law, in common law systems. This is different from civil law systems where legislative enactments are the only things that are binding.

Therefore, the effect is that judges in the common law system have a much more significant role in shaping the law. The judge is who decides which precedents to apply to each case. Thus, the judge really has a very significant role in what becomes the law of the state or federally. That is much different from the civil law system. In the civil law system, the judge's role mostly is to establish the facts and to apply provisions of the code to them. Another major difference is that the judge actively participates in seeking the evidence and questioning of the witnesses. The judge determines what evidence needs to be brought to the court for questioning witnesses.

A major difference between the common law adversarial system and the civil law system is that the judge in the common law is merely an impartial referee. It is the duty of the parties in the common law system under the adversarial system to put together the evidence and present the evidence at trial. That is one of the major roles that the lawyer plays in the common law system. It is up to the lawyers to determine what the appropriate evidence is and how it should be presented in court. And if the lawyers do not present or the parties do not present evidence into court, the evidence will never make it into court.

In the civil law system, it is the judge who actually drives the case—determining what evidence should be brought in and questioning witnesses. It is really something that we need to take note of in terms of determining the differences between the common law and civil law systems.

One of the other major differences between the common law system and the civil law system is the way that the law is perceived. In the common law system, generally everything is permitted except which is expressly prohibited by law. In essence, everything is legal and permitted unless there is a law which specifically prohibits you from doing that. That is very different from the civil law system.

In the civil law system, your rights and your duties are found in the law. If they are not in the law, you do not have them. In the civil law, unless you have the right or the obligation to do something, you do not have it. In the common law, you have all these rights and obligations unless law prohibits you from doing it.

One of the other and most famous differences between the common law system and the civil law system, of course, is that in common law system and in America specifically, we have the widespread use of juries. I know that you have the use of juries in Japan, but we have them in criminal and civil cases. The rights to jury trials are contained in our Constitution in both criminal cases and in civil cases, and that also very much changes the practice of law in a practical way.

We have triers of fact that are the people who decide what happens and what does not happen in the case—the trier of fact. Because our triers of fact are jurors who are not legally trained, we have a much more complicated system of evidence. Since you have a trier of fact who is not a legal professional, you have to control the type of evidence that comes into court.

U.S. evidentiary laws are much more complex than ones in the civil law system and the systems that do not involve juries. Because in those systems it is the judge who is the trier of the fact and there is not as much concern that the judge can not discern what evidence is proper. You will find that when you deal with American lawyers, there are much more evidentiary concerns that they have to deal with.

2. 米国における裁判所制度
Structure of the U.S. Court System

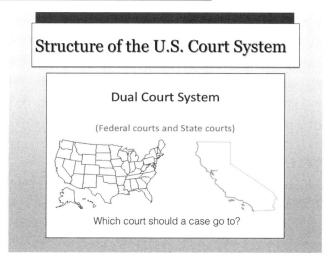

Now, we are going to talk about the court system in general, the basic structure of the American court system. The American court system is a dual system, meaning that we have a system of federal courts and we have a system of state courts. Now, where this came about is going back to our history.

When the country became independent from England, it was initially 13 separate states. While we were trying to build an overall federal power, many of the states were very concerned about not giving too much power over to the federal government and they wanted to control as much as they could, their own affairs.

We have a system that has checks and balances. The U.S. branches of government are the executive branch, the legislative branch and the judicial branch. They check and balance each other because there was a concern that there would be too much power in one branch or another. The states tried to give as little power as they could to the federal government.

The President has the right to appoint Supreme Court justices. That is the President's way of controlling the Supreme Court. Then the Congress or the Senate actually has to approve the nominee.

The last point is that those initial 13 states recognized the powers of the federal Constitution and that federal laws needed to be supreme over the land. We have something in our Constitution called the "Supremacy Clause." Therefore, where there is federal jurisdiction, federal law is the supreme law of the land.

3. 米国における裁判所制度の基礎〜3階層構造
Basic U.S. Court System Structure –Three Tier System

American courts have a three-tier system. The first tier is a trial court of general jurisdiction. That would include torts, personal injury cases, civil cases, criminal cases, and contracts cases. There are certain courts that have limited or special jurisdictions. For instance, there often will be family courts, probate courts, and courts that have to do with inheritances. There are some first instance courts that deal with a certain subject matter.

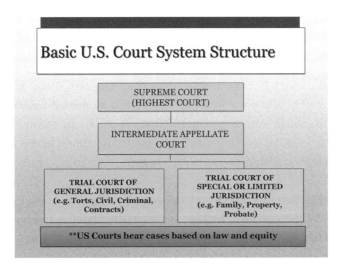

In Colorado, we had separate juvenile courts for minors. Different states have different courts that are specific to certain subject matters. But in general, the system works where we have a first instance court which is the trial court of general jurisdiction.

Then, cases from those courts can be appealed to an intermediate appellate court and cases can only be appealed on matters of law. In the U.S. when there is no retrial of cases, you cannot retry the facts. And so if you bring an appeal to a case, you can only appeal matters of law. You cannot appeal matters of fact. In general, there is an intermediate appellate court.

4. 米国における裁判所制度の基礎〜連邦裁判所と州裁判所
U.S. Court Structure-Federal Courts and State Courts

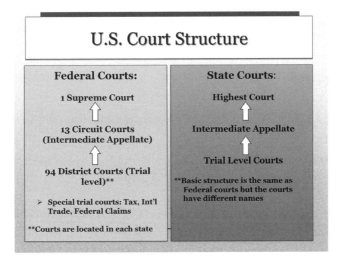

In a state or the U.S. federal system, there is a supreme court or the highest court. We generally have a three-tier system. You have a first instance trial court, an intermediate appellate court and then you have a high court or Supreme Court. What is also a little bit different in the American system from other countries is that U.S. courts hear cases based on law and equity.

We will start with the federal courts. There are 94 district courts in the U.S. These courts are located in each state and sometimes there are a few different districts in the state—there is an eastern district or a northern district. Some states have more than one federal court. The courts of first instance in the federal court system are the district courts and there are 94 of the district courts throughout the country.

There are again some special trial courts that deal with specific issues like tax, international trade and federal claims. We also have some courts which have specific jurisdiction, subject matter jurisdiction. But in general, the 94 district courts are at the trial level.

Then, you have intermediate appellate courts which are 13 circuit courts. For instance, Colorado is in the Tenth Circuit. A circuit court handles the appeals from district courts from several different states. The Tenth Circuit, which Colorado is a participant in—the district courts of Colorado, Kansas, New Mexico, Oklahoma, Utah and Wyoming—handles appeals from those different states.

We have 13 circuit courts and they handle appeals from the states in that circuit. For instance, California, which is the Ninth Circuit and one of the biggest circuits, handles appeals from Alaska, Arizona, Hawaii, Idaho, Montana, Nevada, Oregon, and Washington.

After the circuits hear the case, the next appeal is to the U.S. Supreme Court. The U.S. Supreme Court has jurisdiction over all federal cases. The court decides which cases it will hear, called "certiorari." The court has to decide to hear your case. In general, the court hears cases of novel legal issues, which have not been dealt with before in the courts. What happens often is that you get different decisions on the same issues in the circuit courts.

The circuit courts do not bind on one another. They are termed "sister courts." Therefore, if the Tenth Circuit makes a decision, that decision does not bind on courts in the Thirteenth Circuit or the Twelfth Circuit. The circuits will make decisions based on the same legal issue, but their decisions will be different. And often, those cases go to the Supreme Court, which makes the final decision.

Basically, the structure of the state courts is very similar to the federal courts. But, all the states have their own constitutions. They all have their own court systems. All of them are organized in different ways. The first instance court in every state might have a different name. It could be called a "District Court." It could be called a "County Court." There are many different names, but the bottom line is, they are all trial court levels or courts of first instance.

Then, once again, each state has an intermediate appellate court and then there is the supreme court of that state.

5. 連邦裁判所と州裁判所の管轄権
Federal vs. State Court Jurisdiction

Now, we are going to look at the different jurisdictions. Any of you who will have any cases regarding American law will need to know who has the right to hear your case. Is it a case that needs to be in the federal court? Is it a case that needs to be in a state court? And if it is a state court case, which state does it need to be in?

This is one of the largest issues when you are practicing in the common law systems in the U.S. for which you have to pay very close attention to. You will hear me come back to this issue in different ways throughout this series of lectures because it just touches every different aspect of research, creating your arguments and then writing.

Federal vs. State Court Jurisdiction

Federal Jurisdiction
- Limited Jurisdiction
- Civil and criminal cases based on federal law or the US Const.
- Cases based on federal law or *diversity jurisdiction* (concerning more than one State)
  - e.g. **Discrimination, International Treaties, Interstate Commerce**
- Cannot hear state law or state const. claims (must include fed law issues)
- **Exclusive Jurisdiction:** Admiralty, Maritime, Bankruptcy, Patent, or Copyright

State Jurisdiction
- General Jurisdiction
- Most types of cases are heard in state court
  - e.g. **torts, family, probate, contract**
- Can handle cases based on federal law or diversity actions (however these issues can be appealed through the Federal System)
- **Exclusive Jurisdiction:** cases based on state law or state constitution

I. Federal jurisdiction
a. Limited jurisdiction

Looking at federal jurisdiction, again, it is limited jurisdiction. According to the Tenth Amendment and how the system was set up, unless the federal courts are specifically given jurisdiction over a certain area of law, that jurisdiction goes to the states. Therefore, limited jurisdiction means that it has to be specifically given to the federal courts in the Constitution or in U.S. courts.

Now, we will talk about cases in the federal courts. Our civil and criminal cases in the federal courts are based on either federal law or the U.S. Constitution. If it is a federal criminal case, it usually means that the crime took place in more than one state. A classic federal criminal case might involve transporting minors across borders of states. If you bring the case under federal law or the U.S. Constitution, it will be in the federal court.

b. Diversity jurisdiction

The jurisdiction in federal court is based on again, federal law or what is termed "diversity jurisdiction." What diversity jurisdiction means is that the plaintiff and the defendant or the parties might be from different states. If one person from Colorado is suing someone from California, that is diversity jurisdiction because they are not from the same state. The idea is that the federal court can provide a fair forum so that when citizens from different states bring claims against each other, they are in a fair and impartial forum.

Not only do the federal courts deal with federal laws or cases under the Constitution, they can also deal with cases based on diversity jurisdiction, federal law or the Constitution. For instance, discrimination cases based on federal law are federal cases. Cases involving international treatises are federal cases. Cases involving interstate commerce, meaning business between states, are considered federal cases.

c. Exclusive jurisdiction

Other areas of exclusive jurisdiction for the federal courts are maritime law, so law of the sea, bankruptcy cases, patent cases and copyright cases. These are all the types of cases that specifically are delegated to federal jurisdiction.

II. State jurisdiction
a. General jurisdiction

Federal courts cannot hear state law or state constitutional claims. Everything that the court hears must include federal issues or be based on diversity of the parties. That is important because it differs from state courts. In general, state courts have general jurisdiction. It means that anything which is not specifically delegated to the federal government falls to state jurisdiction. Every other type of case that could arise would be under the state jurisdiction.

b. Most types of cases are heard in state court

In the end, most of your everyday cases are actually heard in state courts. For instance, personal injury cases, torts, family law cases, cases involving probate or contracts, certainly, most criminal law cases—most of those cases are heard in the state court.

As I said, there is one little caveat—there is one little exception here. State courts can handle cases based on federal law or diversity actions. However, if they do handle cases that are involving these federal law issues or diversity actions, those specific issues can be appealed through the federal court system. In that one exception, if there is some sort of federal law or diversity action that is part of a state law claim, the state court can hear it. But the path for appealing those sorts of issues goes to the federal courts.

c. Exclusive jurisdiction

And, once again, the jurisdiction of state courts are cases based on state law and state constitutions. In the U.S., each state has its own constitution and law that must be applied. It is important for you to recognize that because each state has its own law, which means that the state laws are not always consistent with one another.

Example: If you are in California, you need to know the California requirements for your case. This is important because the requirements might be different if it is Colorado versus New York.

6. 米国における訴訟のプロセス
U.S. Litigation Process

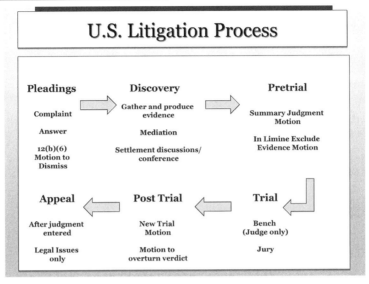

Now, we are going to the litigation process and will talk about it in terms of the legal writing involved in each stage of the process.

Legal Writing Examples During Litigation Process

- ❖ **Pleadings**
  - Complaint
  - Answer
  - 12(b)(6) Motions to Dismiss
- ❖ **Discovery**
  - Legal Memorandums
  - Evidence and Witness Statement/Deposition Summaries
  - Client Opinion Letters and Case Assessments
  - Demand letters/Offer letters/Settlement Agreements
  - Mediation Briefs
- ❖ **Pretrial**
  - Summary Judgment Motion – party entitled to judgment as a matter of law
  - In Limine Motion – request to exclude or limit evidence at trial
- ❖ **Trial**
  - Jury Instructions
- ❖ **Post Trial**
  - New Trial Motion
  - Motion to Overturn verdict in whole or part
- ❖ **Appeal**
  - Appellate briefs – request higher court to overturn verdict based on errors in law by lower court

I am going to speak with the assumption that the claim is in court. Often in cases, there are negotiations or there are back and forth among the parties before anybody brings the case to court. But, what I am going to start talking about here is the point where someone has actually filed papers in court and has initiated a court action.

I. Pleadings

The first area we are talking about is pleadings. What starts the case is called a "complaint." Pleadings are the documents that you file with the court. The complaint is the document that the party files with the court that initiates the case. The complaint has to state all the facts and law that support the claim.

a. Complaint

For instance, you have to state what are called the "elements" of a claim or a cause of action. Every lawsuit has certain elements that you have to prove to successfully recover based on your action. All of the elements must be included in your complaint.

Example: If it is a personal injury case, someone has filed a case based on a car accident. That is what is called a "negligence" case. The elements that plaintiff must prove are that—someone was involved in the car accident—that the defendant was negligent in some way, he did something to cause the accident that the plaintiff was injured as a result of the accident. Those are the elements with supporting facts that you would have to put into your complaint.

The complaint also must set forth the remedy. What are you asking the court to do? What are the damages that you are saying were caused to you? You have to set forth the damages as well.

b. Answer

After the complaint is filed, we come to what is called the "answer." The plaintiff, the person who brings the case, has filed the case and now the person who is being sued, the defendant, has to file an answer. An answer responds to all of the statements that are in the complaint.

In an answer, you would either admit the fact in the complaint or you would deny the fact in the complaint. If you do not have sufficient information, you would say, "I do not have sufficient information at this time to admit or deny that fact." The first part of an answer is to admit or deny facts or say that you need further information to admit or deny. Then you have to state all of your defenses in your answer.

Let's go back to our example where the car accident has occurred and the person has filed suit. The answer would be the defendant might admit that they were driving the car. They might admit that an accident occurred. But they might deny that they were negligent or they did something wrong in causing the accident.

For instance, if the plaintiffs said that they lost work due to the said car accident. And they are permanently injured so they are going to have medical bills for the rest of their lives. Therefore they want to recover those monies. The defendant might admit that the person was injured or they might not admit that in an answer.

They might say, "I do not have enough information right now to know the extent of the injuries. I do not have enough information to know if you have lost work," or anything along those lines. The defenses could potentially be that it was raining and the plaintiffs were driving with their lights off. Therefore, they contributed to this accident or in fact, they actually caused this accident. Those are the types of defenses that you might hear.

c. 12(b)(6) motion to dismiss

The next type of writing that you would see is called a "12(b)(6) motion," or a "motion on the pleadings." A motion on the pleadings or motion to dismiss would state that the complaint failed to state a claim, meaning you did not state all of the elements and supporting facts that you needed to successfully make a claim against the opponent.

You could also file a motion to dismiss because the court lacks subject matter. It means if you bring a case in a state court, but actually federal courts have jurisdiction over these types of cases, this case would be objected to because it should not be in state court based on subject matter jurisdiction.

You could also argue sometimes that the court does not have personal jurisdiction over the case. It means that I am from Colorado and someone is trying to sue me in California where I have no connections with California or that accident that occurred in some other state. There is no basis to sue me in California because the court lacks personal jurisdiction to hear the case.

II. Discovery

After we get through the pleadings, we move to what is called "discovery." Discovery is essentially where you investigate the cases. And, from this list of types of writing, legal writing that occurs during discovery, most of the legal writing that a lawyer does is during the discovery process. Discovery is where you are investigating the cases, which can often go on for years at a time. The most writing that you will do is often during the discovery process.

a. Gather and produce evidence

During discovery you make written requests for information, evidence, documents, and witnesses from the other side with the goal that there should be no surprises at trial. You have the right to ask for all the evidence the other side is going to present at court, any witnesses that the other side might present, what those witnesses are going to say, or any documents that they might be presenting—again, all with the idea that you do not want to have unfair surprises in court.

Some of the other things that happen during discovery are what we call "depositions," which is when you take sworn statements from witnesses. The types of writing during the discovery phase are legal memorandums.

We will discuss how to write legal memorandums in subsequent lectures because it is one of the most common things that lawyers in common law systems do. These are documents where you research legal issues and set out the facts and conclusions based on your research.

Other types of writing that you do are evidence and witness statements and deposition summaries. Meaning that when you are interviewing witnesses to the case, often you will write summaries of what the people told you, or if you have done a sworn statement or a deposition, you will write summaries of the important information.

Another type of writing you prepare is client opinion letters where you write your legal opinion and case assessments.

Then, there are settlement agreements or demand letters when you write to the other side and request certain settlements—amounts of money, depending on the type of case. Offer letters are when you make offers of settlement to the other side. And then, if you are actually successful in settling cases, you would draft what's called "settlement agreements," which is a document that just contains all of the terms that you have agreed upon.

b. Mediation

In the U.S. system, and as well as in Japan, during the discovery phase there is also a mediation that can occur between the parties. You often might put together documents for the mediator saying what your case is—summarizing what your case is and why you think you should prevail.

c. Settlement discussion/conference

Also, we have "settlement conferences." In Colorado for instance, there are retired judges and both parties would pick a retired judge. You would go in front of that judge to see if you can settle the case and the judge would give their legal opinion.

III. Pretrial

The next aspect is pretrial. This means that you have not settled the case and you are going to court and you are going to trial.

a. Summary judgment motion

The kind of documents that you write in pretrial is a "summary judgment motion." A summary judgment motion is a motion that claims after you have gathered all the facts there are no disputes as to the facts so that you are entitled to judgment as a matter of law.

You can file summary judgments based on full claims or parts of claims. It is something that you can use strategically. What you essentially say is that after you have done all the investigation in the case, though there is actually no dispute as to the facts, the courts can decide certain issues as a matter of law.

b. In Limine exclusive evidence motion

The other writing in this phase is called "in limine motions." They are motions that you write to the court in order to get certain evidence excluded or included at trial. If someone is trying to bring evidence to court that you think is improper, you would file a motion with the court and claim that the evidence should not be brought in at trial.

IV. Trial

The next phase is the trial. Trials can be by the court. It means that sometimes the parties agree to have the trial in front of the judge. There is a constitutional right in the U.S. to have trials in criminal cases and civil cases. Therefore, that is often just a strategic decision between the parties whether they want to have a trial to the court or a jury trial.

Trials before judges tend to be less time-consuming in terms of your client's resources. It does not cost as much, while jury trials tend to cost more. Often, the parties will decide whether they want to have a trial to the jury or a trial to the court.

In terms of how the trials proceed, the burden of proof is on the plaintiff or the person who brings the case. The plaintiff or the person bringing the case goes first to produce all of the evidence that they believe will support their claims. Next, the defendant brings in all of the evidence that supports their defense.

Then, there is something called a "rebuttal," which means if the defendant brought in information that the plaintiff wants to contradict or oppose, the plaintiff has one last chance.

There is not much writing during the trials. Usually the only writing that is involved is jury instructions. Before a jury gets a case, the court has to read all of the applicable law to them. The parties will put together what law applies to the case and then, the judge will read the law to the jury in order to guide the jury in making their decisions for how the facts should be applied.

V. Post-trial
a. New trial motion
Then, you have "post-trial motions." After the verdict, whether it is by the court or by the jury, most often by the jury, you can file a motion for a new trial. A new trial is generally when one of the parties argues that there were significant legal errors in the way the trial was conducted, or the jury or the judge came to an incorrect result which was not based on the evidence.

b. Motion to overturn verdict
Motions to overturn the verdict usually are not successful. But there are times when juries award excessive damages, or a punitive damage award which is excessive. There are cases where people will file post-trial motions asking the judge to reduce the damages because the awards were just too high. Those again, are uncommon, but they do occur.

VI. Appeals
Finally, the last part of our litigation process is the appeal process. The writing involved there are the appellate briefs. Appeals are only based on mat-

ters of law. This is the effort to request a higher court to overturn the verdict based on legal errors by a lower court.

第 2 部　米国法の源 ——Sources of U.S. Law

1. 一次的法源と二次的法源 Primary vs. Secondary Sources

> ### Primary vs. Secondary Sources
>
> ❖ Primary sources or **mandatory authorities** in U.S. law are statutes, regulations and cases:
>   - <u>Federal Law</u> – federal constitution, federal statutes, federal regulations, federal cases
>   - <u>State Law</u> - state constitution, state statutes, state regulations, state cases
>
> ❖ Secondary sources or **persuasive authority** in U.S. law are **not law**:
>   - works by scholars or lawyers to summarize primary source information (e.g. legal periodicals, restatements, hornbooks, treatises, etc.). **These are tools to find relevant law.**
>   - "Sister" court decisions

Now we are going to talk about sources of U.S. law. There are primary and secondary sources in all legal systems.

I. Primary sources or mandatory authorities

The primary sources of law in the common law and in the U.S. are the statutes, regulations and cases.

a. Federal law
In federal law, the mandatory authorities—these are binding and are the sources binding on courts—the federal constitution, federal statutes, federal regulations and federal cases.

b. State law
In state law, the mandatory authorities are the state constitution, state statutes, state regulations and state cases.

II. Secondary sources or persuasive authority
The secondary sources of law, called "persuasive authority," means that they are not binding, but the court can consider them in making their decision.

The secondary sources, which are not law but are works by scholars like our law review articles or books that summarize primary source information such as legal periodicals, restatements, hornbooks, treatises—these are always the best tools to find relevant law.

a. "Sister" court decisions
Sister court decisions are also a secondary source. A "sister" court means that it is a court decision which is not from your state. Although it does not bind you, it might be dealing with the same issue. Since the court has decided a similar issue, the sister court decision is not binding, though it could persuade the judges or the judges could use it as part of their decision. This is what a sister court decision is, but those are secondary law and they are not binding.

2. 米国法における4つの一次的法源
Four Main Primary Sources of U.S. Law

4 Main Primary Sources of U.S. Law

1. **Constitutional Law (Federal and State)**
2. **Court Decisions: Common Law**
3. **Statutory Law**
4. **Administrative Regulations**

The four primary sources of law are: constitutional law, the federal and state constitutions, court decisions; statutory law, and administrative regulations.

3. 米国憲法
Constitutional Law

#1: Constitutional Law

U.S. Constitution

- Is the most fundamental law in the U.S.
- Defines the rules to operate the government
- Outlines the fundamental rights of citizens
- Defines the limits of the federal and state governments for passing laws
- Describes the functions of the various agencies of the national government

The U.S. Constitution is the most fundamental law in the U.S. and defines the rules to operate the government, the different branches. It outlines the fundamental rights of citizens. In the U.S., we have the Bill of Rights, the first ten amendments, which form the basis of what we consider our most basic freedoms such as freedom of speech, right to juries, right to a fair trial, and a right to lawyers. It defines the limits of the federal and state governments for passing laws. And, it describes the functions of the various agencies of the national government.

Most common law countries have constitutions and they are very similar to how the Japanese constitution works as well.

4. 裁判所による3種の法創造
Court Decisions : Common Law

> **#2: Court Decisions: Common Law**
>
> **Courts make law in 3 ways:**
> 1. **Through Common Law** – state/federal court decisions become law, and other courts in the jurisdiction <u>must</u> follow
>   – Unless altered by a statute
>   – Possible to change the precedent
> 2. **By Interpreting Statutes** – A judge can interpret an unclear statute, <u>only</u> if the statute is disputed in the case
> 3. **By Judicial Review** – Supreme Court can declare laws unconstitutional
>
> **Precedent** – A judge is <u>required</u> to follow an earlier court decision when deciding a case with similar circumstances
>
> **Persuasive Authority** - Courts are not required to follow sister court opinions

The second source is court decisions. In the common law systems, courts make law in three ways.

I. Common law

First, law is made through common law. The state and federal court decisions become law and other courts in the jurisdiction must follow that law.

It is binding on them. Unless the decision is altered later by a statute or if that case is appealed to a higher court, it is possible that the precedent could be changed by a higher court—but unless it is altered by a statute or it is changed or overturned by a higher court, those court decisions are in fact binding law.

II. Interpreting statutes

The court also interprets statutes. A judge can interpret a statute if the statute is in dispute in the case. Courts interpret statutes that can also become law.

III. Judicial review

Finally, there is "judicial review" in which the Supreme Court can declare laws as unconstitutional. This is one of the main checks that the court system provides on the legislative branch and the executive branch.

As we discussed before, judges are bound by precedent, which means that the judge is required to follow an earlier court decision when deciding a case with similar circumstances. On the other hand, regarding secondary authorities or persuasive authorities, courts are not required to follow the sister court opinions, but they can find them instructive.

5. 制定法
Statutory Law

#3: Statutory Law

Statutes – *Laws passed **by** a governing body created to make laws*

❖ *Includes all laws passed by Congress, State Legislatures, Local City Government or Town Meetings*

The next source of law is statutory law. Statutes are laws that are passed by the governing bodies in the states or federal government or local governments.

6. 行政規則
Administrative Regulations

> **#4: Administrative Regulations**
>
> - **Organizations created by Federal, Local, and State Legislatures for regulating individual activities**
> - Provides an organization with expert knowledge to govern a specific field
> - Congress can end the agency or regulations at any time
>   - Example = Food and Drug Administration (FDA)

Then, there are administrative regulations. They are administrative bodies or organizations that the federal, local and state legislatures create for regulating individual activities.

In essence, it is an attempt to create an organization, which has expert knowledge in a specific field. For example, the Food and Drug Administration issues regulations that can be binding.

第3部 英米法のリサーチにおける戦略
——Strategies for Common Law Research

1. 戦略を実行する〜5つのステップ
Implementing a Strategy –Five Steps

Implementing a Strategy

Step 1: Collect and Analyze the Facts

Step 2: Identify Legal Issues and Search Terms

Step 3: Verify the Jurisdiction

Step 4: Find the Law

Step 5: Read and Update the Law

❖ Always use at least 3 research sources for any issue
❖ Know when to stop researching!

What is the best way to implement a strategy when you face a legal research problem? There are five steps that you should follow. Step one is collecting and analyzing the facts. Step two is identifying legal issues and search terms. Step three is verifying the jurisdiction. Step four is finding the law. And step five is reading and updating the law.

We will go through each one of these steps more specifically. But, let me give you some advice.

You always use at least three research sources for any issue. If you are looking at an issue, do not just look at one legal database and then stop. You should look at three separate sources, which means look at the statutes, look at the digests, and search in Westlaw, Lexis or other legal databases. Make sure that you go to at least three separate sources of law before you stop researching.

That is how you can be thorough; and with legal research you have to be thorough, especially in the common law system because you have to find all the cases that govern your claim. In the civil law, you just look at the law and that is the source for research. In the common law, when you have a claim, you have to make sure that you research different sources to find all cases for the claim.

The second advice is to know when to stop researching. If you go through all the three sources and you keep coming up with the same one or two cases, you can stop there. Just stop researching. Do not go in circles. Do not start researching all minor issues that may not have anything to do with your case. One of the greatest skills is to know when to stop researching. Also when your research starts to repeat itself, or when you start seeing the same cases repeatedly, it indicates to stop researching.

2. ステップ１：事実の収集と分析
Step 1: Collect and Analyze the Facts

I. Collecting facts

Step 1: Collect and Analyze the Facts

Collecting Facts - Separate the facts into categories to determine what is present, what is missing – create a "**map of information**"

WHO	WHAT	WHERE	WHEN	WHY	HOW
Company X, a drug company headquartered in New York	Obtained a patent and approval to sell new cancer medication (CANCEX)	From Food and Drug Admin. in Washington DC -- Patent applies across entire U.S.	April 2015 – patent applies for 10 years	To protect its proprietary interests in the new drug (CANCEX)	By fulfilling the requisite FDA approval and patent process
Company X	Began selling CANCEX for $50/pill	In all 50 US states	From June 2015	For business purposes	By selling to hospitals and pharmacies
Company Y, a drug company headquartered in California	Began selling a generic form of CANCEX, for $15/pill	In California, USA	In December 2015 (exact date unknown)	For business purposes	By selling to hospitals and pharmacies in California
Company X	Sent Company Y a Cease and Desist Letter	At Company Y headquarters in Los Angeles	December 17, 2015	To stop Company Y from violating its patent	By certified mail, hand-delivered and signed for

29

Collecting and analyzing the facts. When you are collecting the facts, how do you go about collecting them? This technique is called a "map of information." You create a map of the important facts of your case: **Who? What? Where? When? Why? How?** You put it into a chart which helps you collect the important facts in your case.

Example: **Who?** Company X, which is a drug company, headquartered in New York. **What?** Obtained to sell a new cancer medication called, "CANCEX." **Where?** They got this patent from the patent office and the Food and Drug Agency ("FDA") . They also received approval to sell it. **When?** In April 2015, and this patent happens to apply for 10 years. **Why?** Which was why they got the patent to protect their proprietary interest in the drug. **How?** They did it by fulfilling the FDA's requisite and patent approval process.

The next fact becomes: **Who?** Company X. **What?** Begins selling their cancer drug at $50 a pill. **Where?** In all 50 states. **When?** They started selling from 2015 in June. **Why?** For business purposes. **How?** By selling in hospitals and pharmacies.

Next: **Who?** Company Y, which is a drug company, headquartered in California. **What?** Begins selling a generic form of CANCEX for $15 a pill. So they were selling for $50 and now Company Y is selling it cheaper for $15. **Where?** They started selling in California—this is important for your jurisdiction where the case might be. **When?** They started in December 2015. **Why?** For business purposes. **How?** They started selling to hospitals and pharmacies in California.

Then again: **Who?** Company X. **What?** Sends a letter to Company Y telling them to stop selling this drug because they are in violation of Company X's patent. **Where?** Company X sent the letter to Company Y's headquarters in Los Angeles. **When?** Company X did it in December 2015. **Why?** To stop Company Y from violating Company's X's patent. **How?** By certified hand-delivered mail.

This is how you start mapping the information. Once you start mapping the information, then you can start analyzing the facts. By doing so, you can start identifying the legal issues.

II. Analyzing facts-questions to answer

Step 1: Collect and Analyze the Facts

Analyzing Facts – Questions to answer
- What remedy/result does your client want?
- What legal questions must be raised and answered to help your client get that remedy/result?
- What law governs the legal questions?
- What are the legally significant facts?

Chart for Analyzing Facts

Parties	Places	Objects	Claim/Basis	Defense	Relief
Company X	HQ – NY; Nation-wide patent	CANCEX	Patent Infringement	Patent was lawfully approved	Injunction to stop selling medication Damages – lost sales
Company Y	HQ – CA; Generic CANCEX sold in CA	Generic CANCEX	No patent violation occurred	Patent Invalidity – why?	Terminate Patent

Once you have collected your facts and you start analyzing your facts, the questions you need to ask yourself are:

What remedy or what result does your client want? If you are representing Company X, you want Company Y to stop selling the cancer medication in violation of your client's patent. What result or remedy do they want?

What legal questions must be raised and answered to help your client get their favored result? You are starting to analyze, "what the client wants. What do I have to prove to get the remedy in their favor?"

What law governs the legal questions? You are starting to identify law that governs your case. In this case, patent law is a federal case, so you would be looking at federal law.

And then, what are the legally significant facts?

The chart above helps you to analyze facts. You are looking at **the parties**, Company X and Company Y. **The places?** Company X's headquarters is in New York but their patent is nationwide. Company Y's headquarters is in California and they sell the drug in California. **The objects?** CANCEX and the generic CANCEX. **The claim—what are you claiming?** You are claiming that Company Y infringed your client Company X's patent. And now Company Y is probably going to claim that they did not infringe the patent. That is their claim or their defense. The defense to the claim is that Company X would be claiming that the patent was lawfully approved, and therefore, they could not infringe upon it.

Company Y, for instance, might be arguing that the patent was invalid. Perhaps Company Y was selling the drug based on false or misleading information that the patent should not have been issued. Therefore, we cannot be said to violate it. Then you are looking at what the relief would be? Company X wants Company Y to stop selling the medication and also potentially to recover money for their sales loss.

On the other hand, Company Y, might claim that the patent was not legally approved and might be asking to terminate the patent. Now you start to analyze the facts and then you put it into the claims. Finally, you put those issues together and combine the facts and the claims.

3. ステップ２：法律問題の選別と用語の選定
Step 2: Identify Legal Issues and Search Terms

> **Step 2: Identify Legal Issues and Search Terms**
>
> You must identify the law, the legal question, and the legally significant facts
> - **Example Legal Issue**: Under U.S. Patent law did Company Y violate Company X's patent when Company Y sold generic CANCEX in CA?
>
> **Chart to identify legal issues**
>
> | | | |
> |---|---|---|
> | Under (Law) | Fill in the statute, regulation or governing doctrine | e.g. Under U.S. Patent Law |
> | Did (Legal question) | Fill in the legal question | e.g. Did Company Y violate Company X's patent |
> | When (Legally significant fact) | Add legally significant facts: if facts change the outcome changes | e.g. When Company Y sold Generic CANCEX in CA |

The next step in your research process is to identify legal issues and your search terms. In order to identify the legal issues, you have to identify the law, what is the legal question, and what are the legally significant facts.

How to do this is organizing it in the following way. Create the sentence "**Under**" first. Then you would fill in the statute regulation or governing doctrine. For example, in our patent case, we would say, "Under U.S. patent law…" "**Did**," and you fill in the legal question—the legal question being "Did Company Y violate Company X's patent?" Then "**When**," being the legally significant fact—you would add it. Now the legally significant fact being, "When Company Y sold generic CANCEX in California."

When you put them all together, you have your legal issue as follows: "Under U.S. patent law, did Company Y violate Company X's patent when Company Y sold generic CANCEX in California?" This is how you build your legal issue. You look at what is the governing law? What is the legal question? And then, what are the legally significant facts?

> **Step 2: Identify Legal Issues and Search Terms**
>
> **Identifying Search Terms**
> - Once the facts are categorized, analyzed and preliminary issues framed, search terms for legal research are easy to identify
> - Researcher must think of synonyms and antonyms and related terms that offer a range of possibilities for a natural language search or an index search
>
> Example Issue: Did Company Y violate Company X's patent?
>
> Search Terms: U.S. patent law; patent requirements; patent violations; patent violation remedies; patent violation defenses; patent invalidity

Once you start identifying the legal issues, you have to start identifying your search terms because now you will answer the question. When your facts are categorized, analyzed and you have those preliminary issues framed, the search terms become much easier to identify. You begin to think of all of the terms that might relate to your case.

Here, in the example we are talking about, "Did Company Y violate Company X's patent?" While you are searching the issues, you would potentially use the search terms: "U.S. patent law," "patent requirements," "patent violations," "patent violation remedies," "patent violation defenses," and "patent invalidity."

After you identify the legal issue, you are simply looking for all of the various issues that you would have to search for in the beginning. Usually you are looking for both words having the same meaning and words having the opposite meaning. It helps you to look into the various sources for searching.

4. ステップ３：管轄の確認
Step 3: Verify Jurisdiction

> **Step 3: Verify Jurisdiction**
>
> - Determine what substantive law applies (ex. Tax, Criminal, Secured Transaction, Patent, etc.)
> - Does Federal Law apply to this area or State Law?
> - Is there a conflict of laws between States on this issue?
> - Is this issue covered in part by Federal Law and in part by State Law
> - Research and answer these questions to determine jurisdiction

Next, and what is a very important stage, is verifying jurisdiction. Again, you have to determine what substantive law applies. For example, if it is a criminal case or secured transactions, or patent—in our hypothetical example, it is patent law. Does federal law apply to this area? Or, does state law apply to this area?

We know that patent law is under federal law, which means you would begin your search in federal law, not in state law.

Look for whether there a conflict of laws between states on this issue? If your claim is governed by state law, do different states have different laws? Do they have different finds and different decisions on this? Then there are certain situations where the issue is covered in part by federal law and in part by state law?

You have to research all of these issues because in the end you have to verify that your claim is in the correct place. When you file your claim, you need to know that you are in the right court. Also, you have to answer the issues and questions while determining whether you are in the correct court.

This is a very important step because if you are in federal law, you are going to focus your research on federal law, federal cases and federal regulations. But if you are in state law or if you are in California, then you are going to focus your research there. If you are in Colorado, you are going to focus your research there.

5. ステップ４：法を調べる
Step 4: Finding the Law

I. Researching the law-where to start

Step 4: Finding the Law

Researching the Law – Where to start
- ✓ Statutes (often Annotated with applicable case law)
- ✓ Treatises
- ✓ Restatements
- ✓ Legal Encyclopedias
- ✓ Digests
- ✓ Computer Research Services (LEXIS and WESTLAW)
- ✓ Shepards
- ✓ ALR and Legal Periodicals
- ✓ PACER - Public Access to Court Electronic Records (PACER) to obtain case and docket information online from federal appellate, district, and bankruptcy courts, and the PACER Case Locator (www.pacer.gov)

Questions to remember:
What is the governing law in your case?
What sources of law have interpreted the governing law?
What court decisions help define the terms of the law or decision?

This is a process that really depends on how much information and background you obtain in that area. If you are familiar with patent law and you know, for instance, that U.S. Code, Title 35 handles or governs all patent law, then you just immediately can start looking at statutes. If you know what law already is governing your case, you can start there.

However, if it is an area of law that you are not familiar with, the best to start is to go to the **secondary sources**. You will find restatements of law or legal encyclopedias or other sorts of resources that summarize laws. When you are not aware of the sources for your law, you can go to the secondary sources as well. They will point you to the correct primary source.

If you do not know what statute applies to your case, also go to those secondary sources. Secondary sources such as restatements of the law are writings by scholars that state the general areas of law.

A digest is a book—it is a system and it identifies points of law. It is organized based on reported cases and by topic. For instance, you can look up patents in those digests and based on key numbers they will define areas of the law by topic and give them key numbers. And then, they will tell you the cases that are relevant to those areas. As soon as you have those search terms, you can go to the digests.

Then, there are computer legal research services like Lexis and Westlaw. You type in your search terms and they will start pointing you in the right direction as well. There are the other periodicals, the American Law Reports and Legal Periodicals—once again, secondary sources that you can look at.

Just to call your attention to something called "PACER," and I have given you the website here, PACER stands for Public Access to Electronic Records. This helps you obtain case and docket information online from federal appellate district and bankruptcy courts, and the PACER Case Locator. If you are dealing in federal courts and you are looking for other parties or something along those lines, this is a good place where you can get that kind of information.

II. Questions to remember

Questions to remember is a last step when you are trying to find the law. These questions are, what is the law that governs your case? This is what you are trying to answer. What sources of law have interpreted the governing law? What court decisions help to find the terms of the law or decision?

6. ステップ５：法の読み込みと通用性の確認
Step 5: Read and Update the Law

> ### Step 5: Read and Update the Law
>
> **Reading the Law – Questions to consider**
> - Does the source answer, advance/expand or amend your preliminary issue statement?
> - What arguments support your case?
> - What arguments are against your case?
> - How should you organize your case/arguments based on the sources
>   - **Example:** first focus on U.S. Code Title 35 – Patents; then move to Federal cases interpreting relevant code sections on violations, remedies and defenses
>
> **Updating the Law**
> - Ensure the law is still "good law"- meaning that the source has been subsequently upheld, not significantly amended by higher courts, or superseded by statute
> - Tools for updating include the legal databases LEXIS, WESTLAW, and Shepards

I. Reading the law

The final step is to read and update the law. We will talk more the next time about how to interpret cases and how to interpret statutes in Lecture Two.

Here are the questions to consider when you are reading the law: Does this source answer or somehow advance or amend your preliminary issue statement? Did this case answer your question? Or did it make you have to change your question? What arguments support your case? What arguments are against your case?

You are beginning now to organize how you should create your case and arguments based on the sources.

For example, back to the patent law case. First, we would focus on Title 35 of the U.S. Code, if we know it deals with patents. Next, we would move on to federal cases that have interpreted the important code sections on violations, remedies and defenses. When you are presenting your argument in this case, you would start with the statute. Then, you would start looking at the cases that have helped define the statute.

When you create arguments that you are presenting in court, that would be the way to organize the law in that situation. You have the federal statute, then you have the federal laws and that is how you organize those.

II. Updating the law

The next matter you have to be very careful about is updating the law. What does updating the law mean? It is to ensure that the law is still what we call, "good law." This means that case has not been subsequently overturned. What happens in the common law system is that cases are appealed all the time and often, you can be looking at a case and you have to make sure that no later higher court actually overturned that case or somehow amended that case.

Therefore, once you find the cases that you think are important for your case, you have to go through this exercise of updating the law to make sure that has not been changed or altered in some way.

The tool for updating the law is called "Shepards," which is a resource that will tell you what later cases cited your case, meaning it mentions your case in their decision. Did it cite the case with approval saying, "We agree with this case?" Did it follow your case? Did it distinguish your case, meaning that they thought their case was a little bit different from yours. And you need to know why they thought it was different and what their holding was to make sure that your law is still good law. Or did it overturn your case?

Shepards will give you this information about what has happened to your case subsequently. That is one tool for updating your case. And the other tools also are Lexis and Westlaw, if you have access to those legal databases, they will provide you with similar information.

第4部　英米法における法律問題の分析
——Analyzing Legal Questions in the Common Law

Now, we are going to talk about analyzing legal questions in the common law. When you start analyzing these legal questions and developing your legal argument, the first thing you do of course is determine the legal authority that is applicable to your case.

1. 自分の事案に適用することができる法的論拠を確定する
Determine the Legal Authority Applicable to Your Case

Determine the Legal Authority Applicable to Your Case

- Determine/Confirm Jurisdiction (Federal/State Court)
- Analyze Facts and Identify Legal Issues
- Identify applicable primary substantive law (e.g. Federal/State constitutions, statutes, regulations, cases)
- Read & Update the law
- Determine positive and negative law for your case

Determine and confirm whether the jurisdiction is federal or state. You have analyzed the facts and identified the legal issues. You have identified the applicable primary substantive law, e.g., the state constitution or the federal constitution, statutes, regulations, or cases. Then, you read and update the law. After that, you determine what is positive for your argument and what is negative for your case. You are determining what law is applicable to your case.

2. 制定法の分析手法
Strategies for Statutory Analysis

> **Strategies for Statutory Analysis**
>
> ❖ Analyze the language of the Law or Regulation on its face
> ❖ Research how Courts have **interpreted** the meanings of any clauses or terms included in the law or regulation that are relevant to your case
> ❖ Analyze whether the language of the law or regulations on its face, or as interpreted by a Court, helps answer the legal questions in your case

Then, you analyze the language of the law or regulation on its face, when you are talking about a law, a statute. You research how courts have interpreted the meaning or any clauses or terms included in the statute that are relevant to your case. Next, you analyze whether the language of the law on its face or as interpreted by a court either helps the legal questions in your case or is against what you are arguing. We will talk about more on how to do this later in the next lecture.

3. 判例の分析手法
Strategies for Case Law Analysis

Strategies for Case Law Analysis

- **Analyze the facts**: compare the similarities/differences of your case facts to the court opinion facts
- **Identify the legal rule** or principle the Court adopts in its decision
- **Assess the court's reasoning** in the opinion and apply it to your case
- **Look at other jurisdictions** for persuasive authority

Strategies for analyzing the case law. When you are reading cases, you want to analyze the facts and you want to compare how similar are the facts to this decision to your case. How are they different? You want to identify the legal rule or principal that the court has adopted in its decision. Then, you are going to assess the court's reasoning in the opinion and apply it to your case.

4. 自分の事案の事実関係に法的論拠を提供する― IRAC 方式
Apply the Legal Authority to the Facts of Your Case –The IRAC Formula

Apply the Legal Authority to the Facts of Your Case

How to Identify Issues, Rules and Facts

The IRAC Formula

IRAC = Issue, Rule, Analysis, and Conclusion

- Forms the fundamental building blocks of legal analysis. It is the process by which all lawyers think about any legal problem. IRAC allows you to reduce the complexities of the law to a simple equation.
  - **ISSUE**: What facts and circumstances brought these parties to court?
  - **RULE:** What is the governing law for the issue?
  - **ANALYSIS:** Does the rule apply to these unique facts?
  - **CONCLUSION:** How does the court's opinion affect the rule of law?

Identifing issues, rules and facts is very important. The well-accepted way to apply legal authority to the facts of your case is through "The IRAC Formula." **IRAC**—I-R-A-C, "**I**" stands for "Issue," "**R**" stands for "Rule, "**A**" stands for "Analysis," and "**C**" stands for "Conclusion."

Essentially, it is the building block for all legal analysis. It is the process that every lawyer goes through when they are analyzing a legal problem. Further, it is the process that you go through—and we will talk about it later when you are organizing legal writing—it is the process that if you are presenting in a conference call to your American colleague, it is the process that you organize your presentation.

You look at the issue. You talk about the rule. You analyze how the rule applies to the issue and then you come up with a conclusion. This analysis is essentially the fundamental analysis that you go through as a lawyer the common law systems.

When we talk about the issue, the issue is what facts and circumstances brought the parties to court. The rule is what the governing law for the issue is. The analysis is how the rule applies to these unique facts. And the conclusion is how the court opinion applies that rule of law.

5. IRACのI：問題点の同定作業
IRAC: Issue Spotting

Now we are going to talk about issues and issue spotting.

> **IRAC: Issue Spotting**
>
> - *"The **facts** of a case suggest an **Issue**."*
> - The key to issue spotting is being able to identify the **facts** that raise legal issues.
>   - The existence or not of one fact (e.g. time of day or whether someone was drinking) can eliminate or add issues to a case and raise a different rule of law.
> - The easiest way to find the legal issue is to look at the chapter headings of the statues or cases
>   - Ex. "Personal Jurisdiction" in Civil Procedure cases or "Offer and Acceptance" in Contracts cases.
> - Often cases will have language that signals the important issue. For instance, the judge will simply state:
>   - *"The case depends on whether...."*
>   OR *"We come then to the basic issue in the case."*

I. The facts of a case suggest an issue

For common law legal practice, it is important that you spot every relevant issue in your case. If you do not catch every issue, you could lose your case.

The key to issue spotting is being able to identify the facts raising issues. For instance, the existence of a fact or the absence of a fact such as the time of day something happened, or whether somebody was drinking that can either eliminate issues in your case or add to issues in your case or raise different rules of law. Then, you have to look at those facts critically.

II. Look at the chapter headings of the statutes or cases

When you are looking at cases, it is actually quite often easy to find the issues in the case because they are essentially set out for you. Cases have chapter heads. For instance it says, "Personal Jurisdiction," if it is a civil procedure case. Literally, the decision has a section that is entitled "Personal Jurisdiction," so you will know personal jurisdiction is an issue in this case. Or, in contracts cases it says, "Offer in Acceptance."

When you look at chapters in books, or statutes, or cases, frequently just looking at the names of the chapters enables you to find the issues that are the most important.

Often cases have language that signals the important issue. For instance, a judge might simply state, "The case depends on whether Company Y breached Company X's patent." This language, "The case depends on whether…" signifies immediately, this is an issue in the case. Often they even say, "We come then to the basic issue in this case."

By reading the case, the issues could essentially jump out at you if you look at how they are written.

6. IRAC の R：何が法か？
I**R**AC: Rule –What is the Law?

> ### I**R**AC: Rule - What is the Law?
>
> ❖ *The issue in your case is covered by a **Rule** of law.*
> ❖ **The rule is the law**. The rule could be common law developed by the courts or a law that was passed by the legislature.
> ❖ **For every case you read**, summarize the rule of law by breaking it down into its component parts.
>   ❖ **Ask the question: what elements of the rule must be proven in order for the rule to be true?**

I. Rule of law

We have already talked about the rule of law or what law is applying to your case. The rules could be either a statute, a constitution, or a court decision.

II. Break down the rule of law into elements

For every case you read, you should summarize the rule by breaking it down into its component parts. They are called the elements. You ask, "What elements of the rule must be proven in order for the case to apply?" When you are looking at the rule, you are also trying to break that down into the essential elements of that rule. If I want to come under that rule, what do I have to prove?

7. IRAC の A：分析ー弁護士の腕の見せどころ
IR**A**C: Analysis- The Art of Lawyering

The analysis part is known as, "The Art of Lawyering."

> ### IR**A**C: Analysis - The Art of Lawyering
>
> - *"Compare the **facts** to the **rule** to form the **Analysis**."*
> - For every relevant fact, you should ask whether it helps to prove or disprove the rule.
> - Check to see if a rule requires that a certain fact exists for the rule to apply, then the absence of that fact helps you conclude that the rule does not apply.
>   - **Example Rule:** all contracts for the sale of goods over $500 have to be in writing. In analyzing a contract for the sale of goods, you must consider two facts: 1) the value of the goods and 2) whether there's a written contract.
>   - <u>Facts that must exist in your case for the rule to be true</u>: 1) goods over $500 and 2) a written contract.
> - **The biggest mistake people make is to spot the issue and just recite the rule without doing the analysis.**

I. Comparing the facts to the rule

Analysis is comparing the facts to the rule. You should ask for every relevant fact whether or not it helps prove or disprove the rule in the case.

Then, you have to check if the rule requires the existence of a certain fact for the rule to apply, or if the absence of that fact would help you to conclude that the rule does not apply.

II. Example rule

Example: For all contracts of sales of goods over $500, they have to be in writing. In analyzing a contract for a sale of goods, you have to consider two facts: The value of the goods and whether there is a written contract.

The existence or the nonexistence—whether you have that fact or you do not have that fact will determine whether the rule applies. If the goods are only worth $400, you do not need a written contract. If it is for $700, you do need a written contract. Do you have a written contract if the sale was worth $700? Those are the facts that you have to go through to determine whether the law applies.

The biggest mistake that people make here is that people spot the issue and state the law, but they will never go through the analysis. The analysis is critical. Without it, how does the law apply to your facts? And, just by merely stating the fact and stating the law but not stating the analysis, you are not doing your job—you are not finishing your job.

You have to show why your case falls under this rule. What are the facts in the case? The biggest mistake law students make as well as young attorneys are just stating the facts and stating the rule, but leaving out the analysis.

8. IRAC の C：結論ー意見を伝える
IRA**C**: Conclusion- Give an Opinion

Last, there is the conclusion—giving an opinion.

IRA**C**: Conclusion – Give an Opinion

- ❖ *"From the **analysis** you come to a **Conclusion** as to whether the **rule** applies to the facts."*
- ❖ The conclusion is the shortest part. It can be a simple "yes" or "no" as to whether the rule applies to a set of facts.
  - The mistake many people make is to never give a clear opinion one way or the other on an issue.
- ❖ **Make sure that your opinion is supported in the analysis.**
  - Remember your opinion is always whether or not the rule applies to the facts of your case.
- ❖ The conclusion should always state a **_probable result_**. Courts differ widely on a given set of facts, and there is usually flexibility for different interpretations.

I. State whether the rule applies to a set of facts

You have your legal question. You have found your facts. You have analyzed them and you have found the law. You have applied the facts to the law. Now, you have to come to a conclusion. The conclusion is really the shortest part. Generally, it is a "Yes" or "No", such as whether the rule applies or not.

Matters that you should be careful about are that many times attorneys do not give a clear opinion on the issue. They discuss the facts one way and they discuss it another way, while they never simply say, "Yes" or "No." When you make an opinion, you have to give a definitive and a certain opinion, such as "Yes it does" or "No it does not," and why?

II. Your opinion supported in the analysis

Your job as a lawyer is to give a clear opinion. You have to make sure your opinion is supported in the analysis. Not only do you give your opinion, "Yes" or "No," but also you have to give a clear analysis as to the rule of law and how the rule applies to your facts.

III. Conclution should state a probable result

The conclusion should always state a probable result. The point is you cannot make guarantees. Use the previous example, the court could "**absolutely**" find that Company Y was in a violation of the patent. You have to be careful not to speak in such definitive terms. You have to give your conclusions in probable terms, such as, "It is **most likely** that the court will find that…" or "We **believe** that the court will find this…"

In this way, there is flexibility in the conclusion just in case there is an issue you missed or there is law or a case that you did not find. This is the reason why you never state your conclusions in absolute terms.

9. IRAC －参考例
IRAC- Example

Now, let us go through an example of how IRAC applies.

IRAC - Example

Facts:
An old man who is very ill and near death makes an **oral contract** with his nephew. The terms of the contract are that the uncle will immediately give his nephew all of his life savings - $100,000 - in return for the nephew's promise to provide food and shelter for the old man **until the man dies**. The nephew takes the money and supports the old man at a cost of $10,000 a year. The old man lives longer than expected and is **still alive after fifteen years**, at which point the **nephew cuts the old man's support**.

Issue:
- Is an oral contract valid after fifteen years?
- *Note that the issue is stated in the form of a question and uses key facts to illustrate the problem.*

Rule:
- Statute of Frauds: A contract must be in writing if it is not possible to perform the contract within one year.

Analysis:
- The Statute of Frauds does not state that the contract **must** be performed within one year. It only states that it must be **possible** to complete the contract within a year. Since a very ill, old man could have died within one year, it is possible that the contract could have been completed.

Conclusion:
- The Statute of Frauds **likely** does not apply in these circumstances, and the oral contract is valid even though it was not completed within one year.
- *Conclusions should be short and put in terms of a probability.*

I. Facts

Facts: An old man who is very ill and very near death makes an oral contract. It is not in writing, but he makes an oral contract with his nephew. The terms of the contract state that the uncle will immediately give his nephew all of his life savings—$100,000—in return for the nephew's promise to provide food and shelter for the old man until he dies. The nephew takes the money and supports the uncle at a cost of $10,000 a year. However, the old man lives longer than he expected and is still alive after 15 years following the oral contract. At that point the nephew cuts off the old man's support.

II. Issue

Issue: Is an oral contract valid after 15 years?

Issues are always stated in the form of a question and you have to use those key facts to illustrate the problem. That is, the old man has lived for 15 years. It was an oral contract. You should use these facts to state the problem.

III. Rule

Rule: In the common law, there is something called the "Statute of Frauds." The statute of frauds states that a contract must be in writing if it is not possible that the contract would not be performed within one year. That is the statute of frauds and it is a common law concept. Now you know the rule.

Next, you are going to do the analysis by applying the rule to your issue.

IV. Analysis

Analysis: The statute of frauds does not state that the contract must be performed within one year. It only states that it must be possible to complete the contract within one year. Since a very ill and old man could have died within one year—meaning that the contract could have been performed within one year—it is, therefore, possible that the contract could have been completed. This is your analysis.

V. Conclusion

Conclusion: The statute of frauds likely does not apply in these circumstances and the oral contract is valid, even though it was not completed within one year.

Here is your conclusion. Since the contract could have been completed in one year, the statute of frauds likely does not apply in these circumstances. Note that conclusions in legal writings and arguments should be short and stated in terms of probability.

This is an IRAC example. What is your issue? What is the rule that applies? How does the rule apply to your facts? And lastly you have your conclusion.

That is how you come up with a legal argument. It is also how later you will structure most legal writing.

The same also applies when presenting to partners or other attorneys on the phone or during meetings. Describe the issues, the rule, how the rules apply, and give a conclusion. IRAC is the most basic, fundamental legal analysis that applies to various areas of lawyering.

10. 事案のセオリーを考える
Theory of the Case

A theory of the case is a detailed and accurate story of the situation. It has to demonstrate why your client is entitled to relief. You come up with your theory as to why your client is entitled to relief and should prevail.

The legal argument is the area of law and then the factual theory is the explanation of how the particular course of events could have happened—this is your theory of the case.

A good theory of the case is based on strong facts and inferences that can be brought from those facts. They should be built on facts that are not subject to much dispute.

When you come up with your theory of the case, you cannot ignore facts or situations which are not convenient for what you are arguing. When you argue the case, you have to include facts opposite to your argument. You cannot just ignore the counter argument. You have to create your theory to be able to explain the good facts as well as the bad facts.

A good theory of the case explains why you should prevail, but it also addresses areas of arguments that are against your case and facts. You have to come up with a coherent or consistent theory that includes all of the facts and all of the applicable law.

11. 事案のセオリーを考える参考例
Example Theory of the Case

For example, let us go back to our patent case and talk about the theory of that case. Company Y is going to claim that Company X's patent was invalid because Company X actually stole Company Y's research and their test results, and submitted it for patent approval under their name. Therefore, they actually misled the patent authorities and they should not have been issued the patent.

The theory of the case for Company Y is, under the U.S. Patent Law, a violation of a patent cannot occur if the patent is invalid. Under the law, a patent is invalid if the party provided false or misleading information to acquire that patent.

Ideally, you would have found case law where other parties have brought cases in which they claim that people have stolen their research and analysis, and the courts have determined that it was actually false and misleading; and therefore, invalidated the patents.

You are arguing that the patent is invalid. Company X stole your client Company Y's research and submitted the research under their name so that their patent is invalid. Therefore, Company Y cannot be held liable for patent infringement. That is the theory of the case. It mixes the law and facts and comes up with a coherent explanation for why they should prevail.

In the end, the ultimate goal of all of your research, analysis and legal arguments should be that you create a theory of your case. Then, that theory will be what you argue in court, it will be what you argue in motions and it will become the basis and the foundation of your case.

第5部　英米法の法務文書における引用形式の基礎
——Basics of Common Law Legal Writing Citation Forms

Finally, let us talk about "Legal Writing Citation Forms."

1. 引用とはどういうことか？
What is a citation?

> **What is a citation?**
>
> - A citation is a reference to legal authorities and precedents such as statutes, cases, regulations and law review articles
> - Citations are used in legal writing to courts, legal textbooks, law review articles and memorandums
> - Citations to legal materials follow a standard format that makes it possible to find any cited legal authority

A citation form is a reference to legal authorities and precedents such as statutes, cases and law review articles. When you refer to them in your writing, a citation is used so that the person who reads your writing can go and find that case or find that authority.

Citations are used in legal writing to courts, in textbooks, law review articles and memorandums. Citations to legal materials generally follow a standard format that makes it possible for people to find any of those cited authorities.

For instance, you would need to put citations into your legal writing when you specify a principle of law. If you state the principle of law in a legal writing, you would need to put a citation to support that principle.

Back to our example of the patent case, a patent is invalid if it is based on false and misleading information, Section 35 of the U.S. Code Number 135. When you state a principle of law, you need to have a citation for that law.

Then, if you quote the language of a law or a statute in your writing, you need to provide a citation for them so that the reader knows exactly where to go if they want to read that quote. Also, you need to provide a citation when you quote a judge's decision or a law review article. As we lawyers say, "We do not plagiarize, we cite." As long as you cite the source, you can actually quote what other people say, but you have to give them credit for it or you have to cite to it. This is what legal citations are.

Citations are very important in legal writing because when judges are evaluating your writing or when other lawyers are evaluating, and you say, "This case applies," or "That case applies," they need to know where to find that case, what you are citing and what you are quoting.

2. 引用－３つの基本パーツ
Citations- Three Basic Parts

Citations

Most legal citations consist of three basic parts:
1) the name of the case, statute, or article (with author for articles)
2) a statement of where the item can be found in a multi-volume set of legal materials written as:
   - volume number name of publication (or set) page number
3) the date of decision or publication

Most legal citations consist of three basic parts: 1) the name of the case, statute or article, 2) a statement of where the item can be found in a multi-volume set of legal materials such as the volume number, the name of the publication and the page number, and 3) the date of decision or publication.

3. 判例の引用
Case Law Citations

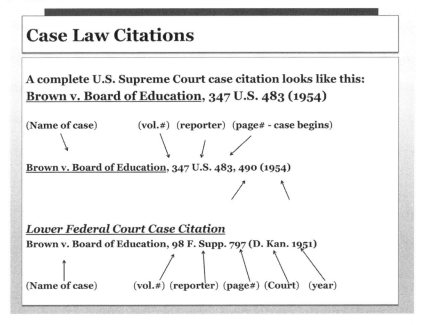

Let us take a look at some of the typical citation forms that you would need to use or read. Again, this is important because while you are researching, if you are reading one case and they are referring to another case, you need to find that other case and these are the citations which would help you find those other cases.

I. U.S. Supreme Court case citations

The top of the slide above shows a very typical case law citation. This is a complete U.S. Supreme Court case citation. One of the most famous cases in the U.S. is Brown v. Board of Education, 347 U.S. 483, 490 (1954), and this is how you read the citation.

The name of the case, Brown versus Board of Education, usually is underlined or in italics. Citation forms are very specific in how they are to be done. Here, you have the name of the case underlined, with a comma, space,

347, which is the volume number of the reporter U.S. This is "U.S. Reports." That is the name of this series of publications—"U.S. Reports." 483 is the page number where the case begins. 490 is the specific page of the quote.

First, you tell the reader the volume number of the reporter and the page of where the case starts. Then, you have a comma and you state the actual page you are talking discussing. The reader is able to know how to go to page 490 in order to find the quote. 1954 is the year of the decision.

There are different reporters for different cases. The U.S. Supreme Court cases are reported in "U.S. Reports." Federal lower court cases are reported in what is called the "Federal Supplement."

II. Lower federal court case citations

Now, we are looking at a typical lower federal court citation. This is the Brown v. Board of Education, 98 F. Supp. 797 (D. Kan. 1951), when it was in the lower court.

Here, once again, you have the name of the case. You have the volume number, volume 98. The reporter is "Federal Supplement." The page number is 797. In parenthesis, the court—District of Kansas, D. Kan. The year of the decision was 1951.

There is something called the "Blue Book." It is very useful because it gives you the format for the various citations.

Lecture 1 Fundamentals of Common Law Research and Analysis

III. Federal code citations

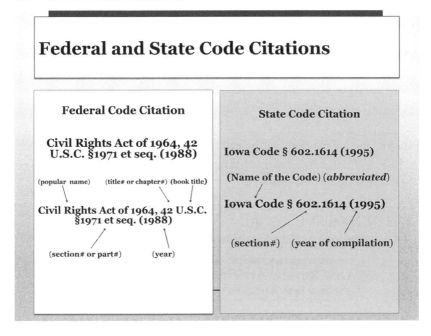

Now we look at federal code citations on the top left. Let us say for instance, the Civil Rights Act of 1964, 42 U.S.C. $1971 et seq. (1988).

You see the Civil Rights Act, 1964 which is the name of the law. The title or chapter number of the U.S. Code is 42. The book Title is U.S.C.—which is an abbreviation of the U.S. Code. All federal laws are inside the U.S. Code. For instance, 35 U.S.C. is the citation for patent law.

Then, you have the section number or part. It says 1971 et seq. "Et seq.," is Latin and means "and following." Now, you know it starts at 1971, though there might be hundreds of code sections. "Et seq." means where it starts, but it can go on further. The year that the law was adopted follows—it was the year of 1988.

IV. State code citations

Move on to the state codes on the top left in the slide. It looks very similar to the previous citation of the Federal Codes. The example is Iowa Code § 602.1614 (1995).

First, the name of the code is the Iowa code. It is the law in Iowa. The section is 602.1614 in the Iowa code. The year of compilation is 1995.

You find the appropriate statute and then under the statute in an annotated code, it will tell you the cases that have interpreted that statute, which is a good starting point for research.

4. 法学雑誌の引用（二次文献）
Law Review Article Citations (Secondary Sources)

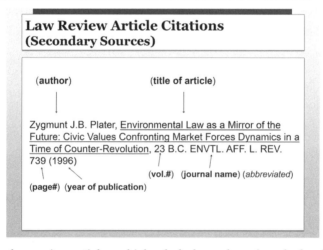

Next, are law review articles, which scholarly works written by legal professionals or academics.

Example: Zygmunt J.B. Plater is the author's name. The title of the article is "Environmental Law as a Mirror of the Future: Civic Values Confronting Market Force Dynamics in a Time of Counter-Revolution."

The article is located in the periodical B.C., volume 23. B.C. ENVTL. AFF. L. REV. is an abbreviation of Boston College of Environmental Affairs Law Review. Again, you can find such abbreviations in the "Blue Book" and other places. #23 is the volume number and 739 is the page number. Lastly 1996 is the year that it was published.

5. 法的引用の参考例
Example of Legal Citations

> **Example of Legal Citations**
>
> The Americans with Disabilities Act ("ADA"), 42 U.S.C. §12101 et seq., is a statute designed to eliminate the long history of discrimination against disabled individuals. 42 U.S.C. § 12101—12213(2000). Title II of the ADA provides broad protection from discrimination by public entities against disabled persons on the basis of their disabilities. Scott v. Garcia, 370 F.Supp.2d 1056, 1073 (S.D. Cal. 2005). Section 12132 states that "no qualified individual with a disability shall, by reason of such disability, be excluded from participation in or be denied the benefits of the services, programs, or activities of a public entity, or be subjected to discrimination by any such entity." 42 U.S.C. § 12132 (2000).

Example: the Americans with Disabilities Act (ADA), which is the abbreviation, 42 U.S.C. §12101 et seq. is a statute designed to eliminate the long history of discrimination against disabled individuals. First, I state the law and cite "The Americans with Disabilities Act."

Now, we are going to talk about certain sections of the law, which is 42 U.S.C. §12101-12213(2000). If I want to prove to the court that this is the legal principle, they can see my citation. The judge can go to 42 U.S.C. §12101-12213(2000) for the information that I stated.

Next, you say Title II of the ADA provides broad protection from discrimination by public and entities against disabled persons on the basis of their disabilities. Once again, I am stating a principle of law that Title II provides a certain protection. Now, I am going to cite a case that has interpreted this law in this way.

Let's see the case, Scott v. Garcia, 370 F.Supp.2d 1056, 1073 (S.D. Cal. 2005). Section 12132 has made this finding that it provides broad protection from discrimination by public entities.

How did I find Scott versus Garcia? It is in 370 of the Federal Supplement 2nd and it starts at page 1056. And where the court actually makes the statement is page 1073. This case is from the Southern District of California, so it is a trial court in California and the decision was made in 2005. And now, I am going to quote a section.

Section 12132 states that—direct quote from the section, "no qualified individual with a disability shall, by reason of such disability, be excluded from participation in or be denied the benefits of the services, programs, or activates of a public entity, or be subjected to discrimination by any such entity."

This is a direct quote from the law, and I am going to cite it for the reader to find it at 42 U.S.C. §12132. It shows that I went to Volume 42 U.S.C. and then I went to Section 12132. This is where I found that quote.

That is an example of how you use citations. It is extremely important when you do appellate briefs or when you write persuasive motions to the court, when you try to persuade the court of one or another, they want to read the cases and the laws that you cite and you have to give them a way to find those cases and laws. That is why citing, while very technical, is important to do in common law practice because case law is binding and plays such a large part in how the law is defined and interpreted.

Lecture 2

弁護士業務における英文リーガルライティングの基礎と応用

◆

Principles of Legal Writing for Lawyers in Common Law Practice

> 弁護士業務における英文リーガルライティングについて習得することを目的として，基礎から応用までを例を挙げながら具体的に解説します。

Let me thank everyone for coming to this second lecture in the six-part lecture series, the "Legal Writing and Professional Lawyering Skills in Common Law Practice." As we talked about last time, this is a series that was organized initially to focus on the fundamental principles that will prepare you to move on later in the series when we are dealing with more specialized writing concepts. For instance, in the first lecture, we talked about strategies for common law research, identifying and formulating legal issues and how to analyze legal arguments.

Lecture Two: Principles of Legal Writing for Lawyers in Common Law Practice

Agenda:
- ❏ Types of Legal Writing
- ❏ Predictive and Persuasive Writing Styles in Law Practice
- ❏ The Legal Writing Process
- ❏ Statutory and Case Law Interpretation and Analysis
- ❏ Practices for Common Law Case Brief Writing

Marc Lassman
Adjunct Professor of Law
Temple University School of Law, Japan Campus
April 28, 2017
18:00 – 20:00

In the second lecture, we are going to focus on the basic principles or fundamental principles of legal writing in the common law system. Today, we are going to discuss the different types of legal writing, the essential steps in the writing process, the basic principles to write legal documents in the common law, strategies and the importance of statutes in case analysis in the writing process and writing case briefs.

Now, after today, our lectures are going to be much more focused on specific areas and types of legal writing, much more specialized. For instance, in Lecture 3, we are going to move on to some more advanced skills related to initial client interviews, how to write letters of engagements for clients, and writing client opinion letters, which are fundamental to all legal practice, but especially when talking about transactional work. In Lecture 4, we will focus on case file management and drafting legal memorandum and case file assessments. In Lecture 5, we will then get to negotiating and drafting contracts. In Lecture 6, we will talk about handling very specialized topics in writing for U.S. common law practice, like preparing communications for information related to attorney client privilege, confidential information, and then negotiating and drafting settlement agreements.

In essence, these first two lectures are the necessary foundation that we will need, because these concepts that we talk about in Lecture 1 and Lecture 2 are going to apply to every other more specialized type of legal writing that we will discuss later on.

第1部 法務文書の種類
——Types of Legal Writing

1. 弁護士の役割に応じたリーガルライティングの類型
The Types of Legal Writing Depends on the Lawyer's Role

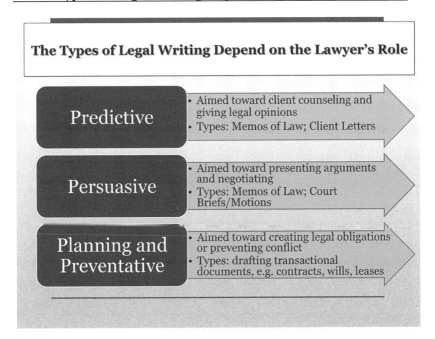

First, we are going to turn to the different types of legal writing, which depends on the lawyer's role.

As a lawyer, you are always going to have as part of your representation, different roles and different points. For instance, there are three basic areas of legal writing: predictive legal writing, persuasive legal writing, and planning and preventative legal writing.

I. Predictive
Predictive legal writing is aimed towards client counseling and giving legal opinions. For instance, the typical types of predictive of legal writing are memorandums of law, client letters, and opinion letters to your clients.

II. Persuasive
Persuasive legal writing is aimed at presenting arguments and negotiating. This is the type of writing that you would normally do when talking about court briefs or memorandums again, and then also if handling matters such as writing cease and desist letters to outside parties.

III. Planning and preventative
And finally, what we call planning and preventative legal writing; this is aimed towards creating legal obligations or preventing conflicts. This is the typical kind of legal writing you might find in your transactional practice, such as drafting contracts, drafting sales agreements, any other transactional documents, wills, for instance.

第2部　実務での法務文書の形式
——Predictive and Persuasive Writing Styles in Law Practice

Let's look more specifically at predictive versus persuasive legal writing. The goals differ between predictive and persuasive legal writing, but you must understand both concepts to improve your legal writing. Lawyers have to play different roles during the course of your representation. At some points, you will do predictive writing, however, you might also do some persuasive writing based on the same case.

1. 弁護士業務におけるわかりやすく説得的な文書作成スタイル
Predictive and Persuasive Writing Styles in Law Practice

Predictive and Persuasive Writing in Law Practice

Predictive writing - legal writing that predicts the outcome of a legal question by analyzing the authorities governing the question and the relevant facts. It explains and applies the authorities, and ends with ***neutral advice and recommendations***.

Persuasive writing – legal writing that persuades a decision-maker (court, tribunal, or mediator/arbitrator) to adopt a specified position. The writer analyzes the issues, argues for one approach to resolve the issue and ***does not present a neutral analysis***.

Predictive Writing	Persuasive Writing
Write factual or descriptive information	Write about your opinion or argument on a topic
Present information as clearly as possible supported by evidence and analysis	Convince the reader that your point of view is the correct one
Enable the reader to understand all perspectives of the case	Predict opposing arguments to your perspective and prepare to counter them accordingly
Provide neutral information necessary to make an important decision	Give reasons why opposing arguments are not valid – analysis is not neutral

Predictive writing is legal writing that predicts the outcome of a legal question by analyzing the authorities governing the question and relevant facts. It explains and applies the authorities, and ends with neutral advice and recommendations. In predictive writing, you write factual or descriptive information that is basic and direct. In this writing style, you present information as clearly as possible supported by evidence and analysis. In predictive writing, you are helping the reader to understand all the perspectives of the case. You are trying to make sure that your client is aware of every possible situation, every possible area of law that applies. You are going to be as inclusive as possible.

Persuasive writing is legal writing intended to persuade a decision-maker. The decision-maker is either the court who will decide the case or a mediator who might decide in the case; or for instance, in your transactional work, if you are writing a cease and desist letter to some company or some party, that will also be the person who would decide the case as to whether to comply with your letter. The goal is to convince the reader of your point of view that is correct or to persuade on a position. You are trying to anticipate the arguments that are opposed to your position and how to counter them. You are not necessarily presenting all of the information in a general way. What you are doing is trying to assert your opinion and predict what the opposing opinion is going to be and then prepare how you are going to counter those opposing opinions.

Finally, the most basic difference between the two styles is that in predictive writing, you are providing neutral information, which is necessary to make an important decision; whereas, in persuasive writing, you are giving reasons why the opposing arguments are not valid. The analysis is not neutral. Rather, you are presenting an opinion here.

2. 弁護士業務におけるわかりやすく説得的な法務文書の類型
Predictive and Persuasive Legal Writing Types in Law Practice

Predictive and Persuasive Legal Writing Types in Law Practice

Predictive Writing	Persuasive Writing
1) **Case Brief** – a written summary of a court opinion 2) **Memorandum of Law** –discusses how the law applies to the client's case/issue 　• key for determining case-handling strategy 3) **Client Opinion Letter/Case Assessment** – advises client how the laws and authorities apply to their specific situation 　• can be in letter or email format 4) **Letter of Intent** - outlines agreements between parties before the finalized contract 5) **Letter of Engagement** - defines the legal relationship between a lawyer/law firm and client(s)	1) **Court Documents - Pleadings, Motions and Briefs** –filed with courts to begin litigation; request court rulings; or bring arguments on appeal 2) **Negotiation Letters** – letters to negotiate terms of a business agreement or settlement, salaries, etc. on a client's behalf 3) **Cease and Desist Letter** – letter sent to an individual or business requesting to stop inappropriate activity 4) **Demand Letter** - letter stating a legal claim, demanding restitution or performance of some obligation

As mentioned above, examples of predictive writing are case briefs, which are a written summary of a court opinion, and memorandums of law, which discuss how the law applies to your client issue. These are key to determine your case handling strategy. Regardless of the situation, when you are trying to advise your clients as to a course of action or whether a deal is a good deal or protecting the client during a deal, memorandums are key to create your analysis.

Similarly, in client opinion letters or case assessments, you are advising your client, essentially, on how the laws and authorities apply to their specific situation. This can be in a letter or e-mail format. The next is letters of intent, which are predictive styles of writing that outline an agreement between the parties before finalizing contracts.

Finally, letters of engagement define the legal relationship between the lawyer and the client. This is essential, especially in common law. In the U.S., when you begin your representation, you must be clear the scope of your representation of the client.

Regarding persuasive writing, most court documents and pleadings and briefs are all related to litigation. Then, we are looking at negotiation letters to do deals or write letters to negotiate terms with another party, whether they are related to settlement or some other aspect of the deal. Cease and desist letters are sent an individual or a business requesting to stop inappropriate activity. In addition, demands letters state a legal claim or demand restitution performance of some obligation. Again, these last two "cease and desist" letters and demand letters are common in transactional work.

第 3 部　法務文書作成のプロセス
── The Legal Writing Process

Now, we are going to talk about the legal writing process. We are going to talk about each one specifically, but in general, in the legal writing process, there is prewriting and outlining, and then, writing and rewriting.

1. 法務文書の作成プロセス
The Legal Writing Process

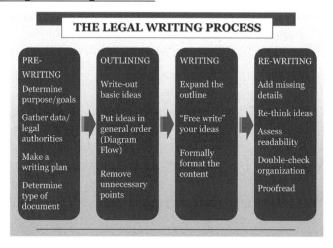

I. Pre-writing

The basic point here is, you must think before you write. You have to do all of your thinking before you start putting words onto the page. Legal documents are not like writing novels or writing poetry. Often, people will start writing without knowing the structure of their writing or their conclusion. You have to plan out your writing beforehand. When you plan and do all of your thinking beforehand, you can include that with the eventual writing, which will be much quicker than if you just start writing straight.

In prewriting, the first essence is to determine the purpose of your documents or the goals. Then, you gather data and legal authorities, and make a writing plan to determine the type of document that you want to write.

II. Outlining

When outlining, you are writing your basic ideas, then putting these ideas in a general order, or a diagram flow, which we will discuss later.

III. Writing

In talking about the writing section, you are expanding your general ideas that you wrote in the outlining process. I want to focus here on what is called "free writing" your ideas. This is a common way begin writing by putting your ideas on the paper. Later you can worry about making the writing grammatically correct and as perfect as possible. It is easier to edit than to write perfectly from the beginning. This is something that they will teach not only in law school but will teach in any kind of writing courses.

IV. Re-writing

Then, we are talking about re-writing. At that point, you should proofread for accuracy and readability. And when I talk about readability, I mean, how easy is it to read this document. That is where you will try to make the documents shorter or simple. If you are producing writing that your reader will not read, because it is too long or too complicated, then the purpose of your document is lost. If you are writing for a client who is a businessperson and you give them a 20-page long document that is full of legalese (technical leagal terms), they will not be able to understand it. They will not read it. Therefore, you have to look at what you are creating, who you are creating it for, and you have to make sure that the document meets the needs of the person you are creating it for.

Talking just quickly about proofreading; if you have the time, proofread the next day or the day after you finish writing. You should try to do all of your proofreading with a fresh mind. Often, if you are writing a document and spending many hours on it, it is always better to do your final proofreading the next day.

2. 作成前の分析：最初に検討すべき要点
Pre-writing Analysis: Important Initial Considerations

Now, we are going to talk more specifically about prewriting analysis, the important initial considerations. You have to know the purpose of your document, understand your audience, and then do your research.

**Pre-writing Analysis
Important Initial Considerations**

- KNOW Purpose
- UNDERSTAND Audience
- DO Research

I. Know the purpose

Initial Considerations: Purpose

What is the <u>purpose</u> of the writing?

❖ Must clearly understand the issue or assignment

❖ The purpose will determine the format of the writing

> **Predictive Purpose**: inform/give objective analysis
>> – ex. memorandums, client opinion letters, case assessments
>
> **Persuasive Purpose**: argue/give opinions
>> – ex. memorandums, court documents, negotiation letters
>
> **Planning/Preventative Purpose**: create legal obligations/prevent conflict
>> – ex. contracts, agreements, cease and desist letters

We are going to look at the purpose. You have to understand the issue or the assignment that you are writing, what you have been asked to do. The purpose will determine the format of the document that you are writing. For instance, if you are writing to inform or give an objective analysis in the form of either a memo or a client letter or case assignment, the question is, are you going to write in e-mail or full letter format. When you are looking at the purpose of the document, you have to understand if you are giving some general advice in the situation, a short summary or is this a complex issue that will require a lot of explaining.

If you are writing a short piece that is only summarizing, then you can write that in an e-mail. That will be the format. That is the purpose of what you are doing. However, if the purpose is writing something that is more complex with many issues involved, then, you cannot put that information into the e-mail. Rather, you would write a letter. You have to understand your assignment and what you are being asked to do essentially. And then, that purpose will help you to determine the best format for your writing.

The different purposes are, for instance, a predictive purpose is to inform and to give an objective analysis. The typical purpose for persuasive documents is to argue and to give opinions. Whereas, writing for planning preventative purposes is to create legal obligations and to prevent conflict.

II. Understand the audience

Initial Considerations: Audience

Who is the <u>audience</u> or reader?
- ❖ **Is the reader a lawyer or a client/party without legal training?**
  - ➤ This will determine how much legal detail to explain
  - ➤ Lawyers do not need minor legal concepts explained but clients or non-lawyers might
- ❖ **How much time and interest does the reader have?**
  - ➤ Appeals judges may be happy to read long legal documents and analysis, but business people will not have the time
  - ➤ Business people will want the information presented as quickly and as easily understood as possible
- ❖ **What is the best way to communicate your points?**
  - ➤ Depending on your purpose and audience this could be writing detailed documents with:
    - Issues/analysis/contract provisions
    - Short summary conclusions or recommendations followed by brief analysis
    - Graphs and charts to show data, e.g. sales or other business trends, property valuations, etc.

This topic is very important for all documents. Who is the audience? Who is going to read the document? Is this person who is going to read your document a client? Is it going to be another lawyer in your law firm? The audience is going to determine the way in which you write the document and specifically the amount of detail you will put in the document.

First, if you are writing to a lawyer, you do not need to explain every small legal detail, because lawyers likely will already understand the issues. But, if you are writing for a client, you may need to explain simple legal ideas to the client. You have to know who you are writing for, because that will determine what to write and how much detail to write.

Second, you should consider the amount of time and interest the recipient has to read the document. For instance, an appeals judge might be more than happy to read the legal authorities page and memos discussing complicated issues; but, a business person is not going to have the time. A business person is going to want you to write a document that they can understand as quickly and as easily as possible. If the writing is for a client who is a business person without a legal background, then your goal is to try to make the writing as easy to read and understandable as possible.

If the writing is to a court, then you are going to be much more formal in how you present the legal arguments. You have to know who your audience is, and how much time your audience is going to have to read what you are writing. I repeat this again, because it is one of the most important points here. If you produce a document that the readers are not going to read, because they do not have the time or inclination to read such a document, then there is no purpose to what you are writing. That is why it is so important to understand your audience and their needs.

Third, you should think about the best way to communicate your points. Depending on the purpose and audience, the best way might be, for example, using the IRAC analysis that we will discuss. If the writing is a short, easy issue, then you may provide a summary of conclusions with recommendations followed by a brief analysis. For example, if you are discussing sales data, talking about property value, then that type of information is much better shown in graphs or charts. Consider the information you are trying to communicate and the best way to communicate it.

III. Do research

> **Initial Considerations: Research**
>
> **What research or information do you need to write effectively?**
> ❖ Must investigate the facts or circumstances of the issue
> ❖ Must determine what information is missing or necessary for you to complete the task
> > ➢ Follow-up with client or boss about obtaining information necessary to handle the issue
> ❖ Must identify the relevant legal authority and sources
>
> NOTE: review Lecture One of this series for effective research tools in common law practice

The next part of the initial considerations after thinking about the purpose of the writing and the audience is the research to write the document. You have to investigate the facts or circumstances of the issue and determine the missing or necessary information to complete the task. Perhaps, you may need to follow up with your client or boss about obtaining the information necessary to handle that issue. Let me give you examples of missing information.

Example: you are advising a client who is in negotiations to acquire another company. You are helping to draft the purchase agreement. However, you do not know the discussions that took place between your client and the other company regarding what will happen to the existing staff of the company. You want to know if the agreement allows the other company to keep the staff; and, if so for what period of time. That is the type of information you are going to need to know while you are drafting the contract, because that is an essential term of the contract. That is an example of missing information. You have to make sure that you have all the relevant information to draft whatever you are working on. If you do not have that information, then you have to get that information.

And then, also you have to talk and think about the relevant legal authorities and sources that govern whatever situation you are working on. If you are doing an acquisition of another company, decide the relevant authorities that relate to that situation. Please refer to the Lecture 1 materials for a discussion on legal authorities. You have to be sure before you start writing that you have done all your research and have all the information.

3. リーガルライティングの基礎
Legal Writing Fundamentals

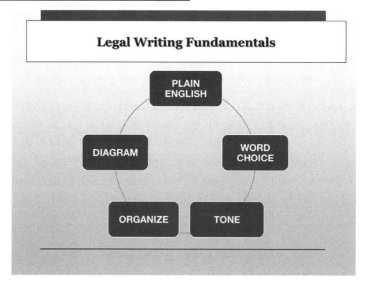

Legal writing fundamentals. These are concepts that will apply to any documents you draft in English in the common law. Now, you have to write in plain English, your choice of words, your tone, how you organize the document, how you diagram the document, and how you diagram the arguments. These are all part of the fundamentals. We will go through these one at a time.

Lecture 2 Principles of Legal Writing for Lawyers in Common Law Practice

I. Write in plain English

You Should: Write in Plain English

- ➢ **Draft in English that is clear and easy to understand**
  - ○ *Bad*: Mr. Jones committed his signature to writing on the document conveying the real estate to the new record title holder.
  - ○ *Better*: Mr. Jones signed the deed to the land, transferring it to Ms. Smith.
- ➢ **Limit using legalese**

Legalese: The parties only agree to the terms and conditions **set forth herein**.	Plain English: The parties only agree to the terms and conditions **in this agreement**.
Legalese: **In the event** that Mr. X defaults on his obligation, he will **forfeit** his rights.	Plain English: **If** Mr. X defaults on his obligation, he will **lose** his rights.

- ➢ **Make short sentences**
  - ○ *Bad*: Holders of the Class A and Class B stock certificates will be entitled to receive on each Payment Date, to the extent monies are available therefore (but not more than the Class A Stock Certificate Balance or Class B Stock Certificate Balance then outstanding), a distribution.

    versus
  - ○ *Better*: Class A and Class B stock certificate **holders will receive a distribution** on each payment date if cash is available for their class.

The most important rule here is you have to draft in plain English. What I mean by plain English is you have to draft in language that your clients are going to understand. You have to remove all the legalese or technical legal terms. Why do you want to draft in plain English? Because it makes your client more comfortable. If you give the client a readable document, the client can understand your advice more comfortably. If you give the client a document that is full of legalese that they cannot understand, the client will not be comfortable. Making readable writing also helps to avoid misunderstandings later on. If you give a document that everyone can understand, then it is less likely later on that there will be some misunderstanding about the terms of the documents or terms of the deal.

Example: Mr. Jones committed his signature to writing on the document conveying the real estate to the new record title holder. This sentence is difficult to understand. It is much better to write: Mr. Jones signed the deed to the land, transferring it to Ms. Smith. The writing should be clear and easy to understand by removing the legalese language.

Generally, with lawyers, it is easy to write legalese because these technical legal terms are convenient for drafting based on what you learned in law school. But, you have to remember that you are working for clients. And, your clients have to be able to understand what you are doing. There is a big movement within the last 20 years in the U.S. to push towards basic English and to move away from complicated legal English.

Here is an example of legalese: The parties only agree to the terms and conditions "set forth herein." This phrase "set forth herein" is just legalese that you do not need. You can change this language to say the parties only agree to the terms and conditions "in this agreement." This language is simple and easy to understand.

Another example of legalese: "In the event" that Mr. X defaults on his obligation, he will "forfeit" his rights. Plain English: "If" Mr. X defaults on his obligation, he will "lose" his rights.

Example: you can change the language of "set forth herein" and "wherein" which are common terms in contracts because lay people or non-lawyers do not always know the meaning of these terms. Plain English is easier for people to understand, and when writing documents, you will have fewer problems in the future.

Make short sentences. This is something that every law student all the way through to becoming an associate in a law firm or partner, this is the point in which writing is criticized. You have to write in short, brief sentences, expressing one idea per sentence. Do not write long sentences that become lost in the idea or topic you are discussing.

Here is an example bad sentence: "Holders of the Class A and Class B stock certificates will be entitled to receive on each Payment Day, to the extent monies is available therefore (but not more than Class A Stock Certificate Balance or Class B Stock Certificate Balance, then outstanding), a distribution." This language is from an actual contract.

A better sentence: "Class A and Class B Stock Certificate holders will receive a distribution on each payment day if cash is available for their class." This language is simple, direct English.

Now, this is something that is very important in contract writing especially, because what happens is the longer your sentences become, and the more complex the number of ideas you try to put in a single sentence, the more confusing as to the meanings of your provisions. And, that will cause problems later on. Larger, complex sentences are difficult to interpret and apply to the situation.

My advice is, do not try to put too many thoughts into a single sentence. One or two thoughts maximum. My rule is when you get to a third comma in a sentence, you have to start thinking that maybe it should be two sentences.

Later on, after you drafted some contracts, for example, there will be lawyers who look for problems in the contract. If there is a disagreement or some dispute between the parties of the contract, the lawyers will look for any vague language or anything in that contract that they can use to get out of the contract or interpret it in a different way. The vast majority of problems that come out of contracts are the fact that they were written poorly to begin with. Always remember that your writing should be clear and it should not be open to various interpretations. Short sentences, clear sentences, direct sentences.

II. Write in the appropriate tone

You Should: Write in the Appropriate Tone

	Examples
➢ Be conversational but professional. Use your natural speaking voice ➢ Do not use **slang words** or **contractions** and limit use of **idioms** ➢ Be concise but thorough in talking about the issues ➢ <u>Do not</u> personalize your writing	○ **Bad**: There is <u>no way</u> the tenant will agree to leave the premises. (slang) ○ **Better**: The tenant <u>will not</u> agree to leave the premises. ○ **Bad**: The landowner <u>won't</u> sell. (contraction) ○ **Better**: The landowner <u>will not</u> sell. ○ **Bad**: <u>I do not believe</u> that the purchase price is reasonable. (do not personalize writing) ○ **Better**: The purchase price is not reasonable.

I will speak briefly about the appropriate tone. You should always be conversational but professional. What I mean by that is to use your natural speaking voice. When you write, try to write as you would speak. Often people try to write very differently from how they would actually say something. It is always easier to read a document if you write it as if you are speaking. Try to use your usual speaking voice. Do not use slang or contractions and limit use of cliché phrases or idioms.

For example, bad language is, "no way" that the tenant will agree to leave the premises, because that is slang. It is better to write: the tenant "will not" agree to leave the premises. The landowner "won't" sell. Contraction: it is better to write the landowner "will not" sell.

You should be concise. You should always make sure that you cover everything as concisely as possible, and then, something that people often will do is personalize their writing which you should never do. What I mean by personal is, "I do not believe" that the purchase price is reasonable. If you are writing on behalf of your client, law firm, or group, you never talk about "I believe." You always should write in the generalized point of view.

Example: You would not say "I don't believe the purchase price is not reasonable." You would say "the purchase price is not reasonable." Remove "I" because you are not talking about yourself personally. Rather, you are giving legal advice on behalf of your firm or client.

III. Organize your writing

> **You Should: Organize Your Writing**
>
> ➢ **Structure issues from most important to least important**
>   o State your conclusions first, then move to analysis/support
> ➢ **Explain the structure of your writing**
>   Sample language includes:
>   o <u>First</u>, we will discuss the issue of...
>   o <u>Then</u>, we will discuss the question of...
>   o <u>Finally</u>, we will turn to...
> ➢ **Clearly indicate/recommend future actions in the matter**
>   o Explain the outcome or result
>   o State your future action or what will happen in the legal matter
>   o Provide the reader with instructions or recommendations for next steps

This is one of the most important parts in all types of legal writing, which is the organization of your writing. You should structure your issues from the most important to the least important. And, one area that is different in legal writing than any other type of writing is that you should state conclusions first. Then, move to your analysis and your support. Often when people are writing articles or any other type of novels, etc., you go through your arguments and analysis, and then, finally at the end of your document, you come to your conclusion.

In legal writing, when you are handling matters for your clients, you have to put your conclusions first. You put them in front. Do not place your most important points at the end of your document. Make them easy to find. Do not make your reader work to understand your main points. Again, this goes back to your audience and how much time they have for this document.

If it is a business person or client, you cannot force them to read through some 10-page document to finally find your main point at the end. When the reader looks at your writing, they want to know what you are saying. People might not have the time to read your document or they only have a limited amount of time; and if you put your main points at the end of the document, they might never get there. They might just take a look at your 10-page document and decide not to read it because it is not useful to them.

In structuring your writing, tell the reader exactly what you are going to do in the document. Specifically, if you are doing predictive writing, first, we will discuss the issues. Here is the sample language you can use: "First," we will discuss the issue of dischargeability of debt in bankruptcy. "Then," we will discuss the question of... "Finally," we will turn to... so that it is a roadmap. The person who is reading your document knows exactly what you are going to talk about, how you are going to talk about it, and your roadmap of where you are going in the discussion. The reader should be able to know from your writing, the structure and organization of your document.

Also, you should clearly indicate future activities and explain the outcome or result. As you are going through the discussion or point, you should state your follow-up actions. And then, you provide the reader with the instructions or recommendations for next steps.

It is important to make sure that your document is structured in a very simple way to follow. Use headings, for instance, like next steps or issue or legal analysis so that the reader can jump to them if they want to. If it is a 10-page document, your client wants to know the next steps. You want to make it clear in your document so that the client can go directly to the next steps section or recommendations section. You want to make sure that you organize the document in a way using the headings and bullet points to make sure that it is easy to understand how to find information in your document.

IV. Diagram the flow of your document

You Should: Diagram the flow of your Document

- When organizing your writing, you should first <u>diagram</u> the flow of your document. It can be in outline form or as a map like below
- There is no need to use complete sentences or thoughts when diagramming your flow. You only need to organize your structure
- <u>Example</u>: Client Opinion Letter to determine a fair purchase price for Company X, which is in bankruptcy

Issue/Intro: What is a fair purchase price for Company X?

Question: How much of Company X's current debt can be discharged in Bankruptcy

Conclusion: As most of Company X's debts are unsecured loans, under Chapter 13 they can be discharged

Analysis: Set out language in Bankruptcy Code defining dischargeable debts. List main cases interpreting the relevant statutory provisions and any other authorities supporting conclusion

Next steps: Discuss what the action plan is to confirm whether there are any other potential debts or liabilities of Company X that you are not currently aware of

The next step in the pre-writing part of the process is called diagramming the flow of your document. When organizing your writing, you should first diagram the flow of your document, meaning how to organize this document. Some professionals create an outline form or some make a map such as the example above. These are called mind maps business analysis in MBA programs because you have a central idea and show the flow of the argument.

The above example is mapping a client opinion letter to determine a fair price for Company X, which is in bankruptcy. Perhaps the client is thinking about buying Company X and that company is in bankruptcy. You are trying to determine the fair price for this company. You are advising the client on this issue and will diagram the way that the document should be organized.

The question is how much of Company X's current debt can be discharged in the bankruptcy because you are trying to evaluate their purchase price.

Then, maybe you would talk about most of Company X's debt being unsecured loans under Chapter 13 in that they can be discharged. Next, you would do, for instance, an analysis, or you would set out the language in the bankruptcy code defining dischargeable debts by listing the main cases interpreting the statutory provisions and any other authorities supporting those conclusions. Finally, list the next steps, for instance, discussing what the action plan is to confirm whether there are in any other potential debts or liabilities of Company X that you are not currently aware of.

This slide above an example of how you diagram the flow of your document. Think about the question you want to answer. Here is the conclusion upfront with the analysis and next steps. There is no need to do complete sentences or thoughts when diagraming your flow. You only need to organize your structure and basic ideas. You are not writing full sentences and full paragraphs at this point. All you are doing is making sure that the organization of your document makes sense.

4. リーガルライティングの構造
Legal Writing Structure

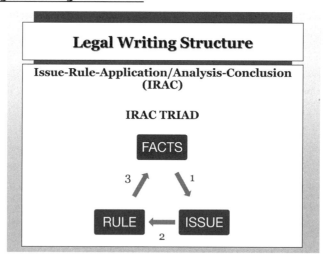

We will go back to a topic we talked about in Lecture 1 because it is the basic rule in legal analysis and writing, and further shows the way to structure documents: issue, rule, application analysis, conclusion—IRAC triad.

5. IRAC 方式
IRAC Format

> **IRAC Format**
>
> 1. Articulate the important legal issue or question
> 2. State and explain the relevant legal rule
> 3. Apply the rule to your facts
> 4. Conclude by explicitly answering the question

This is the basic IRAC format, articulating the important legal issue or question, explaining the relevant legal rule, applying the rule to your facts, and then concluding by specifically answering the question.

6. IRAC 方式による参考例
Legal Writing Example: IRAC in Action

Legal Writing - IRAC in Action

Excerpt from an Opinion Letter to a client (Tokyo Rubber Company):

In July 2016, Tokyo Rubber Company sold John Johnson of Big Apple Rubber Products Corp. (*Big Apple Rubber*) $1 Million of raw rubber for his business, which manufactures household rubber products. John Johnson of Big Apple Rubber has been a customer for many years of Tokyo Rubber Company, and has made many similar purchases in the past. Unfortunately, this invoice has not been paid, even after several written and oral requests to the company....

The issue we must consider as we decide next steps is whether under New York law, if *Big Apple Rubber* cannot pay the invoice, can we hold John Johnson personally responsible for the debt since he both exclusively ran the company and owned all the shares in it? (ISSUE)

....The New York Court of Appeals has established a high barrier as to when it is possible to pierce the corporate veil. While courts must assess each case based on its own unique circumstances, there are two key factors in making this determination: (1) "complete domination of the corporation in respect to the transaction attacked," (2) which "was used to commit a fraud or wrong against the plaintiff which resulted in plaintiff's injury." *Morris v. Dept. of Taxation*, 82 N.Y.2d 135, 141 (1993). (RULE)

In our situation, although Mr. Johnson clearly has complete domination over Big Apple Rubber as the sole director and shareholder, there has been no information uncovered to suggest that he used this domination in a manner "to commit a fraud or wrong" against Tokyo Rubber Company. (ANALYSIS)

Consequently, it is unlikely that Mr. Johnson can be held personally liable for the debt. (CONCLUSION)

Here is IRAC in action in a specific example. This is a portion of an opinion letter to a client. Your client is Tokyo Rubber Company, which in 2016 sold to John Johnson of Big Apple Rubber Products or Big Apple Rubber, $1 Million worth of raw rubber for his business that manufactures household rubber products. John Johnson has been a customer of Tokyo Rubber for many years and has made many similar purchases in the past, but unfortunately, he has not paid for this invoice. And, there have been several contacts between the companies both in writing and orally, but the invoice has not been paid. You are now advising your client on what they should do.

Next steps: John Johnson a few years ago actually created a corporation where he previously was a sole proprietor. The question is if John Johnson or Big Apple Rubber is unable to pay the invoice, can you actually get the money from John Johnson personally? Let's say that is the problem. You are advising your client. This is the opinion letter and IRAC analysis in action.

First, you are going to set out the relevant facts of the case. Example: In July 2016, Tokyo Rubber Company sold John Johnson of Big Apple Rubber Products $1 Million of raw rubber for his business which manufactures household rubber products. John Johnson of Big Apple Rubber has been a customer for many years of Tokyo Rubber Company and has made many similar purchases in the past. Unfortunately, the invoice has not been paid, even after several written and oral requests to the company. Make brief, direct sentences, and do not use any legalese.

The first 10 years, Mr. Johnson ran his business as a sole proprietor. However, in December 2015, Mr. Johnson's accountant recommended that he form a company to carry on his business. A new company was duly registered with the name Big Apple Rubber Products Corp. with Mr. Johnson as a sole director and a shareholder.

Now, you are going to talk about the issue. Example: The issue we must consider as we decide next steps is whether under New York Law, if Big Apple Rubber cannot pay the invoice, can we hold John Johnson personally responsible for the debt since both exclusively ran the company and owned all the shares in it? So there is your issue. You set out the issue, which is how we were talking about formulating legal issues in the first lecture. These are the important legal facts.

Next explain the rule of law. Example: It is well established that a shareholders' corporation has liability for the debts of the corporation if they are bound to the requirements set out by the state law and the company's own bylaws. However, there are exceptions in the law where shareholders can be personally liable, called "piercing the corporate veil". The New York Court of Appeals has established a high barrier as to when it is possible to pierce the corporate veil. While courts must assess each case based on the unique circumstances, there are two factors in making the determination: "complete domination of the corporation in respect to the transaction attacked" which "was used to commit a fraud or wrong against the plaintiff which resulted in the plaintiff's injury." This comes directly from the case by the

New York Supreme Court. The citation is here with the page number that this actual quote comes from.

The next step is to talk about the analysis, which is how the rules apply to the facts. Example: In our situation, Mr. Johnson clearly has completed the domination of Big Apple Rubber because he is the sole director and shareholder. There has been no information to suggest that he used his domination in a manner to commit fraud or wrong against Tokyo Rubber Company.

Your analysis is that you have no information that Mr. Johnson was actually trying to commit a fraud here. Therefore, the conclusion is that it is unlikely that Mr. Johnson can be held personally liable for the debt. There is your conclusion. That is IRAC. Please note in the conclusion what we were talking about in the last lecture, you are to state a position. You cannot say, for example, maybe this is correct or maybe that is correct. You have to take a definitive position.

In this conclusion, you have taken the position that he cannot be held personally liable, but you do not speak in absolute terms. Consequently, it is **unlikely**. You always have to make sure, because later on you might find out that there was fraud or wrong doing. You cannot say, consequently, that it is **impossible** that Mr. Johnson can be held personally liable. Do not use that sort of absolute language, because you never know what the situation is going to be. Consequently, it is unlikely that Mr. Johnson can be held personally liable for the debt.

This is how IRAC works in action. Of course, this is a much shorter document than you would normally write, but I want to show you in basic terms how IRAC works in action, how you should think about writing such documents.

第4部 法と判例の解釈と分析
──Statutory and Case Law Interpretation and Analysis

Next, we are going to talk about statutory and common law case interpretation and analysis, and how this applies to your practice in business transactions.

1. 事業取引に関する制定法と判例の分析
Statutory and Case Law Analysis in Business Transactions

Statutory and Case Law Analysis in Business Transactions

❏ Statutory and Case Law Analysis is often used when advising a client on the benefits or possible risks of a business transaction

  Examples:
  - Valuing companies for potential purchase that are currently in bankruptcy (debt dischargeability in bankruptcy defined in statute and case law)
  - Assessing purchase price for land that may have environmental contamination (when does seller or buyer have to pay clean up costs – defined in statute and law)

❏ Statutory and Case Law Analysis is necessary when determining what provisions to include in specific types of contracts

  Examples:
  - What provisions are necessary for IP licensing agreements; sales of real property to include the underground mineral rights; etc.

Analyzing statutes and case law is often used when you are advising a client on, for instance, benefits or possible risks of a business transaction. Here are some examples.

Example: You are valuing a company for a potential purchase we were talking about before that is currently in bankruptcy. The issue is the debt dischargeability of that company in bankruptcy, but that is defined in statute and case law. For instance, in the U.S., if a company has created debt and that is a result of their own fraud, then there is a chance of that debt might not be dischargeable in bankruptcy.

If you are advising a client as to what the value of a company might be and you are looking at that company, you are looking at what debt that company has and what can be discharged in bankruptcy. One issue you have to think about is the statute and case law you will rely on to determine what exactly will be dischargeable in bankruptcy. Statutory and case law interpretation is not only relevant in litigation, but also is relevant in transactional business. Even in your basic transactional work, you need to know the law that is applying to your situation when you are giving advice.

Here is another example. You are assessing the purchase price for land that may have environmental contamination. For instance, I think people are aware of Toyosu Market here. This is an issue that is being faced right now. There was a sale of land that had some environmental contamination. Let's say three or four years in the future you are looking at buying land that might have some environmental contamination.

The question becomes for your client when does the seller or the buyer have the obligation to pay cleanup costs. Because those costs will determine how much you are will pay, or how much you are going to sell for, you need to know what the cost will be for any potential cleanup. Where you are going to find that type of information?

In the common law, you will look to statutes. More specifically, you are going to find that in case law as well. Therefore, you will need to analyze case law and the applicable statutes before you write the contract. This is an extremely important point especially regarding case law, because if you are writing, for example, the purchase contract, you want to make sure that the language in those provisions protects your client in the event that later on, they find out that there is environmental contamination on that land.

You want to know the correct language that has been successful in a contract to protect people in the example situation. And, if you are not finding that in the statute, such specific types of information will be in the case law. You need to find cases that are similar in circumstances where the court was perhaps reviewing contracts that were for the sale of property, but had a contamination issue. You look at the language of that contract in the case law and check the court's decision or result. Then, you copy that favorable language into your contract. That is how you can find information in case law. And, that is how you will be able to write potential contract provisions to protect your clients. That is one example about why statutory case law analysis is important in business transactions.

The second example is when it is necessary to determine the provisions that should be in specific types of contracts. Let's say you are writing a contract for an IP licensing agreement. You will need to look at the cases that have interpreted the laws to make sure that you have all of the necessary provisions in your contract.

Example: Sales of real property to include underground mineral rights. I am a lawyer from Colorado. In Colorado and in many oil producing states, Texas and other such states, the law in Colorado is when you sell property, you can sell the surface rights and you can sell the underground mineral rights separately. Many states have that law in states that are oil producing. You need to know that whenever you sell property or you buy property, if your client is going to buy property in Colorado, you need to make sure that the contract includes not only the sale of the surface rights, but it also includes any subsurface rights, or you are going to have some oil company next to your land drilling under your land for oil. This is something that you will only find in the statute or case law in Colorado. These are the sources that are absolutely necessary even when you are doing business transactional work. You have to do this type of research and case law analysis, and the statutory analysis to protect your client. That is why I am talking about this statutory case analysis with regard to business transactions to make sure that you give appropriate advice to your clients.

2. 制定法 — 典型的な構成
Statutes — Typical Structure

Statutes -Typical Structure

1. Definition Section – defines important terms
2. Purpose section – describes scope of statute
3. Substantive Legal Provisions - states the law
4. Enforcement Issues - methods for ensuring proper application of the statute
5. Effective Date - when the law comes into effect

We are going to talk about statutes and how to understand and interpret statutes. Your typical statute will have a definition section, which means, it is going to have a section to define the important terms in that statute. The statute will have a section that describes the purpose of the statute. The purpose of this statute is to define the relations between the parties. Then, we will have the substantive legal provisions, which will state the law. Next, we will have a small section on enforcement issues, meaning methods for ensuring the proper application of the statute. There always is a section about the effective date showing when the statute comes into effect.

3. 制定法を分析するためのツール
Tools for Analyzing a Statute

Tools for Analyzing a Statute

Primary Sources

Statutory Definitions - Many statutes contain a "definitions" section that sets forth and defines the key terms used in the statute.

Case Law - Often courts have already analyzed and interpreted the statutes at issue. Court decisions may have discussed alternative interpretations of the statute and why the court either approved or rejected those alternatives.

Administrative Regulations or Decisions - agencies in charge of administering the statute issue regulations or guidelines to clarify how that statute should be interpreted and applied. **Administrative regulations can be found in the Code of Federal Regulations (CFR).**

Secondary Sources

Dictionaries and legal encyclopedias - can provide additional guidance on how to interpret a statute.

Legislative history - committee reports and hearings, floor statements from members of Congress, proposed amendments, etc., can give guidance on statutory meanings.

In analyzing statutes, you have primary sources and you have secondary sources.

I. Primary sources

The primary source for statutory analysis is the definition section within that statute. Most statutes will have definitions in them stating that the words in the statute have a certain meaning. This section will define all of the important words in that statute. But also, once again, which is something that is unique to common law that you have to be very careful about, is that we have case law that often defines, analyzes, or interprets the statutes that you are dealing with. They discuss alternative interpretations of the statute or have agreed to approve or disapprove of certain statutory interpretation. You have to remember that the case law, the common law is binding law. In common law, you must analyze case law. That is when you will see specific discussions about a statute's meaning, and you must be sure that your interpretation is consistent what the case law says. I mean, also you are going to have administrative regulations or decisions that will talk about how statutes should be applied or interpreted. For example, you must check the case law on how to interpret statutes regarding environmental cleanups or regulations that come from our EPA, Environmental Protection Agency. Many regulations are located in what is called the Code of Federal Regulations or the CFR.

II. Secondary sources

The secondary sources that you can look at in interpreting the statutes are either dictionaries or legal encyclopedias, which provide additional guidance on how to interpret the statute. Another unique source is legislative history, which are the committee reports on the hearings in Congress or the state legislature from the members' discussions when they drafted the statutes. This can be persuasive to judges because you can look at the legislative history that shows the intent of the drafters.

III. U.S. federal statute example

U.S. Federal Statute Example

U.S.C. Title 42 - THE PUBLIC HEALTH AND WELFARE
CHAPTER 103 - COMPREHENSIVE ENVIRONMENTAL RESPONSE, COMPENSATION, AND LIABILITY
§9614. Relationship to other law
(c) Recycled oil

(1) Service station dealers, etc. No person (including the United States or any State) may recover, under the authority of subsection (a)(3) or (a)(4) of section 9607 of this title, from a service station dealer for any response costs or damages resulting from a release or threatened release of recycled oil, ...if such recycled oil —

    (A) is not mixed with any other hazardous substance, and....

(2) Presumption. Solely for the purposes of this subsection, a service station dealer may presume that a small quantity of used oil is not mixed with other hazardous substances if it—

    (A) has been removed from the engine of a light duty motor vehicle or household appliances by the owner of such vehicle or appliances, and....

(3) <u>Definition</u>. For purposes of this subsection, the terms "used oil" and "recycled oil" have the same meanings as set forth in sections 1004(36) and 1004(37) of the Solid Waste Disposal Act [42 U.S.C. 6903(36), (37)] and <u>regulations promulgated pursuant to that Act [42 U.S.C. 6901 et seq.]</u>.

(4) <u>Effective date</u>. The effective date of paragraphs (1) and (2) of this subsection shall be the effective date of regulations or standards promulgated under section 3014 of the Solid Waste Disposal Act [42 U.S.C. 6935] that include, among other provisions, a requirement to conduct corrective action to respond to any releases of recycled oil under subtitle C or subtitle I of such Act [42 U.S.C. 6921 et seq., 6991 et seq.].

Lecture 2 Principles of Legal Writing for Lawyers in Common Law Practice

I want to show you a portion of a typical statute. Example: This statute is about compensation in liability for environmental damage. This statute relates to recycled oil and gas service stations. There is the definition section, which defines what "used oil" means and what "recycled oil" means, and where you can find the meanings in the larger law. The statute also talks about regulations promulgated (created) pursuant to this law. You need to know how this law applies. The statute also shows where these regulations are located. The next section is the law itself, which is the substance of the law. Finally there is the effective date, which tells you when this law has come into effect. This is a very typical looking statute. The statute also organized to try to make it easily understandable.

You should know the basic rules in common law for how to interpret a statute.

4. 制定法を解釈する際の基礎的ルール
Basic Rules for Statutory Interpretation

Basic Rules for Statutory Interpretation

Plain Meaning - Courts generally assume that the words of a statute mean what an "ordinary" or reasonable person would understand them to mean. **Whole Act Rule** - when a term or phrase is used multiple times in a statute, that term or phrase should be interpreted in the same way. **Avoid Extra Words** each word or phrase in the statute is assumed meaningful and useful. An interpretation that makes a word or phrase repetitive or meaningless should be rejected.	**Example**: The Securities Act of 1933 <u>defines</u> the term **"prospectus"** as "any prospectus, notice, circular, advertisement, letter, or communication, written or by radio or television, which offers any security for sale or confirms the sale of any security." If the term "communication" was interpreted to include any type of written communication, **the words "notice, circular, advertisement, letter" would serve no independent purpose in the statute**. However, if "communication" were interpreted to include oral statements made through radio or television, **then all the words in this section of the statute would contribute something to it's meaning, and none would be considered "surplusage."** <u>Gustafson v. Alloyd Co.</u>, 513 U.S. 561, 577-78 (1995).

The most basic rule is the plain meaning rule. Courts will always assume that the words of a statute mean what ordinary or reasonable persons would understand them to mean. Whenever a court is reading a statute or you are reading statute, you should always try to read it based on what a normal person would understand that statute to mean. It is the most basic premise in common law statute interpretation.

There is something that is called the "whole Act Rule", which means that when there is a term or phrase that is used multiple times in the statute, that term or phrase should be interpreted in the same way. You should always assume that it has the same meaning throughout the statute.

You should always avoid interpretations that would create extra words. The idea is that each word or phrase in the statute is assumed to be meaningful. Interpretation that makes words or phrases repetitive or meaningless should be rejected.

Example: You have to interpret the statute in a way that makes sense. Here is the perfect example of the securities law of 1932. This is from a U.S. Supreme Court case in 1995 where the court is talking about the Securities Act. The Security Act defines the term prospectus as "any prospectus, notice, circular advertisement, letter or communication, written or by radio or television, which offers any security for sale or confirms the sale of any security." The issue in this case is what does the word "communication" mean? If the term "communication" is interpreted to mean any written communication, then that might mean that the terms "notice, circular, advertisement, letter," would serve no independent purpose in the statute, because you could simply say communication. If the communication meant every written communication, there is no reason to list in the statute the words "notice, circular, advertisement, letter," because all of these words are included in the one "communication."

However, if you interpret "communication" to mean any oral statements, all the words in the section of the statute would contribute something to its meaning and nothing would be considered "surplusage" (useless meaning).

The point being that if you interpret communication just to mean anything that is written, that will mean all these other terms become useless. But, if you interpret communication to mean any oral communication, then the other terms now have a meaning. The courts are always going to interpret a statute to make sure that all the words are meaningful.

This is the most basic rule of statutory interpretation. Plain meaning, is that the same term has the same meanimg throughout the statute, and you have to interpret the statute to make sure that every word has a meaning. You cannot interpret the statute in a way that makes certain portions of the statute make no sense at all. The statute must have a consistent meaning. That is how the court, how you should interpret the statutes.

I. Legal writing example-statutory analysis in action

> ### Legal Writing - Statutory Analysis in Action
>
> **Example: Excerpt from a Memorandum to Partner**
>
> As our client, Tokyo Department Store Corp., begins its due diligence to purchase land on the outskirts of Denver, Colorado to build a new "Tokyo Outlet Super Mall", there is one unique feature of Colorado law that they must be aware of. Colorado Revised Statutes § 38-35.7-108 (2016) states in part:
>
> > "The surface estate of [p]roperty may be owned separately from the underlying mineral estate, and transfer of the surface estate may not include transfer of the mineral estate. Third parties may own or lease interests in oil, gas, or other minerals under the surface, and they may enter and use the surface estate to access the mineral estate." C.R.S. § 38-35.7-108(1)(a) (2016).
>
> Consequently, in Colorado, the sale of property does not automatically include any mineral rights to the subsurface of the land unless it is specifically stated in the sales agreement. It is not uncommon for property sellers to split the surface property rights and the sub-surface mineral rights, and sell or lease the rights separately. Prior to finalizing any purchase, Tokyo Department Store Corp. must confirm that the seller has rights to both the surface and sub-surface of the property, and that the sales agreement specifically conveys the sub-surface mineral rights as part of the agreement.

I want to give you an example of what we are talking about related to statutory analysis in action. Example: I am going back to the example I was talking about in Colorado where I am a seller of property. You can have the surface rights and you can have the mineral rights.

This is a small portion of a memorandum to a partner in a law firm. The client is the Tokyo Department Store Corporation. They are hoping to buy some land outside of Denver because they want to build Tokyo Super Outlet. They want to buy some land to build a large outlet or mall just outside of Denver. You are advising them on how to proceed.

You researched the revised statute on sales of property—section 38-35.7-108, which was enacted in 2016. The statute states in part: "The surface of state property maybe own separately from the underlying mineral state and trends of the surface state may not include transfer of the mineral estate. Third parties may own or lease interests in oil, gas or other minerals under the surface, and they may enter and use the surface estate to access the mineral estate." There you have the specific site to that section of the statute.

This is the situation where you have to go through and interpret the statute as it relates to your client interest. You are trying to advise your client Tokyo Department Store, as to what they should do, and then you learn that there is an actual law in Colorado. The surface land and the mineral can be sold separately and that if it is sold separately, the owner of the mineral estate can actually go on to the land to mine the minerals. They can enter the surface to access to the mineral estate.

You are writing to the partner, and interpreting this legal research to the client. Consequently, you are giving the advice that in Colorado, the seller of property does not automatically include any mineral rights to the subsurface of the land, unless it is specifically stated in the sales agreement. It is not common for property sellers to split the surface property rights and subsurface property rights, and to sell or lease the rights separately. It is not common for them to sell the top of land and to sell the underground separately.

Therefore, you have to advise your client, Tokyo Department Store, that they have to confirm that the seller actually has the rights to both the surface and the sub-surface, and that the sales agreement specifically conveys both the sub-surface and the surface rights as part of the agreement. This is the statutory analysis in action, because you have to make sure that your client has within that agreement, the rights to both the surface and the sub-surface. Otherwise, your client will be in the situation later on that they build an outlet and some oil company has come in, and they are actually drilling under the land. You do not have the provision in your contract to prevent that. That is why you have to go through the statutory analysis when you are giving advice even in transactional situations. This is the example of statutory analysis in action. You explain what the situation is for your client. You go through the statute and now you are talking how the statute applies to your advice to the client.

5. 判例の解釈と分析――事案の読み方――着目すべき事項
Case Law Interpretation and Analysis

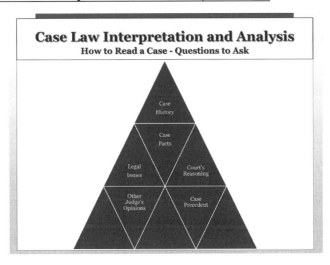

Next, we are going to talk about case law interpretation and analysis, which is essentially, how to read a case. You need to look at case history and case facts, legal issues, court reasoning, precedent and other judge's opinions.

Most court opinions in U.S. common law are very long. The main point you have to remember is that the specifics of the law are not only found in statutes, which set forth general principles of law. Once you are looking for how a specific situation should be covered under the law, you have to go to case law to determine that. For example, you have a 25-page court opinion that you are reading; and the question is how do you analyze it and what is the best way to approach it. You start reading the case and these are the questions to should ask yourself to understand the case.

> ## Case Law Interpretation and Analysis
> ### How to Read a Case - Questions to Ask
>
> 1. **What is the background/history of the case?**
>   - Where is the case located? Is it federal or state? If a federal case, what circuit?
>   - When was the case decided?
>   - At what level is the case? Is it a district court case, circuit court case, or Supreme Court case?
>   - Are there any legal terms in the case that you don't understand?
> 2. **What are the facts of the case?**
>   - Who is the plaintiff?
>   - What is the plaintiff claim or legal injury?
>   - What kind of remedy is plaintiff seeking from the court?
>   - Who is the defendant?
>   - What are defendant's arguments against plaintiff's claims?
>   - What side did the court find more convincing? Even if the court's explanation of the facts seems relatively neutral, can you identify points at which a close question of factual interpretation went one way or the other?

I. What is the background/history of the case?

You want to look at where the case is located. Decide if this is a federal case or state case. If it is a state case, then identify the specific state court, such as the district court, circuit court, or the state's high court. In addition, you should know when the case was decided. Finally, always look at the legal terms in the case that you do not understand, because then you have to research and decide the issues in the case.

II. What are the facts of the case?

Next, you look at the facts of the case. You have to identify the parties in the case. For example, you should know who is the plaintiff (person or entity) bringing the case and what is the claimed injury. Basically, you should know the problem or issue in the case and the remedy the plaintiff is asking for. The same is true of the defendant and the defenses to oppose plaintiff's claims.

You have to look at which party's argument the court finds more convincing. Even if the court seems relatively neutral in its analysis, you are looking for points where there is a close question or factual interpretation one way or the other. The court in its analysis will reveal the arguments that are the most persuasive.

Case Law Interpretation and Analysis
How to Read a Case - Questions to Ask

3. **What is the legal question in the case and how does the court answer it?**
   - What legal question is the court centering its analysis on?
   - What legal question is the key determining factor in the court's decision?
   - How does the court answer this legal question? With a yes/no answer or with a specific test that it suggests for future courts to use?

4. **What reasoning supports the court's decision?**
   - What essential issue(s) is the case really about?
   - What arguments does the court use to justify its answer to the legal question you've identified?
   - What other cases does the court cite for support? Does it distinguish other cases? On what basis does it rely on some cases and distinguish others?

III. What is the legal question in the case?

Next, you are looking at the legal question in the case. You look at the facts, what everyone is claiming, what is the basic question that the court being asked to answer, how the court will answer that question, and what is the issue the court is identifying. Often it is quite easy to define, because it will literally say "issue presented." And then, you have to look at the court's answer to that issue. Again, as we often do with conclusions, they are "yes" or "no" answers. Is the defendant liable for this? Yes or no Conclusions should often be yes or no, and then you should look to see if the court set out some sort of specific test or interpretation of, how these decisions should be made in the future.

IV. What reasoning supports the court's decision?

The next point you are looking at is the court's reasoning, which is the court explaining its rationale for its decision. Ask questions, such as: What argument did the court use to justify the decision? What other cases did the court cite for support? Does it say that other cases are different or the same? You have to look at those other cases to determine whether those cases fit the facts of your specific case or are they different from the facts of your case. It is important to look at the cases that the court cites for support, because they are the ones you will apply to your facts, whether you are representing a client during the transaction or giving advice, this is where you are going to find the more specific information that applies to your issue.

Case Law Interpretation and Analysis
How to Read a Case - Questions to Ask

5. Are there any separate opinions?

<u>For Concurrences</u> (judge agrees with outcome in majority decision):
- How is the concurring judge's view different from the majority's view? What facts or legal issues give rise to the disagreement?
- Where are the areas of agreement? Why does the judge still agree with the outcome in the case?

<u>For Dissents</u> (judge does not join in majority decision):
- Does the dissenter interpret the facts the same way as the majority? Does the dissenter identify the legal question in the same way?
- How does the dissenter's legal reasoning differ from that of the majority?
- What responses does the dissenter have to the majority's reasoning?
- Does the majority address the dissenter's reasoning?

6. How does the decision fit in with other cases?
- In what way does this case address issues you have seen before? What cases do the facts or legal issues remind you of?
- To what extent does this case extend or modify legal reasoning in earlier cases?
- Does this case leave issues unresolved?

V. Are there any separate court opinions on the issue?
a. Concurring opinions

Often in common law cases, you have to look at whether there are separate court opinions in the same case. Sometimes we have what is called "concurrent opinions," which means a judge agrees with the end result, but has different reasoning to reach the result. The judge writing the concurring opinion agrees with what the court has decided, but has different reasons for the decision. You have to look at what their reasons are for making their decision, where do they agree, where do they disagree, because again, you are looking to see if there is a judge's reasoning that could apply to your issue.

b. Dissenting opinions

Then, there is the dissenting opinion, which means these are the judges who are disagreeing with the court's majority opinion. You have to look at why they disagree, what facts they disagree about, and what legal reasoning they disagree about.

If you are writing a contract and using certain language in the contract, you want to make sure that the language is supported by the courts. Examine the dissenting opinions, because there are judges out there who may have found that your language is problematic, and even though the opinion is a dissent, perhaps you should try to use different language. When drafting the contracts or giving advice, the point is to manage or reduce potential problems.

VI. How does the decision fit with other cases?

Finally, you should decide whether the court opinion and reasoning matches other case law. Often, cases align with other cases even though slightly different issues are being decided. You should check to see the way in which the court opinion you are researching and reading is similar or dissimilar in addressing the issues that you are dealing with. Essentially, you are checking to see consistency in court precedent.

VII. Sample case

> ### Sample Case - Breakdown per Questions
>
> *Lucy v. Zehmer*, 196 Va. 493; 84 S.E.2d 516 (1954)
>
> **1. Procedural History:** Supreme Court of Virginia decision. Lower court ruled that Plaintiffs failed to establish a right to specific performance and dismissed their claim (this is where the court erred).
>
> **2. Facts**
> - J.C. Lucy & W.O. Lucy (Plaintiffs) vs. A.H. Zehmer & W.O. Zehmer (Defendants). D's sold a lot of land to Lucy for $50,000 on Dec. 20, 1952. They were out drinking and at the bar, Zehmer drafted up a contract on back of a bar receipt specifying the land, the amount, and title satisfactory to buyer.
> - Defense – writing was prepared as a bluff, the whole matter was a joke, the writing was not delivered to Lucy, and made NO binding contract.
> - Defendant Zehmer had conflicting stories saying that he "was as high as Georgia pine" but testified about what was said and done. It is a fact that Zehmer was not so intoxicated that he did not know what he was doing. Evidence shows that he wrote two agreements, no mistakes in spelling and re-wrote it to get away from the "singular."
> - *Resemblance of a serious business offer – 40 minute discussion, Lucy's objection to just one signature (the ensuing re-writing), what to be included, provision of the examination of the title. Not until after the deal was done was there an semblance of a joking offer.*
> - Lucy's Defense, showed that he thought it was a legit contract, next day had brother put up ½ the money, day after that had an attorney examine the title.
>
> **3. Issue:** Did the contract represent a serious business transaction and a good faith sale and purchase of the farm?
>
> **4. Holding:** Yes. **Rule:** In contracts "we must look to the outward expression of a person as manifesting his intention rather than to his secret and unexpressed intention."
>
> **Reasoning**
> - No time prior to the execution had Zehmer indicated to Lucy by WORD, or ACT that he was not serious about selling the farm.
> - Only jesting was about paying $50,000 that night.
> - Good faith offer and good faith acceptance and delivery of a written contract.
> - Mutual assent is obviously a stipulation of a legit contract, however, the law imputes to a person an intention corresponding to the reasonable meaning of his words and acts...Judged by a reasonable standard (manifest and intention to agree).
> - It is immaterial what may be the real but unexpressed state of his mind....It is what is on the outside, implied that counts.
>
> **Disposition:** Reversed and remanded for judgment for specific performance....Requiring the D to perform the contract.

Now, I want to give you the specific examples that I was talking about in a court opinion—how to understand and analyze the case. This is a summary example of a case.

Lucy v. Zehmer, is one of the most famous cases U.S. law school students study. When you are reading this case, you are looking at the procedural history. This is a case from the Supreme Court of Virginia and on appeal from a lower court decision.

Facts: The case involved a sale of property. These two people were in a bar. They were very drunk and one person agreed to sell land to another person. He wrote a contract on the back of a restaurant bar receipt. The amount of the "contract" was $15,000 dollars. He specified the land, the amount to be paid, and defined the titles. The next day, buyer thought this was a contract and tried to proceed with the sale. The question becomes, is this actually a contract?

The defendant seller said, "I was just joking. This was a joke. I thought we were kidding. This wasn't the contract." The issue that the court is analyzing, as you would define it, is whether the "transaction" was a joke, which would not make this a binding contract. Another factor is that the seller said that he was so drunk that he could not understand what he was doing and should not be responsible for the contract, which is what "High as a Georgia Pine" means.

The question becomes for the court, is this a valid contract? Then, the court analyzes whether this situation resembled a serious offer. The two guys in the bar had a 40-minute discussion about what to do about this contract. In fact, the contract was written twice. The seller asked for changes in the contract, as did the buyer. The seller actually threw away one napkin, got another napkin, and changed the terms that the seller requested. The buyer asked for the wife also to sign it. The seller's wife was there as well. The seller changed the agreement to include the wife's signature. The next day the buyer had his brother give half the money and his lawyer examined the title of the land.

Issue: Did the contract represent a serious business transaction in a good sale on the purchase of the farm?

Holding: The court's holding is yes, it did because this was a contract. The court indicated that parties must look at the outward expression of the parties and their actions in making the contract. You cannot try to guess the intention of the parties or what is in someone's mind that they never stated. If the seller truly believed that this was a joke, he never said anything. In fact, he acted in a way that implied this was the contract. The court is holding that in contracts we have to look at the outward expression of a person as evidencing his intention rather than his secret unexpressed intention.

Court reasoning: Here is the reasoning, which states that at no time prior did the seller indicate to the buyer he was not serious. This was a good faith offer and acceptance delivering a written contract. The law will impose on a person the intention that corresponds to their words and their acts, which is judged by the reasonable person standard. When you are looking at the parties as to whether they intended to do something or not, look at what they said and what they did. That was the reasoning of the court. The court reversed the lower court's decision and sent it back to that court to enforce the contract.

This is how you breakdown or read a case. You are looking at how the case got to where it is. What caused the dispute? What is the plaintiff claiming? What is the end remedy? What does the plaintiff want from the court? What is the defendant saying in response? Then, you are looking at the court's ruling based on the arguments and the court's reasoning.

That is a basic outline on how you attack reading a case. Analyzing case law is an important part in your transactional work, because this is what is going to guide you in making decisions, advising your client, or drafting specific provisions of contracts.

第５部　ケースブリーフの作成
——Practices for Common Law Case Brief Writing

Next, we will talk about common law case briefing.

1. ケースブリーフの基礎
Case Brief Basics

What is a case brief? Essentially, a case brief is a summary of a court opinion. These are essentially your personal notes of the case. Case briefs should be no longer than one to two pages. The question is why should you write a case brief, especially for a transactional sort of work? It helps you focus on the important information in the case and summarize what you have researched and read. If you are summarizing the case in your own words, then you can truly understand the important issues of the case. If you can summarize it in your own words, then you will understand the court's holding, and you can explain the opinion to your client or supervisor. Making a case brief also helps you keep track of the legal research that you did and helps you to write the formal memos or briefs later on. Case briefs are extremely important in a process of helping you provide guidance to your client during business transactions or litigation.

> **Case Briefs -Basics**
>
> **What is a case brief?**
> - A case brief is the summary of a court opinion
> - They are your personal notes of the case
> - Case briefs should be no longer than **1-2 pages**
>
> **Why write a case brief?**
> - It helps you focus on the most important information in a case and summarize what you read
> - Summarizing the case facts, analysis and holdings in your own words helps you increase your understanding of the case and ability to explain it to others
> - It helps you to organize and keep track of research you did
> - It helps you to efficiently write memos and briefs using cases you briefed
>
> **Case briefs are extremely important in the process of helping you properly provide guidance to your client during their business transactions**

Again, going back to the Toyosu Market example, what happens if you write a contract, and maybe two years later there is a problem. You are writing these case briefs and the information you need from that case brief goes into your work file. Perhaps, you will need that information six months, one year, or two years later; or, you have worked on 15 other legal matters. That is why it is important to condense the information and keep it, because you will have it when you need it. And, you may not remember the specific details of each legal matter, for example, why you gave some opinion or why you made the contract in some way. There are good reasons to write case briefs.

2. ケースブリーフの書式と内容
Case Brief Format and Contents

Case Briefs - Format & Contents

1. **Case name, citation, court, year**
2. **Facts**
3. **Issues**
   - **Evidentiary facts** - what happened that caused plaintiff to sue defendant, including material facts (facts court used to decide case) and any helpful background facts.
   - **Procedural facts** - History of how the case got to the court that wrote opinion (usually an appellate court i.e. include what trial court held, grounds of appeal). Discuss questions court decided to resolve the claims.
   - *Write separate issue questions if court decided more than one issue. Use "under-did-when" formula discussed in <u>Lecture One</u>.*
4. **Holding**
   - Court's ruling on the issues. Brief should answer the questions posed in statement of issues. There should be a holding for each issue.
5. **Reasoning**
   - Rules that the court applied and the court's reasoning for how decision was reached. Show how court applied rules to facts.

Here is the basic format and contents of a case brief.

Case name, citation, court, year: The first thing is, of course, you have to do is you list the case name, the citation of where you can find it, the court, and the year of the decision.

Facts: Then briefly explain the facts of the case. You saw the last example that I gave you about the contract case. You summarize the important facts and ones that will help you immediately to remember the case. This is a good way to trigger memories.

Issues: Then, you have to remember is that cases do not only deal with one issue. Often, there are four or five issues involved in the case. Sometimes, it is jurisdiction and the contract provisions, and then remedies that are being sought, or there is a punitive damages issue. You should summarize and breakdown each issue.

And now going back to Lecture 1 where I talked about using the "under-did-when" formula to summarize issues.

Holding: This should be the court's holding related to each issue. Provide an answer to the questions posed in the issues section. Begin with a statement of "yes" or "no" to each issue question. For example, yes, the court found that the contract was valid and enforceable.

Reasoning: Finally, you want to list the court's reasoning for its holding. The reasoning is the rule of law that the court applied to the facts and why the court reached its decision. Again, this is all going back to the IRAC analysis. You are listing the issue, stating the holding, and explaining the court's reasoning and conclusion. You always apply the same structure of legal analysis.

3. ケースブリーフの例
Sample Case Brief

Sample Case Brief

Benn v. Thomas, 512 N.W.2d 537 (Iowa 1994)

Procedural History: Benn's executor sued defendant for Lora Benn's injuries and his death in 1989 after defendant's vehicle rear-ended the van in which decedent was a passenger. The estate requested a jury instruction based on the "eggshell plaintiff" rule, but the trial judge denied the request and gave a general charge instead. The jury found $17,000 in injuries for plaintiff but did not find defendant liable for his death. The court of appeals reversed the trial court's judgment and remanded the case based upon error in the jury instruction.

Facts: Benn died of a heart attack 6 days after suffering a bruised chest and fractured ankle in a car accident caused by defendant's negligence. Benn had a history of coronary disease and insulin-dependent diabetes. He had a heart attack in 1985 and was at risk of having another.

Issue: Is the eggshell plaintiff rule relevant in determining proximate cause and/or damages?

Rule: The "eggshell plaintiff" rule requires the defendant to take his plaintiff as he finds him, even if that means that the defendant must compensate the plaintiff for harm an ordinary person would not have suffered.

Analysis: Because the eggshell plaintiff rule rejects the limit of foreseeability that courts ordinarily require in the determination of proximate cause, the defendant can still be found liable for defendant's death in a case where his negligence causes the death, even if the death would not have occurred in an ordinary person.

Conclusion: The trial judge erred in not giving instruction on the "eggshell plaintiff" rule. Affirmed the court of appeals decision and remanded for a new trial.

This is a sample case brief and is bit shorter than the full case brief. This is a case called Benn v. Thomas, from the Iowa Supreme Court in 1994. The citation is 512 N.W.2d, which means that is the location where you would find the court opinion. The page number of the case is 537.

Procedural History: First, we are looking at the case procedural history. Benn's executor means the person who is representing a person who is deceased. Clearly, Benn has died and is suing the defendant for injuries resulting from a car accident in 1989, where the defendant's vehicle hit the back of the van in which Benn was a passenger. The plaintiff requested a jury instruction based on what we call the "eggshell plaintiff rule" in Tort law. However, the trial court denied the request and gave a general instruction on the law. The jury found in favor of plaintiff for $1,700 dollars in damages based on the injuries, but did not find the defendant liable for Benn's death. The court of appeals reversed the trial court judgment and remanded the case by sending it back down to the lower court for erring in giving the jury instructions. This case is on appeal to the Supreme Court.

The point is to explain the basic arguments and court procedure, including the court judgments to show and understand the history of the case in proceedings.

Facts: Then, you are looking at the facts of the case. The facts here are that the person died of a heart attack six days after suffering bruises and a fractured ankle in a car accident. The person suffered minor injuries in the car accident. The plaintiff had a history of heart disease and diabetes, and he had a heart attack a few years before the accident. He was always at risk of having another heart attack. This plaintiff had previous medical conditions, but the accident was fairly minor and plaintiff actually ended up dying as a result of his injuries. Those are the important facts and what you would need to remember.

Issue: The issue relates to a legal doctrine called the eggshell plaintiff. The idea of an eggshell plaintiff means a plaintiff who is sensitive in some way, usually having a pre-existing sensitive medical condition. The plaintiff can be injured easily in the same way that eggshells can break easily. The issue in this example is whether Benn was an eggshell plaintiff due to his previous medical condition to determine liability or damages in this case.

Rule: The rule in this example is that in a case involving an eggshell plaintiff, the defendant must take the plaintiff as he finds them, even if that means the defendant has to pay the plaintiff for harm an ordinary person would not have suffered. The idea is that, defendant is responsible for injuries to plaintiff from the car accident even though the defendant did not know or could not anticipate that Benn would actually die from a minor car accident because of a prior heart condition. Defendants are liable for damages to eggshell plaintiffs even though some other medical condition may have contributed to the injury. That is the rule of law that the court cited.

Analysis: In the analysis section, discuss the court's application of the rules to the facts. The analysis as explained above is that courts will find the defendant responsible for injuries to eggshell plaintiffs, even in the cases where death would not have occurred to the normal person. That is the analysis in this situation because of the eggshell plaintiff rule of law. Even though know one would ever expect that a person would die from minor injuries in a car accident, courts will find the defendant responsible for that because you take your victim, so to speak, as you find them.

Conclusion: Finally, state the conclusion. In this example, you write that the trial court erred in not giving the proper jury instruction regarding the eggshell plaintiff rule. The Supreme Court affirmed the court of appeals decision and remanded the case down to the lower court for the new trial.

The purpose of this case brief is to summarize the key points of the court opinion. Here, you have a one-page overview of a case that you can use.
Again, just to reiterate these are the ways of writing in common law practice that lawyers always do throughout their legal practice. Writing case briefs and memos are not only reserved for junior lawyers. Rather, senior lawyers also prepare such writings as part of their everyday practice. For instance,

if I am trying to advise a client during a conference call and I had this case brief in front of me, it is easy for me to look at this brief and refer to it during the call. These summaries are useful in your law practice.

Lecture 3

依頼者に対して提示する文書の作成において求められるライティングコミュニケーションスキルの基礎と応用

◆

Professional Lawyering Skills for Written Communications with Clients

> 弁護士が依頼者とのやり取りを英文で行う際のライティングコミュニケーションスキルを習得することを目的として，基礎から応用までを例を挙げながら具体的に解説します。

Welcome to Lecture Three of the six-past lecture series, the "Legal Writing and Professional Lawyering Skills in Common Law Practice." Tonight during lecture three we will discuss professional lawyering skills for written communications with clients. Communications with clients is probably one of the most important parts of your job as an attorney. And, communicating with clients in English, I think, is probably one of the largest challenges, and I hope that tonight is an interesting lecture for you.

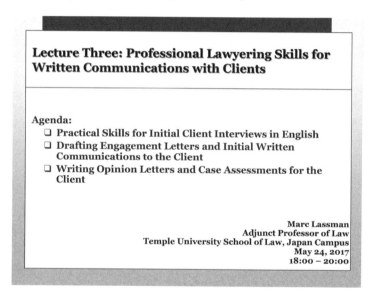

Tonight on the agenda we will talk about three main topics: Practical skills for initial client interviews in English, drafting engagement letters and initial written communications to the client, and writing opinion letters and case assessments for the client. Much of what I will talk about tonight will highlight the fact that in most situations when you are dealing with foreign clients or foreign lawyers, their expectations might be a bit different than what you are used to in terms of the amount of communication or the types of communication. The lawyers might have different ideas of how much communication should be between you and them or with the clients.

Lecture 3 Professional Lawyering Skills for Written Communications with Clients

第1部　英語で初回法律相談を実施する際の実践的スキル
——Practical Skills for Initial Client Interviews in English

The first subject we will discuss tonight is practical skills for initial client interviews in English.

1. 到達点と目的
Goals & Purposes

For initial client interviews, the first matter to consider is your goals and purpose for the interview. Essentially, there are six goals and purposes that you are going to think about during that interview.

The first one is to know the client and assess credibility. When first meeting a client, you need to understand their needs and problems. Assessing credibility means you should have an idea of how much information your client is willing to share with you or do you need to go deeper by asking more questions to obtain all of the information. You want to assess how open your client is being towards you, which will inform you as to whether you have all of the facts.

The next important goal is to understand the client's goals and priorities. This is about what the client wants and what is the problem, which helps your strategy for the legal matter or case. The third is to obtain the facts. This is your opportunity to talk to the client for the first time and to understand what is happening, again what the client wants, and what the client would like to see as an outcome and there are several strategies that I will offer tonight on how to do that in the most effective way. The next goal is building trust. You are assessing the potential client and they are also assessing you. As the attorney, you are the person who may represent them. Building trust with the client, therefore, is important in order for the client to feel that you can handle their business.

If applicable, during the first interview you should explain the fee arrangements. Some legal practitioners here are working for law firms and working as in-house counsel, and perhaps the situation of explaining fee arrangements is not a part of your regular business. But, if you are in charge of such situations, it is important to do so in the beginning of the representation. Finally, you will offer a preliminary assessment of the problem and define the next steps.

2. 事情聴取のプロセス
Interview Process

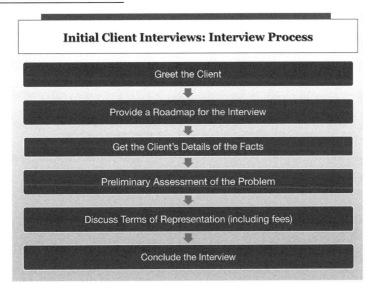

The initial interview goes through a process, and we will talk about each step more specifically. The first step is greeting the client. Then, you will provide a roadmap for the interview by informing the client of what will happen in the interview, when it will happen, and how long it will take. The next parts are probably the most important of your interview, which is obtaining the client's details of the facts, understanding the problem and the client's needs. Then, you give a preliminary assessment of the problem based on your interview. Again, only if applicable under the circumstances, you discuss terms of representation. And, finally, conclude the interview.

I. Greet the Client

Interview Process: Greeting the Client

Goal: Motivate the Client's Participation – develop a connection so the client can talk freely

- ❖ Clients may hesitate to talk because topics are sensitive or difficult
- ❑ How to build a connection:

Technique	Sample Language
✓ Start with casual conversation to put the client at ease before moving on to more specific topics	➤ Sample language for casual conversations: • The weather has been (hot/cold/rainy) recently hasn't it? • Was the traffic bad getting here? • How was your weekend/holiday?
✓ Use active listening techniques: ○ good eye contact ○ head nodding ○ use phrases of reassurance	➤ Sample phrases of reassurance: • I understand • Of course • You make a good point

First we will talk about greeting the client. Your goal in this initial greeting of the client is to motivate the client's participation. You want to develop a connection so that the client feels like they can talk freely. Clients sometimes will hesitate to talk about topics that are sensitive or difficult. Particurarly, if they think there is a problem or a mistake is made, you need to at the outset, create an environment where the client feels comfortable to talk to you.

The first technique that I want to suggest is to start with casual conversation to put the client at ease before you start moving on to more specific topics. When I say casual conversation, I am talking about topics, such as the weather or weekend activities—basic small talk. You want to have the client relax and feel calm because you may not know their feeling or mindset, for example, if they are excited or angry.

The second technique is to do "active listening." When talking to the client, make good eye contact and pay attention by head nodding using phrases of reassurance. And, when I say phrases of reassurance, I mean saying, for example, "I understand," "of course," or "that's a good point." You are confirming what the client is saying and showing understanding. Reassurance techniques are important because you want the client to talk and tell their story. Those are the techniques that are commonly used to build connections initially with clients during the interview process.

II. Provide a Roadmap of the Interview

Interview Process: Provide a Roadmap of the Interview

Goal: Outline for the client how you intend to conduct the interview

- Explain how long the interview will likely last
- Explain your goals (i.e. that you will be asking questions initially and taking notes)
- Explain when the client will be able to ask questions
- **Emphasize that what the client says during the interview will remain confidential (ABA Model Rules of Conduct 1.6)**
- Explain that you will discuss your preliminarily assessment at the end of the interview and suggest potential options/solutions
- Explain that you will discuss fee arrangements at the end of the interview (if applicable)

Next, after small talk, provide a roadmap of the interview. Your goal is, at this point, to outline the way in which you intend to conduct the interview. Explaining how long the interview will last by saying, "we'll probably be here for about 30 minutes." Explain the goals and mention that you will ask questions and take notes so the client feels that you are paying attention. Let the client know when they can ask questions. For example, the client sits down, and you say,

"All right, initially we'll be here for about a half an hour, and I just need to hear what the situation is and why you're here. I'll take notes during this time and first I want to hear from you. After you tell me everything, then if you have some questions for me, you can ask."

One important point is to emphasize to the client that what they say during the interview will remain confidential. The most basic tenant as a U.S. lawyer is confidentiality, lawyer-client confidentiality. The American Bar Association is the largest voluntary bar association in the U.S., and it created the Model Rules of Professional Conduct for U.S. lawyers. Model Rule 1.6 cited is regarding the lawyer-client confidentiality rule. Explaining the confidentiality rule to the client also helps the client feel more comfortable to talk freely. Finally, explain to the client that you will provide a preliminary assessment at the end of the interview, and suggest some potential options or solutions based on what you discussed initially.

III. Getting the Client's Details of the Facts

Interview Process: Getting the Client's Facts (1)

Getting Started: Ask the client for a general description of the transaction/event that brought them to you and the remedy they desire

- **Use only open-ended questions at this point**
    - <u>Examples of open-ended questions</u>: How can I help you?/Can you tell me what happened?/ Tell me what the problem is?/ What would you like to have done about it?/ What would you like to see happen?
- **Let the client tell the story in their own words – get a chronological step-by-step description of the situation**
    - Use open-ended questions like "What happened next?"/ "and then what?"
- **When the client has finished their initial description summarize your understanding of the situation**
    - <u>Useful expressions</u>: To summarize, what happened was…/ From what I understand, you are saying that… / Am I correct that…

In this initial phase of the client interview, you want the client to explain their purpose for coming to consult with you. Important information the client should give is to explain the issue, the purpose, what the client would like from you as the lawyer, and the desired outcome. To obtain this information from the client, you should use "open-ended" questions. These types of questions are designed to allow the client to talk.

For example, questions such as: "How can I help you?" "Can you tell me what happened?" "Tell me what the problem is?" "What is your goal here?" "What is your main priority?" "What is most important to you?" "What would you like to have done about it?" "What would you like to see happen?"

These are open-ended questions that allow the client to talk. Your goal as the lawyer, at this point, is to listen to what the client wants and what is important to the client. If the attorney asks too many questions at this point, you will not obtain the necessary information from the client. The most important point is to let the client tell their story without interruption. Another key point of the initial interview is to let the client explain the issue in their own words. You want to ask questions that elicit the client to give a chronological and step-by-step description of the situation.

For example, you would ask questions such as, "Okay, what happened next?" "And then what?" to keep the conversation going and to get information. After the client finishes giving their initial description of the issue, you should then give your summary of the situation to make sure that your understanding is correct. The examples in the slide are useful expressions to summarize information: "What happened was...," "From what I understand, what you are saying is...," or "Am I correct that..." These are expressions to check your understanding of what the client has told you.

> **Interview Process: Getting the Client's Facts (2)**
>
> **Getting the details**: After hearing the initial explanation from the client, you must fill in the necessary details required to assess the matter
> - ❖ You will need to use **narrow or closed questions** to get the specific details you require for your work
>   1) **Narrow questions** – select specific aspects of the topic (ex: What was the employee compensation offered?/Who was involved in the initial negotiations?)
>   2) **Closed questions** – Yes/No questions (ex: Did the company get patent approval yet?/ Was the company able to get start-up funding?)
>   - *Note*: Closed questions can sometimes be "leading questions," which means they potentially suggest an answer (ex: You were not involved in the initial negotiations were you?)
> - ❖ **Leading questions should only be used to confirm information the client has already given you or to get information the client may be hesitant to give**

After you learn the basic story from the client and summarize your understanding, you next should get specific details of the issue. In this situation, using "narrow or closed" questions helps you obtain the information necessary to make a preliminary assessment. The narrow questions in the slide are examples to elicit detailed information from the client: "What was the employee compensation offered?" or "Who is involved in the initial investigations or the initial negotiations?"

There are also closed or leading questions, which are basically "yes" or "no" questions to control the information you want clarified. For example, "Did the company get patent approval yet?" The client will give a yes or no answer. "Was the company able to get start-up funding?" Yes or no. Closed questions are useful when trying to determine specific facts. "You were not involved in the initial negotiations, were you?" That question suggests an answer. "You weren't involved in the initial negotiations, were you?" The answer is no or yes. Leading questions should only be used when you are trying to confirm information that the client has already given you or to get information that the client may be hesitant to give you.

The initial interview progresses by beginning with you asking open-ended questions, and then moving to more narrow questions to get additional details, and finally asking closed questions to confirm information.

Interview Process: Getting the Client's Facts
Use Questioning Techniques Appropriate for your Purpose

Type of Question	Purposes	Examples
Open-ended	<ul><li>Allows the client to talk openly and freely</li><li>Gets information in the client's own words</li><li>Best for initial portions of interview</li></ul>	<ul><li>Tell me why you are here?</li><li>What happened (next)?</li><li>What would you like to see happen in this situation?</li></ul>
Narrow	<ul><li>Allows you to get more specific information on an important topic</li><li>Best when you are trying to clarify details of what the client told you initially</li></ul>	<ul><li>What was the company valued at?</li><li>Who was at the initial meeting?</li><li>When did the bank make the loan?</li></ul>
Closed/leading	<ul><li>Yes/No questions that may sometimes suggest an answer – gives lawyer more control over questioning</li><li>Used only for confirming information the client already gave you or may be reluctant to give you</li></ul>	<ul><li>Did the bank agree to extend the deadline?</li><li>Did you research the property title?</li><li>You had difficulty finding funding for the project didn't you? (ex. of area of possible client reluctance)</li></ul>

To summarize, during the interview process use question techniques that are appropriate for your purpose. Open-ended questions are useful when your purpose during the interview is to allow the client to talk freely and to get information in your client's own words. Then you move to narrow questions when trying to get more specific information on an important topic. Finally, move towards closed or leading questions, which are yes or no questions that give you more control over the questioning when you need specific details. Please remember to use these types of questions and to think about your purpose at that point of the interview and try to use the appropriate questions.

IV. Preliminary Assessment of the Problem

> ### Interview Process: Preliminary Assessment of the Problem
>
> **Develop and Verify Theories**
> - Based on the information obtained in the initial portion of the interview, the lawyer can begin to create theories supporting possible legal actions
> - Consider all plausible claims or courses of action and then obtain the relevant information that might support or negate the claim/course of action from the client/witness
> - Pursue all questions that occurred to you while the client/witness was going through their overview, and obtain greater detail on relevant facts
> - Be clear about what the client wants when developing legal options, for example:
>   1) are they concerned with their reputation
>   2) continuing a future business relationship
>   3) protecting a specific interest they have in certain property like the ability to remain as a tenant after a sale

At this point in the initial interview, you want to give a preliminary assessment of the problem. During this time, you should develop and verify theories of the case or matter. For example, if dealing with a contract matter, you want to know the terms, the problem, and applicable law. Based on the information in the initial portion of the interview you received, you will think about creating theories to support possible legal actions or next steps.

Points to consider are the possible claims or courses of action, and obtaining the relevant information from your client that would either support or negate the claim or course of action. I say this because you will not get all information from your client during the first interview or the first two times you talk to your client. As the case or matter goes on, you will need to follow up with your client about the additional information you may need. Therefore, during this initial interview you should think about trying to get as much information as possible to limit the number of times you have to go back to your client for more information or requests. Finally, you should

be clear about what the client wants when you are developing the legal options. Here are some examples:
1. You are talking to your client and their biggest concern may be about their reputation. A business deal happened and if there is a problem that becomes public, then others in the market will begin to have a negative impression. As their attorney, you are thinking about next steps and about the most important issues or potential issues to the client.
2. Your client wants to continue a future business relationship with another party. The most important issue to the client is ensuring that they maintain a good relationship, or during negotiations for a contract, the client wants to be tough but also leave a good relationship with the party to have future negotiations.
3. The client has a specific interest, such as selling some property but also wanting to remain as a tenant. It is essential that during that initial interview, you understand the client's needs and priorities; and only then can you start to develop your legal options to meet such priorities.

V. Conclude the Interview

Interview Process: Concluding the Interview

- Give the client a brief summary of the law and/or legal conclusions you have come to that relate to the issues that you have spoken about during the interview
- **Be clear that what you are giving is a <u>preliminary assessment</u> based on what you have been told**
    - **Sample language**: Preliminarily, I believe that… / What I can say at this point is… / Based on what you have told me, I think that…however we still need to…
- Advise the client what further research or investigation you will need to do prior to giving a final opinion or taking further action
    - **Sample language**: Before I can give a final opinion, we will need to… / As a next step, we will have to…
- **Tell the client what you will do next/ Confirm what the client should do (if applicable)/Tell the client when your next contact will be**

Finally, we will discuss concluding the interview. You have gone through this process and now you want to end the interview. At the end of the interview, you want to give the client a brief summary of the law or legal conclusions regarding the issues discussed. Be clear that you are only giving a preliminary assessment based on the client's explanations. Why is this important? Often, clients will withhold information or do not tell you everything. Sometimes the clients do not know all the relevant information at the initial interview.

Sample language in English that you can use to explain this point is, "Preliminarily, I believe that...," "What I can say at this point is...," "Based on what you've told me I think that...however, we still need to...." These are expressions that you can use to reflect the fact that you have only received a certain portion of the information. You are explaining to the client or whoever is in front of you, the other lawyer, that the assessment is based on limited information that might change later, which could completely change your opinion or decision on what to do next.

Also, it is important to explain your next steps as the attorney to the client. For example, you may need to conduct further research or investigation prior to giving a final opinion. You may need to review other documents or talk with other people before you can develop a final opinion. Useful language is, "Before I can give a final opinion, we will need to...," "As a next step, we will have to..." These are good expressions for you to use.

Finally, when concluding the interview, tell the client what you will do next. Confirm what the client should do if anything, and always tell your client when your next contact will be. For example, "Okay we'll be back in touch in two weeks. I'm going to research the property title. You should get a copy of the sales agreement and provide it to us."

One of the big mistakes lawyers can make is not doing that and if clients do not hear from you, or if they do not have a clear idea of when you are going to communicate with them next, that is an issue that creates mistrust.

Therefore, let them know, "Listen. We're going to need to do... (this). We're going to need to do this research but it generally takes a few weeks so we'll be back in touch at the end of the month."

第 2 部　委任契約書の作成と依頼者との最初の文書でのやり取り —— Drafting Engagement Letters and Initial Written Communications to the Client

Next, we are going to discuss drafting engagement letters and initial written communications to the client. Specifically, we are talking about engagement letters or retainer letters as we call them, and initial written communications to the client.

1. 委任契約書とは何か？
What is an Engagement Letter?

What is an Engagement Letter?

*An **Engagement Letter** (also called a **"Retainer Agreement"**) is a written document between the lawyer and client that sets forth the duties of the law firm, the lawyer, and the client*

- The letter identifies what the lawyer will—and won't—do for the client
- Always give the client the opportunity to think about the engagement letter before signing
- **In-House Counsel (you are the client)**: your external counsel will create an engagement letter when you hire them to handle a legal matter

- The engagement letter should also:
  - **Identify** the nature of the legal issue (e.g., merger negotiations with Company X –or– purchase of Disneyland)
  - **Name** the expected adverse or related parties
  - **Set forth** important dates if they are a trigger for a deadline (like a Statute of Limitations or a required action under Corporate By-laws)
  - **Define** the attorney-client relationship - when it begins and ends, what happens during the process, and receiving and storing documents/information
  - **Describe** fees (e.g., an hourly rate, a flat fee, a contingent fee), what other expenses will be paid by the client, provide an estimate of the fees, and how fee disputes will be settled
  - **Outline** the obligations of both the client and the lawyer

What is an engagement letter? Often this document also is called a retainer agreement. Engagement letters are written documents between the lawyer and the client that sets forth the duties of the law firm, the lawyer and the client. The engagement letter will identify the scope of the lawyer's representation, including what the lawyer will and will not do. It is essentially the formal acknowledgement that you will represent the client.

If you are an in-house counsel and hire external or outside counsel, often you will receive engagement letters from the outside counsel as well. Not only do you prepare engagement letters for your clients, but you also may receive engagement letters from outside counsel.

The engagement letter should always identify the nature of the legal issue. For example, merger negotiations with Company X or purchase of Disneyland, depending on whatever it is that you are handling. The letter should name the expected related or adverse parties. In addition, the engagement letter should set forth important dates, such as the time limit of the lawyer's representation, deadlines or some important dates in which action is required, or statutes of limitation, meaning if you only have a certain amount of time under the law to do something. Make sure those dates are in the engagement letter because you can avoid problems later with misunderstandings or miscommunications on the scope of the representation.

A crucial part of the engagement letter is to define the attorney-client relationship, including the time period, the specific terms of the services to be provided, a document retention policy, and fees.

2. 委任契約書はどうして重要なのか？
Why is an Engagement Letter Important?

> **Why is an Engagement Letter Important?**
>
> - ❖ **THE ABA STANDING COMMITTEE on Lawyers' Professional Liability** released data on legal malpractice claims from 2008 to 2011, reporting that nearly <u>16 percent of all claims against attorneys had been caused by poor client communications</u>
>
> - ❖ To avoid such problems, lawyers should start their relationship with a client by having a thorough discussion about the goals and terms of the engagement and the responsibilities of the attorney and client
>
> - ❖ The *ABA Model Rules of Professional Conduct* "prefer" written engagement letters and require written agreements where a contingency fee is permitted (Rule 1.5(c)) or where the fee charged may be considered entering into a business transaction with a client (Rule 1.8(a))
>
> - ❖ It is "desirable" for an attorney to provide the client with a memorandum or statement containing "the general nature of the legal services to be provided, the basis, rate or total amount of the fee and whether and to what extent the client will be responsible for any costs, expenses or disbursements in the course of the representation" (Rule 1.5(c), Comments Section)

Why is an engagement letter so important? The American Bar Association (ABA) has a standing committee on lawyer's professional liability, which means when lawyers are defending themselves against claims from clients and other sources. The ABA released data on claims against lawyers from clients for three years between 2008 and 2011, and nearly 16 percent of all claims against lawyers by clients came from poor client communications.

The source of a majority of the claims that lawyers had to deal with from clients was based on poor communications. And, that is why it is important to have these engagement letters upfront. For foreign lawyers that you are dealing with, that is the environment that they work in. When American lawyers are writing engagement letters or processing the case, the fact that clients can make claims against lawyers and that they could be held responsible is something that lawyers are always thinking about.

The ABA committee says, to avoid such problems, lawyers should start their relationship with a client by having a thorough discussion about the goals and terms of the arrangement and the responsibilities of the lawyers and clients. Based on the ABA Model Rules of Professional Conduct, written engagement or retainer letters are preferred for basic agreements. Written agreements are required if the legal matter involves contingency fees, meaning the lawyer would get a certain percentage of any recovery or where a fee might be charged to enter into a business transaction. The Model Rules also state that for engagement letters, you should explain the general nature of the legal services to be provided, the basis, the rate and total amount of the fee, and to what extent the client would be responsible for costs or expenses. In general, this is why engagement letters are important.

3. 委任契約書の要点
Essentials of an Engagement Letter

Essentials of an Engagement Letter: Identify the Client

- The engagement letter should 1) identify the client whose interests are being represented and 2) define those *whose interests are not being represented by the attorney*
  - In representing a business organization, take care to explain to the directors and staff that the *organization is the attorney's client* especially where the interests of the organization may not be aligned with those of the directors, staff or outside consultants
    - i.e., the attorney represents the company during a sale and not the CEO personally, who may benefit individually from the sale
    - i.e., the company hired an outside accounting firm to value the company being bought

Sample Language:

The purpose of this letter is to confirm, based on our conversation of May 1, 2017, that the Tanaka Law Firm will represent Tokyo Chemical Inc. in its purchase of Ohio Chemical Industries. Our representation will extend solely to Tokyo Chemical Inc. during the sale/purchase process, and not to any Directors, employees or any other staff of Tokyo Chemical Inc., in their individual capacity or any independent contractors or consultants hired during the sale/purchase process.

I. Identify the Client

Now, we are going to talk about the essentials of these engagement letters. What is essential in the engagement letter is to identify the client. You want to make clear in this letter who your client is and, more importantly, define who your client is not. Why is that important for people doing transactional work? Because you are usually representing corporations. If you are representing a business organization like a corporation, your client is the corporation. It might not be the individual CEO or the individual staff member or, for instance, if they hire outside consultants. Therefore, you have to make it clear in your initial engagement letter that you are representing the company and not any individuals.

For instance, if a company is being sold, there is a possibility that the CEO will personally benefit from the sale; however, the CEO might not be your client. You have to make it clear that you are representing the company in the sale and not the CEO personally. Another example would be if you are selling companies or merging, that company might hire an outside accounting firm to value the company. Perhaps there is some outside expert that the company has hired that will also be part of the sale process, but you are not representing that outside company. Make sure that you identify who you are representing and identify who you are not representing.

Here is some sample language to express this point.
> "The purpose of this letter is to confirm, based on our conversation of May 1, 2017, that the Tanaka Law Firm will represent Tokyo Chemical in its purchase of Ohio Chemical Industries. Our representation will extend solely to Tokyo Chemical during the sale/purchase process and not to any directors, employees or any other staff of Tokyo Chemical in their individual capacity or any independent contractors or consultants hired during the sale/purchase process."

The important language here is, "...in their individual capacity." We are not representing any directors, employees, or other staff in their individual capacity, which is an expression to use when you are trying to refer to someone personally. If you are saying, we are representing the company, but we are not representing the president personally, the expression that you use is, "...in their individual capacity."

II. Define the Scope of Representation

> ### Essentials of an Engagement Letter: Define the Scope of Representation
>
> - The letter should contain a plainly worded provision setting forth the scope of the services to be performed by the attorney
> - If the intended engagement does not include certain activities, the engagement letter should say so
>   - Ex: representation in any court proceedings
> - An engagement letter with a loosely defined scope of the work included can expose an attorney to potential liability outside the range of services he/she intended to perform
> - If the ongoing representation expands beyond its original scope, a simple amendment to the original letter/agreement is acceptable
>
> **Sample Language**:
>
> *We will provide legal services related to the negotiation, due diligence, asset and stock purchase, and final sale agreement for the sale of Ohio Chemical Industries to Tokyo Chemical Inc. Our services will not extend to representation in a court of law in any potential future legal proceedings that may occur related to this sale.*

The next important aspect is to define the scope of representation. You should be clear as to what your responsibilities are and what they are not. If you are not extending your representation to a specific area, you should be clear about this point in your initial engagement letter. For instance, it should be plainly worded as shown in the sample language.

"We will provide legal services related to the negotiation, due diligence, asset and stock purchase, and final sale agreement for the sale of Ohio Chemical Industries to Tokyo Inc. Our services *will not* extend to representation in a court of law in any potential legal proceedings that may occur related to this sale."

A good expression is, "...services will not extend to..." If you are in a situation where you will represent the client during the negotiation, drafting, and closing process of the deal; however, you will not represent them if there is a court proceeding. You must put that language in the initial document.

When defining the scope, use clear language rather than general or vague language because being unclear can expose an attorney to potential liability outside the range of their services offered. A mistake that people make is thinking that if we write a general or vague explanation of the services, then the attorney will get more work. This type of strategy is a way of trying to get more work, but you also may be open to potential claims in what you are saying you will do. And, if you have ongoing representation and your representation expands beyond the original scope, you can amend or supplement the letter to reflect the new or ongoing services.

III. Define Terms of Payment

Essentials of an Engagement Letter: Define Terms of Payment

- ❖ The engagement letter must also set forth the monetary terms of payment and should include the frequency of payment, and a definition of the expenses for which the client will be responsible

- ❖ If it is anticipated that the compensation detailed in the engagement letter will change during the representation, the attorney should advise the client in the engagement letter of these potential circumstances

Sample Language:

Attached for your use is information on our billing and reporting procedures. Our fee is [insert dollars/yen per hour] for services performed by lawyers of this firm and [insert dollars/yen per hour] for services performed by our non-lawyer staff. You also will be billed for any expenses incurred on your behalf. Our office will bill you approximately monthly depending upon the amount of work that was done on your file during that period of time. Our office will advise you before undertaking any procedures that will substantially increase the amount of fees.

Be clear to define terms of payment, such as your hourly billable rate. It is also important to explain any expenses. If the client will be responsible for certain expenses, such as closing fees, then your engagement letter should include that information. Good sample language here is, "You will be billed for any expenses incurred on your behalf." That is a very common expression that you would use to describe expenses.

IV. Define Staff Representation

Essentials of an Engagement Letter: Define Staff Representation	
❖ Let the client know which attorneys will represent them ❖ The engagement letter should identify the attorneys the initial drafter anticipates will be involved, and should reserve the right to staff appropriately the work to best represent the client	**Sample Language:** *Your primary contact for this matter will be [insert lawyer's name]. If you have any questions about your case, you should contact him/her directly. Depending on the needs during our representation, our law firm may also assign other appropriate lawyers or staff to this case to carry out specified duties.*

Next, you need to define staff representation. The letter should explain who will be the primary contact for the client, who is the lawyer handling the case. The general sample language that you use in this situation is, "Your primary contact for this matter will be [insert the lawyer's name]." You might use other staff members or other lawyers depending on the matter, and therefore, you want to have a statement regarding other staff in the engagement letter as well. For instance, "Depending on the needs of our representation, our law firm may also assign other appropriate lawyers or staff to this case to carry out specified duties." You want to make sure that the client knows that others may work on the matter depending on what needs to be done.

V. Define Client Communication and Terms of Document/File Retention

Essentials of an Engagement Letter:
Define Client Communication and Terms of Document/File Retention

CLIENT COMMUNICATIONS	Sample Language:
❖ The engagement letter should state the frequency and way in which the attorney will give status updates to the client **DOCUMENT AND FILE RETENTION** ❖ The engagement letter should direct the client to safeguard documents ❖ Few jurisdictions give precise guidelines on how long an attorney must maintain client files ❖ The engagement letter should outline the attorney's document retention policy	We will send you documents, correspondence, and other information throughout the case. These copies will be your file copies. <u>Please retain them.</u> We also will keep the information in a file in our office, which will be our file. When we have completed all the legal work necessary for your case, we will close our file and return original documents to you. We will then store the file for approximately (**insert number of years**) years. We will destroy the file after that period of time unless you instruct us in writing now to keep your file longer.

You should define client communications, meaning explain how often and the manner in which you will communicate with them. Also, the engagement letter should set forth your document and file retention policies. In the U.S., some states will give specific guidelines for the period that an attorney is required to retain files. Most law firms have an internal policy as to how long they keep files. Sample language is, "Please retain them," which is a good expression to tell the client to keep their files.

In the engagement letter, you should include language about what will happen to the files and documents after concluding the legal work on the case. For example, "...we will close our file and return original documents to you and we will store documents for approximately [insert number of years]

years." You are also explaining that you will destroy the file after a certain period unless stated otherwise. If the client wants you to keep the files or documents for a longer period, they should inform you in writing.

VI. Define Obligations of Lawyers and Client

Essentials of an Engagement Letter: Define Obligations of Lawyer and Client

❖ The letter can outline the obligations of both the <u>client</u> and the <u>lawyer</u> (Optional) **For example:** o The **lawyer** can agree promptly to return all phone calls within 24 hours, correspond on a regular basis about the progress of the case, and provide court decisions promptly o The **client** may agree promptly to return all phone calls, respond to all correspondence, cooperate with the lawyer, meet with the lawyer when requested, and advise the lawyer of any changes in his/her situation	**Sample Language:** *Tanaka Law Firm agrees promptly to return all phone calls within 24 hours, correspond on a regular basis about the progress of the case, and provide all relevant documents and court decisions promptly. Tokyo Chemical Inc. agrees promptly to return all phone calls, respond to all correspondence, cooperate with the lawyers, meet with the lawyers when requested, and advise the lawyers of any changes in their situation.*

This is optional, but the engagement letter can also define other activities that the lawyer will do, such as the lawyer agreeing to return all phone calls within 24 hours and correspond on a regular basis. This is something that some law firms like to include. You can also give terms about the client's responsibilities. Language in this situation would be that the client agrees "to return all phone calls, respond to all correspondence, cooperate with the lawyer, meet with the lawyer when requested and advise the lawyer of any changes in his or her situation." In the engagement letter, you can put language in there explaining the lawyer's tasks and making sure that the client is diligent in their cooperation with the lawyer during the case.

VII. Discuss Potential Conflicts of Interest

Essentials of an Engagement Letter: Discuss Potential Conflicts of Interest	
❖ If it is apparent that an actual or potential conflict of interest exists, the manner in which the conflict is being handled should be set forth in the engagement letter	**Sample Language**: As discussed during our meeting on May 24, 2017, Tanaka Law Firm represented Ohio Chemical Company 15 years ago during a minor labor matter. The firm has not represented Ohio Chemical since that time and will not undertake any legal representation of them currently or in the future. The attorney who represented Ohio Chemical at the time is no longer with Tanaka Law Firm, and **will have no contact** with or involvement in our current representation of Tokyo Chemical Inc.

There may be times when doing your initial intake of the legal matter that there is a potential conflict of interest. If there are potential conflicts of interests, you should put that in the engagement letter to describe the conflict and then the manner in which you will handle the issue. Here is an example. I am assuming that you represent Tokyo Chemical during a purchase of Ohio Chemical. You realize that, 15 years ago, you handled some legal work for Ohio Chemical. There may be a potential conflict of interest, but you never represented them again and will never do so in the future. In the engagement letter, the sample language to explain this potential conflict is:

"As discussed during our meeting on May 24, 2017, Tanaka Law Firm represented Ohio Chemical 15 years ago during a minor labor matter. The firm has not represented Ohio Chemical since that time and will not undertake any legal representation of them currently or in the future. The attorney who represented Ohio Chemical at the time is no longer with the Tanaka Law Firm and will have no contact with or in-

volvement in our current representation of Tokyo Chemical."
The point here is, if there is a potential conflict of interest, make sure in your engagement letter that you describe potential conflicts and explain why there is no problem in the representation.

4. 委任契約書・リテイナー条項の例
Sample Engagement Letter/Retainer Agreement

Sample Engagement Letter/Retainer Agreement: New Client

ENGAGEMENT LETTER AND FEE ARRANGEMENT (Date)

Dear (Name):

The purpose of this letter is to confirm, based on our conversation of May 1, 2017, that the Tanaka Law Firm will represent Tokyo Chemical Inc. in its purchase of Ohio Chemical Industries. Our representation will extend solely to Tokyo Chemical Inc. during the sale/purchase process, and not to any Directors, employees or any other staff of Tokyo Chemical Inc. in their individual capacities, or any independent contractors or consultants hired during the sale/purchase process.

We will provide legal services related to the negotiation, due diligence, asset and stock purchase, and final sales agreement for the sale of Ohio Chemical Industries to Tokyo Chemical Inc. Our services will not extend to representation of Tokyo Chemical Inc. in a court of law in any potential future legal proceedings that may occur related to this sale.

Attached for your use is information on our billing and reporting procedures. Our fee is [insert dollars/yen per hour] for services performed by lawyers of this firm and [insert dollars/yen per hour] for services performed by our non-lawyer staff. You also will be billed for any expenses incurred on your behalf. Our office will bill you approximately monthly depending upon the amount of work that was done on your file during that period of time. Our office will advise you before undertaking any procedures that substantially will increase the amount of fees....

Finally, we will discuss two sample engagement letters in this presentation. The first is for a new client and the second is for the same client, but for a new legal matter.

In the new client engagement letter, the example shows the important phrases that you should include. "The purpose of this letter is to confirm, based on our conversation of May 1, that [you will be represent them]..." You are confirming the agreement to represent the client. Then describe the subject of the representation, such as, "...we will represent Tokyo Chemical

Lecture 3 Professional Lawyering Skills for Written Communications with Clients

in its purchase of Ohio Chemical Industries."

Next, you are defining the scope. "Our representation will extend solely to...." In this agreement, you are identifying the client and the nature of the representation. This is the language we were discussing previously but I will highlight certain language, such as, "We will provide legal services related to...." That is how you introduce the scope of work, the legal services you will provide and a description of the work you will do. For example, "...the negotiation due diligence, asset, and stock purchase and final sales agreement for the sale of Ohio Chemical Industries to Tokyo Chemical. Our services will not extend to..." This is the situation again where you are defining what you will do and what you will not do. If there is legal work that you will not perform, this is where you list it. "Our services will not extend to representation of Tokyo Chemical in a court of law in any potential legal proceedings that may occur related to this sale...."

Here, we are talking about fees. "[A]ttached for your use is information on our billing and reporting procedures..." Explain the billing procedures and then attach them to the engagement letter. In addition, here is the language that you use describing the hourly rates for the lawyers and staff working on the case, and how often the client will be billed.

> **Sample Engagement Letter/Retainer Agreement: New Client (cont'd)**
>
> **ENGAGEMENT LETTER AND FEE ARRANGEMENT** (Date)
>
> ....Your primary contact for this matter will be [insert lawyer's name]. If you have any questions about your case, you should contact him/her directly. Depending on the needs during our representation, <u>our law firm may also assign other appropriate lawyers or staff</u> to this case to carry out specified duties.
>
> We will send you documents, correspondence, and other information throughout the case. These copies will be your file copies. Please retain them. <u>We will also keep the information in a file in our office, which will be our file</u>. When we have completed all the legal work necessary for your case, we will close our file and return any original documents to you. <u>We will then store the file for approximately</u> (insert number of years) years. We will destroy the file after that period of time unless you instruct us in writing now to keep your file longer.
>
> We have included a copy of this letter for your review, signature, and return to us in the postage-paid envelope. If any of the information in this letter is not consistent with your understanding of our agreement, please contact us before signing the letter. Otherwise, please sign the enclosed copy of this letter and return it.
>
> On behalf of the firm, we are happy to represent you in this matter. If you have any questions, please contact me at your convenience.
>
> Very truly yours,

As we continue looking at the engagement letter, the next section in the above example states the client's primary contact for the matter. Give the lawyer's name or other staff. And, again depending on the needs of the representation, use language such as, "Our law firm may also assign other appropriate lawyers or staff..." Make sure the letter states that you may assign other lawyers, junior lawyers, associates or staff depending on the needs, so that the client is not surprised about the individuals working on the matter or billing.

Now, we will talk about correspondence and the document retention policy. You are discussing sending information to the client throughout the case, and that the client should retain any documents. In addition, you are explaining your responsibilities by saying, "[W]e will also keep the information in a file in our office." Provide the client with a file number and explain the retention policy using language such as, "...then we will store the file for approximately" [x] number of years...."

In essence, this sample is the basic engagement letter or retainer agreement that you use for new clients.

Sample Engagement Letter/Retainer Agreement: Same Client, New Matter

ENGAGEMENT LETTER AND FEE ARRANGEMENT   (Date)

Dear (Name):

The purpose of this letter is to confirm, based on our conversation of May 20, 2017, that the Tanaka Law Firm will represent Tokyo Chemical Inc. in its purchase of **California Chemical**. Our representation will extend solely to Tokyo Chemical Inc. during the sale/purchase process, and not to any Directors, employees or any other staff of Tokyo Chemical Inc. in their individual capacities, or any independent contractors or consultants hired during the sale/purchase process. We will provide legal services related to the negotiation, due diligence, asset and stock purchase, and final sales agreement for the sale of **California Chemical** to Tokyo Chemical Inc.

All attorney fees, non-attorney fees, reimbursable costs, and billing and reporting procedures shall be the same as those set forth in our mutual **ENGAGEMENT LETTER AND FEE ARRANGEMENT**, which was agreed, signed and dated on May 10, 2017....

All obligations for document retention; return of original documents at the close of the case; destruction of our case file at the end of the case; and periodic updates from Tanaka Law Firm shall be the same as those set forth in our **ENGAGEMENT LETTER AND FEE ARRANGEMENT** of May 10, 2017....

Very truly yours,

In looking at what you might use for of the same client, but a new matter, most of the initial language is the same or similar to what you use in a new client matter. In the first paragraph, describe the purpose of the letter, which is confirming the representation and describing the new matter.

When it is a new matter for the same client, you do not have to go through all of the fee arrangement discussion again. You can say, "[A]ll attorney's fees, non-attorney's fees, reimbursable costs, billing and reporting procedures shall be the same as those set forth in our mutual engagement and fee arrangement letter, which was agreed and signed on May 10." When talking about costs and fees, you can refer to the original engagement letter without explaining the same information again, unless the arrangement will change. In that case, explain the new fee schedule.

And, when talking about the obligations for keeping documents, returning original documents, closing the case, and destroying the documents, you can use language saying, "...shall be the same as those set forth in the engagement letter." If it is a new matter for the same client, you do not need to go through a full explanation of the document retention policy.

5. 依頼者とのその他の文書によるやり取り — 情報や資料を求める文書
Other Written Communications to Clients: Letter Requesting Information or Documents

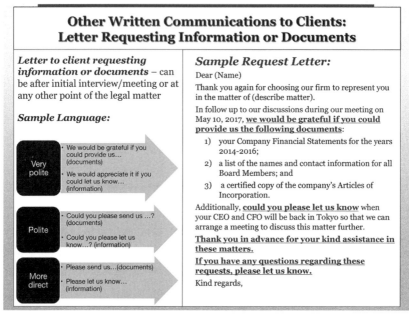

We will next discuss other types of communications with clients. The first type is making requests for additional information or documents. During the course of your representation, you may have the situation where you need to request additional information or documents. The sample language to use depends on the type of communication, such as e-mail or formal letter. We will look at ways to use very polite language, polite language, and direct language. When to use these different types of language depends on whether you are writing a letter or an e-mail.

In the case of a new client, you want to be more polite and use more formal language. If you are trying to obtain documents, for instance, you would say, "We would be grateful if you could provide us..." That is a very polite expression to ask for documents. If you are requesting information, you would say, "We would appreciate it if you could let us know..."

You can use polite language if this is a client that you have had some contact with and you know them well, but you still want to be polite. For example, "Could you please send us..." or when talking about information, "Could you please let us know...." Again, this is polite, but not overly polite language.

I recommend using direct language in situations where you have had multiple contacts with the client that you know quite well or when you are writing e-mails. In that situation, such as when writing an e-mail, "Please send us...," is appropriate direct language to use. "Please send us the sales agreement" or "Please let us know when you can meet us." This language is more direct and I would recommend this style when you know the client or person well or when writing e-mails because e-mails tend to be a little more informal than writing informal letters.

And, you have to use your discretion as to which one is appropriate for your situation. Here is a sample request letter. "Dear [name], Thank you for choosing our firm to represent you in the matter of... [the purchase of Ohio Chemical]. In follow up to our discussions during our meeting on May 10, we would be grateful if you could provide us the following documents." This is an initial contact with a new client, which means that you should use very polite language. Then you can list the documents or categories of information you are requesting.

Finally, when ending a written request for information or if you are asking someone to do something, you can use common polite language such as, "Thank you in advance for your kind assistance in this matter." Then conclude by saying, "If you have any questions regarding these requests please let us know" or "please feel free to let us know."

6. 依頼者とのその他の文書によるやり取り—業務終了にあたって提供する文書
Other Written Communications to Clients: Closing Letter

Other Written Communications to Clients: Closing Letter

Closing Letter – sent after the matter has concluded or at the end of the legal representation ***Important matters to note in letter:*** • Any final matters the lawyer will be taking care of • Any final matters the client should take care of • Remind client of document retention obligations • Remind client of firm's legal matter file destruction policy • Return all original documents to client	***Sample Closing Letter:*** Dear (Name): We wish to take this opportunity to thank you for allowing us to represent you in the (describe) matter. **In order to complete this matter, we will (outline any final matters you will take care of). In addition, you will need to (outline everything the client is responsible for at this time).** Since this matter is now closed, **we suggest that you keep all information relating to the matter in a safe place where you can easily locate it. We are closing our file and are returning your original (records, documents) related to your case.** As we discussed in our initial interview, our firm will store your file for (number of years) years from now. **The file will then be destroyed unless you request that we store the file for a longer period of time.** If you wish us to store the file for a longer period of time, you must instruct us to do so in writing within five (5) days of the date of this letter. **We hope this matter has concluded to your satisfaction.** Thank you for allowing us to represent you in this matter. If we can be of further assistance on this or any matter, please let us know. Very truly yours,

---

The closing letter is the last letter you send when closing the file or when the matter is concluded. You are informing the client that the matter is finished and the file will be closed, and that your representation has concluded. The important information to include in a closing letter is a list of any remaining issues or details that the lawyer will handle to close the matter. For example, "We will send a copy of all the agreements to the Board of Directors" or something that you are going to do to close the matter finally. If there is anything that the client should do, also list that information in the letter such as, "please be sure to retain copies of the agreements."

Remind the client of the document retention obligations, meaning that they should keep copies of all the agreements and other documents given to them related to the matter. In addition, remind the client of your policy for destroying files. Finally, you should always return original documents to the client at the end of the representation.

Here is a sample closing letter with the important expressions highlighted. "We wish to take this opportunity to thank you for allowing us to represent you in the Ohio Chemical sale matter. In order to complete this matter we will...," and then list whatever it is that you will do. "In addition, you will need to...," which is a good expression to outline whatever it is the client needs to do. "Since this matter will now be closed, we suggest that you keep all information relating to the matter in a safe place where you can easily locate it. We are closing our file and returning your original records or documents related to the case." These are sample expressions that you can use. "The file will then be destroyed unless you request that we store the file for a longer period of time." Another good expression to let them know what your document retention policy is and then finally politely say, "We hope this matter has concluded to your satisfaction."

第3部　依頼者に向けた意見書や事案評価書の書き方
——Writing Opinion Letters and Case Assessments for the Client

1. 意見書・事案評価書とは何か？
What is an Opinion Letter or Case Assessment?

What is an Opinion Letter or Case Assessment?

Opinion Letters or Case Assessments provide a client:

- ❏ Information about the law
- ❏ An analysis of how the law applies to their case/situation
- ❏ An opinion or legal advice as to how the client should proceed based on your analysis
- ❏ A report on the progress in the legal matter (i.e. Progress Report)

All Opinion Letters or Case Assessments should:

- ✓ **State the question or issue presented** in the opening paragraph or sentence
- ✓ **Give a factual background** relevant to the question or issue
- ✓ **Inform the reader how the law applies to the facts**
- ✓ **Provide/Recommend next steps or actions**
- ✓ **Minimize** citations to the law

Opinion letters or case assessments provide the client with a legal analysis of their case or situation, an opinion or a legal advice as to how the client should proceed, and a report on the progress of the legal matter.

All opinion letters or case assessments should state the question or the issue presented in the opening paragraph to explain immediately the issue that you will discuss in the letter or assessment. You need to give a factual background relevant to the issue, inform the reader how the law applies to the facts, and provide recommendations on next steps or actions.

An important point to remember is to minimize the citations to law in these types of documents, which is very different from writing legal memos. Opinion letters and assessments usually are written for the client who will not need to know many legal citations to cases or statutes. The purpose of the writing is to advise the client on the law; and therefore, minimizing legal citations and technical legal terms is the most appropriate form and tone of this writing type.

2. 意見書・事案評価書の例
Opinion Letter/Case Assessment: Sample Template

Opinion Letter/Case Assessment - Sample Template

Opinion Letter/Case Assessment regarding (add subject of advice here)*(Date)

  *The advice must contain a subject heading, underlined and in bold

Dear (add name here)*

  *Remember to address the advice to the person whom the client has nominated as the recipient

Introductory Paragraph*

  *The first sentence of the advice should acknowledge the request; state who in the client's office made the request; who in your office received it; and the date on which the request was received.

❖ The Introductory Paragraph should also contain:

  o A clear and direct statement of the question or issue you are providing an opinion on (**Sample Language:** *The question you requested advice on was…*);

  o A clear statement of where the facts you are relying on came from (**Sample Language:** *We are basing our opinion on the information you provided during our meeting on May 25, 2017…*)

  o A clear statement of all documents reviewed and relied upon prior to giving the opinion (**Sample Language:** *Prior to giving this opinion we reviewed the following documents, which you provided on…*)

  o A clear statement of any assumptions you made as part of your opinion, for ex. the authenticity of documents or signatures (**Sample Language:** *For the purposes of our opinion, we have assumed the following…*)

Now, we will go through a sample template for an opinion letter or a case assessment. First, create a subject heading stating the type of writing, opinion letter or case assessment, and the topic. For example, "This is an opinion letter regarding the sale of property."

Remember to address the letter to the person that the client has told you should be the recipient of the letter. For instance, the company CEO may ask you to send the opinion letter to the in-house counsel directly.

The introductory paragraph should acknowledge the request for advice, state the person who made the request, who in your office received it, and the date upon which the request was received. This paragraph should also contain a clear and direct statement of the question or the issue. Sample language is, "The question you requested advice on was...," and then give a description of what has been requested.

You should also give a clear statement of the facts you are relying on in giving your opinion. Why is this important? Because, often you do not always get the full facts from your client and you need to be careful when giving these opinions to let them know the basis of the facts you used. Make it clear in your advice that, "We are basing our opinion on the information you provided during our meeting on May 25, 2017." The same is true for references to documents. You should make a clear statement in the initial paragraph of which documents you relied on. Sample language is, "Prior to giving this opinion, we reviewed the following documents, which you provided on May 25," and then list the documents. Therefore, be clear about the facts you used and where you obtained your facts and documents to come to your opinions.

State if you made any assumptions as part of your opinion, for instance, assuming facts about the authenticity of documents or signatures. The client gives you documents that you assume the person who signed it had the authority to sign; however, later you find out the person actually did not have the right to sign that document for the company, but you did not know that information. You simply list the information you are assuming in making the opinion. Good phrases to use are, "We are basing our opinion on the information you provided during our meeting on..." "Prior to giving this opinion, we reviewed the following documents, which you provided..." listing the documents. "For the purposes of our opinion, we have assumed the following...."

Again, lawyers from the U.S. or other common law jurisdictions are used to this situation because you have to make sure that the clients do not say later on that you gave incorrect opinions or advice, and it is revealed that the client did not show you documents or you were not informed of all the relevant facts.

Opinion Letter/Case Assessment Template (cont'd)

Background

❖ Provide a summary of all the relevant facts upon which you based your opinion. Begin your summary with language like the following: "***Based on the information provided to us, we understand that...***"

> ➤ **This language is intended to protect the attorney in case the client did not give full or accurate information that might change the attorney's opinion or advice**

Discussion/Analysis

❖ Explain to the client in simple and clear language the relevant law that applies to their situation. **Minimize the use of legal citations and legalese.**

❖ Explain how the law applies to the facts of the situation presented by the client

Conclusions/Recommendations

❖ Give a clear, concise, and direct answer to the legal issue that you have been asked to advise on. Conclusions should be framed as ***Yes or No*** responses. Stay away from absolute language in giving opinions and conclusion (i.e. do not say that something is impossible – *See Lecture One re: IRAC Analysis - Conclusions*)

❖ Provide advice to the client on next steps or actions

The next part of your opinion letter is the background section. At this point, you need to provide a summary of all the relevant facts upon which you are basing your opinion. The summary begins with language such as, "Based on the information provided to us, we understand that...," and then you give a summary of the facts.

After you have summarized the information and the facts, you will have a discussion or analysis section. And again, the structure of this section goes to our earlier lectures on IRAC legal analysis writing: Issue, Rule of law, Analysis, and Conclusion. Here the background is essentially the issue. Then explain to the client in clear and simple language, the relevant law that applies to the situation. When possible, minimize the use of legal citations and technical legal terms. At this point, you are explaining how the relevant common law or statutes that you are basing your opinion on applies to the facts of the situation that was presented by the client.

Finally, you have the conclusions and recommendations based upon your analysis. In this section, give a clear, concise and direct answer to the legal issue that you have been asked to advise on. The conclusion should be framed as a "yes" or "no" response. In writing your answer, try not to use absolute language such as, "it will *never* be possible for [x] to happen" or "we are *100 percent* certain that [x] will happen."

3. 意見書・事案評価書における留意点
Opinion Letter/Case Assessment: Points to Remember

Opinion Letters/Case Assessments: Points to Remember

- ❖ It is essential to analyze ***all relevant legal arguments - including those that are adverse* to your client, or which you ultimately reject**, because otherwise the legal advice will not be comprehensive

- ❖ The client must be presented with **all the pros and cons of their legal position** so that they can make fully informed decisions about what course of action to adopt

Since it is a rare situation that lawyers can give legal advice with absolute certainty, all opinion letters and case assessments should frequently include such phrases as:

- *"in our opinion..."*
- *"it is our view that..."*
- *"although an argument could be made to the contrary..."*
- *"although a court might find otherwise..."*
- *"we think it more likely than not that..."*
- *"it is probable that..."*

➤ <u>Remember to include these qualifying phrases in any short answers you may give at the start of the advice</u>

Here are points to remember when writing these case assessments. You should include in the case assessment or opinion, all the relevant legal arguments, including those that might not be good for your client or adverse to what your client is trying to accomplish or which you might ultimately reject. The point is that you have to be thorough by explaining the positive and negative points to the client so that they can make an informed decision. Otherwise, you are not giving full and complete advice. The examples in the slide are the kinds of expressions that you can use in these letters to avoid making absolute statements.

**Opinion Letters/Case Assessments:
More Points to Remember**

❖ **Please refer back to Lectures One and Two related to:**

- Strategies for Common Law Research

- Analyzing Legal Questions in the Common Law

- Statutory and Common Law Case Interpretation and Analysis

- The Legal Writing Process

Please refer to the original two lectures in this series because they are applicable when writing strategies for legal research, analyzing legal questions, statutory and common law case interpretation and analysis, and the legal writing process. All of these skills are fundamental writing effectively in the common law.

4. 意見書の参考例
Sample Opinion Letter

> **Opinion Letter – Sample**
>
> **SAMPLE OPINION LETTER**
>
> May 24, 2017
>
> Re: Purchase of property in Denver, Colorado
>
> Dear Ms. Takagi,
>
> **We appreciate the opportunity to advise you regarding the potential purchase by Tokyo Department Store Inc. of land in Denver, Colorado,** in order to build an outlet mall complex, which we discussed during our meeting on May 10, 2017. At that time, **you requested our advice on whether** the seller could under Colorado law sell Tokyo Department Store Inc. only the rights to the surface of the property, and retain the right to sell or lease the subsurface mineral rights to another party for the purposes of mining or other natural resource exploration.
>
> **We are basing our opinion on the information you provided** during our meeting on May 10, 2017, **along with our review of a seller's disclosure form and a proposed property sales agreement that you provided at that time....**

Here is a sample opinion letter that we will discuss. This is an opinion letter regarding the purchase of property in Denver, Colorado, U.S. We are dealing with the issue of subsurface land rights. In the initial paragraph, you are identifying immediately the matter you are being asked to give an opinion on, which in this case, is to build an outlet mall complex. In this paragraph, state the legal issue, when the request was made, and who made the request. In the sample, we are talking about the ability of a seller to only sell the surface rights and to try to retain the subsurface rights to sell for mining or other natural resource exploration.

In the next paragraph, state the facts and law that you are relying on to make an opinion. For example, "We are basing our opinion on the information you provided during our meeting on May 10th." I am basing my opinion on the facts given during the meeting along with a review of certain documents. The next portion of the letter sets forth the facts and documents reviewed in making the opinion. In this type of writing, you should identify any documents by date or any other identifying information.

> ## Opinion Letter – Sample (cont'd)
>
> **Background**
>
> **Based upon the information you provided us at the meeting, we understand that** Tokyo Department Store Inc. has been negotiating with Denver Land Co. for the purchase of a large plot of land on the outskirts of Denver, Colorado for the purposes of building an outlet mall. After the parties informally agreed on the sale, Denver Land Co. provided Tokyo Department Store Inc. a Sellers Disclosure Statement and a proposed Property Sales Agreement.
>
> After reviewing these documents, Tokyo Department Store Inc. found a similar clause in both documents stating that Denver Land Co. proposed only to sell Tokyo Department Store Inc. the rights to the surface of the property, and intended to retain the right to sell or lease the mineral rights to the subsurface of the property to a third party for the purposes of mining or exploring the natural resources on the property. As the deal has not been finalized yet, Tokyo Department Store Inc. is solely interested in advice on whether selling only surface rights to land is legal under Colorado law.
>
> **Short Answer**
>
> **The short answer to your question is yes. Based on our review, we believe** that Colorado law allows sellers separately to sell the rights to the surface and subsurface of property, reserving for themselves the right to sell or lease the subsurface mineral rights to third parties for the purposes of mining or other exploration.

Now, we are looking at the background section of the opinion letter. The language, "Based on the information you provided us at the meeting, we understand that...," introduces a summary of the facts. Next, you set forth the facts of what occurred during the negotiations in this matter. In this case, they made an agreement to sell the land and when they received a seller's disclosure statement, it was revealed that the seller only wanted to sell them the surface of the land and keep the subsurface land. This information is a recitation of the relevant or important facts, but not all facts that may have occurred. At the end of the background, you are reciting the question or issue. "As the deal has not been finalized yet, Tokyo Department Store is solely interested in advice on whether selling only surface rights to land is legal under Colorado law."

The next section of the letter is the short answer, which begins the legal analysis of the situation. You are giving a clear and concise answer to the question the client asked by stating "yes" or "no". However, in the answer, you are trying to not be absolute by using language such as, "Based on our review, we *believe*...." The short answer is useful, particularly when the client or reader may not have a lot of time to read the entire opinion letter. If the client needs a quick understanding of the issue, the short answer helps to summarize the legal analysis.

Opinion Letter – Sample (cont'd)

Discussion/Analysis

The seller's right to separate the surface and subsurface rights to property for sale or lease is a well-accepted practice under Colorado law. *See* Mitchell v. Espinosa, 125 Colo. 267, 243 P.2d 412 (1952). To implement this policy and protect potential buyers, Colorado passed a law in 2016 that requires sellers to disclose to potential buyers that:

> "The surface estate of [p]roperty may be owned separately from the underlying mineral estate, and transfer of the surface estate may not include transfer of the mineral estate. Third parties may own or lease interests in oil, gas, or other minerals under the surface, and they may enter and use the surface estate to access the mineral estate." C.R.S. § 38-35.7-108(1)(a) (2016).

Consequently, it appears clear that in Colorado, the sale of property does not automatically include any rights to the subsurface of the land unless it is specifically stated in the sales agreement. Moreover, it is not uncommon for property sellers to split the surface property rights and the sub-surface mineral rights, and sell or lease the rights separately.

Following the short answer is the discussion or legal analysis section of the opinion letter. In this example, the "seller's right to separate the surface and subsurface rights to property for sale or lease is a well-accepted practice under Colorado law." An important expression to highlight is, "well-accepted practice" or "well-accepted law." You use that expression in situations where after you have done your legal research and analysis, it is clear that there is no conflict in the law to be applied in the situation or that the principle of law is consistently applied in similar situations as the present one. In your research, you may find many statutes or case law that has similar law and facts as your issue. If there is no question about the way in which the law is applied to this factual situation, then the expression is useful and clear. Please note that you should have some reliable legal authority to support your opinion—case law, statute, regulatory opinions. However, you do not need to cite many legal authorities because the citations are technical and may not be understood by the client or reader. In this example, we quote case law and the statute that allows the client to adopt a certain legal argument to support what the client is trying to do.

Finally, you give your legal analysis conclusion. "Consequently, it appears that in Colorado, the sale of property does not automatically include rights to the subsurface...."The language used in the example is a bit softer or indirect so that you are not making absolute statements.

Opinion Letter – Sample (cont'd)

Conclusions/Recommendations

Since Denver Land Co. properly disclosed their intention to only sell the surface rights to the property to Tokyo Department Store Inc. in both the Sellers Disclosure Statement and the proposed Property Sale Agreement, they are more than likely acting within their rights under Colorado law. However, in our opinion, as the deal was never finalized, Tokyo Department Store Inc. is not under any obligation to continue with the purchase.

Moving forward, we believe that Tokyo Department Store Inc. is free to continue negotiating with Denver Land Co. to determine if an agreement can be made for the surface and subsurface rights to the property. You may also choose to discontinue negotiations with Denver Land Co. and search for other potential properties.

If you have any questions or require any clarifications, please feel free to contact us.

Sincerely yours,

Note: This is merely a sample letter for educational purposes and is not intended to serve as actual legal advice.

The final section of the letter summarizes the points of law and your advice in the conclusions or recommendations section. In the example, we are saying that the client's actions are most likely appropriate under Colorado law because they put language of their intentions regarding the land rights in the disclosure statement. Another part of the analysis is that the deal was never finalized, which means that Tokyo Department Store is not under any obligation to continue with the purchase. Another good expression to discuss next steps is to say, "Moving forward, we believe that...." You are explaining the client's options and the points they should consider during the negotiations.

Now, aside from client opinion letters, case assessments are very similar, which is why they are grouped together for this lecture. The essential template is the same for both types. You are defining the issue, explaining the applicable law and applying the law to the facts, and then giving an assessment of the issue. If dealing with a transactional matter, then the name of the document is an opinion letter. If you are dealing with an insurance company, they may be called case assessments. But, the elements and writing structure are the same.

5. 依頼者に対する業務報告書の参考例
Sample Progress Report to Client

Progress Report to Client – Sample

Progress Report – updates the client on the status of their legal matter	**Sample Progress Report to Client:**
	Dear (Name),
Sample Language:	We would like to update you on the status of our efforts to finalize the closing documents for the purchase of Ohio Chemicals.
(Intro) • We would like to update you on the status of (describe matter)	As you are aware, we have already agreed on June 30, 2017, as the final closing date for the purchase and sale of Ohio Chemicals. The document signing will take place in our conference room at 10:00 am.
(Completed Tasks) • Currently, we have finalized… • We have completed… • We have already…	Currently, we have finalized the Purchase and Sale Agreement based upon the terms agreed with Ohio Chemical. Additionally, we have completed all appropriate documents to transfer 100% of the shareholder stock to Tokyo Chemical.
(Uncompleted Tasks) • We are still in the process of… • At present, we have yet to complete… • We have not…yet. • We expect…to be completed by…	At present, we are still in the process of completing the Articles of Incorporation for the new company to be formed, as well as the corporate by-laws. We expect these to be completed by May 30, 2017.
	Please let us know a date and time during the week of June 12, 2017, that you are available to meet so that we can review all final documents with you.
	Regards,

Finally, we will discuss progress reports. It is important to have continuous client contact by updating them on the status of the legal matter you are handling. To maintain good communication with the client, regular progress reports are crucial. The client usually determines how often they want to receive updates. In certain instances, you may give frequent updates; in others, periodic updates will suffice.

Here is sample language for progress reports. These updates can either be e-mails or letters depending on the manner you communicate with the client. E-mails tend to be more informal compared to letters. If the report will be presented in a formal meeting, such as to the board of directors, then it is better to be more formal. If you have a quick meeting and you need to update your client on the progress of that meeting, then a short e-mail is appropriate. The way to structure the report will depend on the purpose.

In the sample, begin with a statement stating that this is an update or progress report on the matter you are handling. "We would like to update you on the status of..." This is your opening sentence. When discussing completed tasks or matters that are finished, you can say, "Currently, we have finalized...," and then you list what is completed. For tasks that are not completed yet, the expressions that you would use are, "We are still in the process of..." This is a polite way of saying you have not done something yet. Then, a bit less formal is, "We have not..., yet." For example, we have not set the meeting yet or we have not met with the CEO yet.

In the sample, "We would like to update you on the status of our efforts to finalize the closing documents for the purchase of Ohio Chemicals. As you are aware, we have already agreed on June 30 as the final closing date for the purchase and sale of Ohio Chemicals. The document signing will take place in our conference room at 10 a.m." Here, we are talking about some agreement that is already completed. And, next we are talking about the tasks that are finished. "Additionally we have completed all appropriate documents to transfer 100 percent of the shareholder stock to Tokyo Chemical."

Next, discuss the items that are still in progress. "At present, we are still in the process of completing the Articles of Incorporation for the new company to be formed as well as the corporate by-laws." It is always good practice to put an expected completion date using expressions such as, "We expect these to be completed by May 30, 2017."

Usually, in progress reports, the last part is to ask for information or set a time for future meetings or reports. You can use polite language such as, "Please let us know a date and time during the week of June 12, 2017, that you are available to meet…"

This is a sample progress report with sample language that you can use for an informal report to the client in an e-mail as opposed to a formal document that you would send to boards of directors, etc. Most of your progress reports are going to be more informal and on a periodic basis. However, if you are writing a longer progress report, then you can use a more formal style.

Thank you for your attention during this lecture about the practical ways to write for clients.

Lecture 4

依頼者を除く内部関係者に対して
提示する文書の作成において求められる
ライティングコミュニケーションスキル

◆

Practical Writing for Legal Office and Case Status Memoranda

弁護士が依頼者以外の内部関係者（共同受任者や事務所内スタッフなど）とのやり取りを英文で行う際のライティングコミュニケーションスキルについて，例を挙げながら具体的に解説します。一案件について作成されるであろう法務文書（概要，覚書，契約書，証言の内容，事実確認の文書等）をどのように整理し，効率的に情報共有を図るかという点についても説明します。

Welcome to our fourth lecture in our six-part series. Tonight, we will discuss practical writing for legal office and case status memoranda.

The three parts sections we will talk about are 1) drafting legal memoranda in the law office, 2) drafting in-house attorney communications, 3) and preparing case status memoranda.

Lecture Four: Practical Writing for Legal Office and Case Status Memoranda

Agenda:
- Drafting Legal Memoranda in Law Practice
- Drafting In-House Attorney Communications
- Preparing Case Status Memoranda

Marc Lassman
Adjunct Professor of Law
Temple University School of Law, Japan Campus
June 9, 2017
18:00 – 20:00

Drafting legal memoranda is probably the most common type of writing that would be done by any transactional or litigation attorney. And, as we will see, it is some of the most important work that you do as a lawyer and when you are giving value as a lawyer.

In this lecture, we also will speak about in-house attorney communications. We want to focus on the typical communications for in-house attorneys. But, much of this also applies to law firm attorneys.

Finally, we will talk about preparing case status memoranda, which are crucial for client relations and also law firm practice. The status of a file is always an important issue. When doing typical file management as a lawyer, someone should be able to open that file at any moment in time and understand exactly where the deal is, where the case is. It is essential to have proper case file management and good case status memoranda in the file.

第1部　弁護士業務におけるメモランダムの作成
——Drafting Legal Memoranda in Law Practice

1. メモとは何か？
What is a Memo?

What is a Memo

- The memorandum of law (memo) is an internal office document comprised of legal research that analyses the law as it applies to the facts of a client's case and offers an unbiased evaluation
- A memo includes both helpful and damaging information/legal sources
- It suggests solutions to a legal problem or predicts the outcome of a dispute

Memos are the basis of informed decision-making about the case

---

First, we will talk about drafting legal memoranda. A memo is an internal office document comprised of legal research that analyzes the law and applies it to your client's case and then offers an unbiased evaluation. As we spoke about in previous lectures, memos are predictive, which means positive and negative information goes into these memos, because the information will become the basis for decision-making in the case. Therefore, you have to look at the whole situation of the legal matter and evaluate it in a fair and unbiased way based on the legal resources to advise your client and make appropriate decisions. A memo typically will suggest solutions to a legal problem or predict the outcome of a dispute.

2. メモを作成する目的は何か？
Purpose of a Memo

Purpose of a Memo

- ❖ A memo can serve many purposes, which will determine how extensive the research should be, what the nature of the analysis should be, and how to write it

- ❖ Write memos for the **specific purpose** for which it was requested

Reminder: Know your Audience!!

Sample Purposes
- **Decide** whether to accept a legal matter
- **Evaluate** the merits of a legal matter
- **Present** recommendations on how to proceed
- **Identify** legal theories for the case
- **Inform** on case status
- **Prepare** for negotiations
- **Draft** contracts, wills, settlement agreements, corporate papers
- **Decide** whether to settle a case or go to court

A memo can serve many purposes which will determine how extensive your research should be, what the nature of your analysis should be and how to write it. You should always be careful to write the memo for the specific purpose for which it was requested and not go beyond what is being asked of you. In all legal writing, it is to remember your audience. Who is going to read this memo? What do they need this document for? And, then you construct the document to meet their needs.

Memos are useful for many purposes, such as to decide whether to accept a legal matter or a deal. There are memos to evaluate the merits of a legal matter, present recommendations, and identify legal theories of the case. Additionally, memos can inform on case status, aid in preparing for negotiations, and provide information to draft contracts, wills, settlement agreements, or corporate papers. Finally, in litigation, memos can function to decide whether to settle a case or go to trial proceedings.

3. メモランダムの書式
Memorandum Format

Memorandum – Traditional Format

Memorandum

To: Recipient
From: Writer
Date: June 9, 2017
Re: Topic

I. Issue(s)/Question(s)

II. Brief Answer(s)   **[Within the first 1.5 pages]**

III. Facts

IV. Discussion

    A. Sub-section(s)

V. Conclusion

Next, we will discuss the formats of memos. Please note that I have given you two different formats for memos—traditional and modern. I will go through both of them, but you will get the sample language for the modern format because it is probably more likely that people will use the modern format as opposed to the traditional format.

The traditional format gives basic information related to the sender, recipient and topic of the memo. The first substantive aspect of the memo is the "Issues" or "Questions" section. Then, you have your "Brief Answer" and "Facts." Please note that these three sections all should be written in the first page and a half of the document. And what that means is, these sections need to be short. This is the area where if your client is not going to read a 20-page memo, but they need the essential information in the first page and a half to do a quick read and understand the point of the memo.

After you give the overview of the issues and facts, the next section is the "Discussion" section of the different issues. Usually, memos will address more than one issue. Therefore, the discussion section will have sub-sections that deal with the specific issues. Finally, you will have the "Conclusion" section.

Memorandum – Modern Format

Memorandum

To: Recipient
From: Writer
Date: June 9, 2017
Re: Topic

I. Facts

II. Issue [Within the first 1.5 pages]

III. Short Answer

IV. Analysis/Argument
    A. Sub-section(s)

V. Conclusion/Recommendations

Now looking at the modern memo, you will note that in terms of the organization, first you see the facts and then the issue. Next, is the short answer. The modern memo is a bit different than the traditional memo because the traditional memo has the issues and questions, brief answer and then the facts. The modern memo tends to be closer to the way that you would explain something if were sitting down with someone in person. First, you would talk about what happened, then you talk about the issue, and then you would give an answer. The modern memo evolves the way it did because it tracks a little bit closer to the logic in the way most people would make a presentation to a client or senior partner.

After the short answer, then you have the analysis or the argument section, which includes the sub-sections, conclusions and recommendations. I will discuss each section of the modern format and talk about what should be there, but also suggest good language to use.

4. メモランダムの重要ポイント
Essential Parts of a Memorandum
I. Facts

Essential Parts of a Modern Memo
Facts

- **Tell the background story**
  who are the parties, what is their relationship, and what is the problem
- **Include all relevant facts**
  be sure they include those referenced later in the memo
- Draft the facts in context of the **legal issues**
- **Describe past** court proceedings or important meetings (if applicable)
- **Keep the story short**, but thoroughly discuss the factual issues
- Organize facts in a **logical manner**

Sample Language*
Facts

Julie Larson purchased a house from the Randalls. After moving in, she discovered a graveyard in her backyard. An appraiser and realtor stated that the graveyard decreased the value of the house at least $27,000 below the purchase price.

Prior to buying the house, Larson visited the property but saw no graveyard. The house has a long, narrow backyard that extends behind the house. When she visited the property, the yard had a small patio, a grassy area, and several flower and tree areas. The remainder of the yard was wooded and overgrown. Larson walked briefly around the patio area, but she never went to the overgrown area where the graveyard was located.

During her visit to the house, Larson spoke with the Randalls. Although she asked specific questions about the house, she did not ask about the backyard. The Randalls' said the backyard garden was tranquil, but nothing about a graveyard. After discovering the graveyard Larson contacted the Randalls, who said they didn't know anything about it.

*Note: Excerpts of Sample Memo taken from: http://www.law.duke.edu/curriculum/coursehomepages/Fall2004/160_02/writSamples/sample_e.pdf

---

First, we will talk about the Facts section. Here is a sample memo as part of these materials. Basically, we have a client, Julie Larson, and she bought a house from the Randalls. After Julie bought the house, she discovered that there was a graveyard in the back of the house that the Randalls never told her about. The graveyard significantly lowers the value of the house. She is saying that the Randalls failed to tell her about the graveyard and that this was fraud on their side. And they are claiming that they did not know about the graveyard in the back of the house. This is a simple set of facts that we will use as an example.

When setting forth the facts, you have to be sure to tell the background story. The main facts to discuss are the parties, their relationship and the problem. You want to make sure that you list all of the important information to make a legal determination. In this situation, for fraud is what claims, it is important to know the Randalls communicated to Julie regarding the graveyard on the property? How many times did she ask about the backyard? What did the Randalls tell her? Did they say it orally or in writing? In this legal situation, whenever you have the facts, you should list every fact that has to do with any communication between Julie and the Randalls—the buyer and the sellers—because it will be relevant for the legal analysis. Make sure that you are including all the relevant facts and then showing how the facts are important in the context of the legal issues.

If you have a case that has already been in court or had a legal proceeding, you should list those. If you are talking about doing a deal and there have been important meetings, discussions or negotiations as part of that process, you should state those details in the Facts section. Try to keep the memo short, but you also must thoroughly discuss the important factual information. In the case example, every communication that the buyers had with the sellers should be stated in the memo.

For instance, what can happen is facts and information might come later that you did not know about and your opinion might change. In this situation, maybe we find out later that the buyer knew that there was a graveyard because they wrote a letter to a friend talking about the graveyard. But you did not know this imformation when you wrote this memo. Make sure to include all of the relevant information that you have at the time.

Finally, organize the facts in a logical manner. And, logical manner usually means in chronological order—what happened first, what happened second, what happened third. But, it is not always the case that chronological order is the most logical way. For instance, in the example, the first fact that I mention is that she bought the house. That is the most important fact. Then, I go back and talk about the process by which she bought the house.

Some facts technically happened before she bought the house. I want to emphasize that you should make sure to put forth the facts in a logical manner. Usually, you try to do it in the order in which they happened. But it is not always true that chronological order is the most logical way. Another example, is if you are talking about a deal, First, mention that the deal was done. Then, if necessary back and talk about the negotiations, and when they happened, and how they happened.

II. Issue

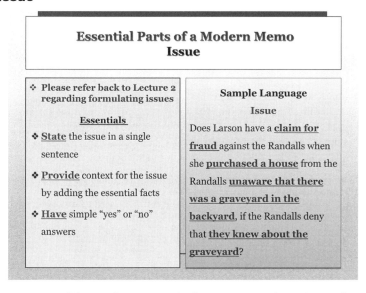

The next part of the modern memo is the "Issue" section. Please also refer back to Lecture 2 when formulating legal issues for your research. We use the same principles here when writing about an issue. The essentials are to state the issue in a single sentence. The issue should be a simple "yes" or "no" question. You have to provide the context for the issue by adding essential facts, which means by reading the issue, the reader should know exactly what is the problem and what needs to be answered.

Here is the example. The issue with regard to the sale of the house: 'Does Larson have a claim for fraud…when she purchased the house from the Randalls unaware that there was a graveyard in the backyard, if the Randalls deny that they knew about the graveyard?' This tells me the context of the facts, the leagal issue and the answer or conclusion we will reach by the end of this memorandum.

III. Short Answer

Essential Parts of a Modern Memo Short Answer

	Sample Language Short Answer
❖ Please refer back to Lectures 2 and 3 regarding formulating Short Answers or Conclusions **Essentials** ❖ **Make** the answer "brief" and begin with a simple "Yes" or "No" ❖ **State** the answer concisely in one to three sentences explaining your reasoning ❖ **Include** the relevant facts that connect to the legal issues involved ❖ **Don't use absolute language** in your Answer	<u>No</u>, Larson **probably does not have** a claim for fraud against the Randalls. **A fraud claim requires a false representation or concealment of a material fact**. A defendant must know a representation is false, or that a material fact is being concealed, and have an intent to deceive. Here, while Larson may have reasonably relied on the Randalls' representations and suffered damages, **it does not appear** that the Randalls made any false representations, concealed any material facts, or that they intended to deceive Larson.

Again, when drafting the short answer, you begin with a "yes" or "no." You should not say "maybe." Rather, you should come to a clear conclusion or answer to the issue. Please note that when stating "yes" or "no," you do need to be careful in the language that you use in expressing that conclusion. State the answer concisely in one to three sentences and include the relevant facts that connect the legal issues so that you are applying the facts to the law. But, do not use absolute language in your answer, such as "absolutely" or "never."

Example: our Short Answer is 'No. Larson probably does not have a claim for fraud against the Randalls. A fraud claim requires a false representation or concealment of a material fact.' For fraud that means you need to show that someone, on purpose, lied about something that was very important that would have changed the person's mind. For instance in this situation, if Ms. Larson knew that there was a graveyard in the backyard, she probably would not have paid that price for the house. You would have to show that it was an important piece of information—i.e., the seller purposely did not tell the buyer; Julie relied on that information; and the Randalls did it with the intention to deceive her or to defraud her.

Here is the statement of the law: the fraud claim requires a false representation or a concealment of a material fact. 'A defendant must know a representation is false, or that a material fact is being concealed, and have an intent to deceive.'

Next is the analysis, which applies the law to the facts. In this situation, 'while Larson may have reasonably relied on the Randalls' representations and suffered damages, it does not appear that the Randalls made any false representations, concealed any material facts, or that they intended to deceive Larson.' This statement is your analysis.

The IRAC structure of writing is throughout every aspect of the memo—Issue, Rule, Analysis, and Conclusion.

IV. Analysis/Argument Essentials

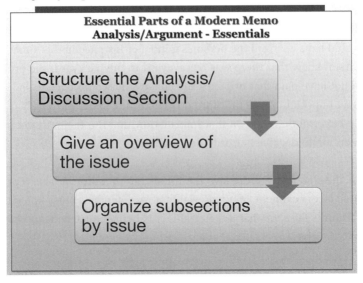

The "Analysis" section is the next topic we will cover. In terms of structure, the first portion of the analysis section should give an overview of the issue. Then, the various issues are organized by subsections.

Essential Parts of a Modern Memo
Analysis/Argument – Essentials
Discussion/Analysis Overview

Start your Discussion/Analysis with an Overview, which should:

- ❖ **Provide a roadmap of the issues** and the order in which they will be discussed
- ❖ **Begin with a broad discussion** of the law
- ❖ **Mention what stage the case is in** procedurally (if applicable)
- ❖ **Discuss standard of review** or burden of proof (if applicable)
- ❖ **Talk about any undisputed issues**

✓ Always begin your Discussion/Analysis by <u>asserting your conclusion in the heading</u>

a. Discussion/Analysis Overview

The overview of the discussion or analysis section will be the first paragraph and should provide a roadmap of the issues in the order in which you will discuss the issues. Begin with a broad discussion of the law, and mention the procedural stage of the case or the deal, if applicable. If the matter is a litigation case as opposed to a deal, discuss any standards of review the court will apply and any burdens of proof of the parties. Next, talk about any disputed issues.

Set out the issues and the order of discussion. For the rest of the memo, such as Issue number 1, Issue number 2, etc. The remaining parts of the memo will be, for example, sub-section 1 relates to Issue number 1. At the end, give the conclusion based upon your analysis. The overview will essentially be a roadmap of the memo.

b. Discussion/Analysis — Sample Language

Essential Parts of a Modern Memo
Analysis/Argument – Essentials
Discussion/Analysis Overview

Discussion/Analysis Overview - Sample Language

[Heading] **LARSON PROBABLY CANNOT RECOVER FOR FRAUD SINCE THERE IS NO INDICATION THAT THE RANDALLS KNEW ABOUT THE GRAVEYARD IN THEIR BACKYARD WHEN THEY SOLD THEIR HOME TO LARSON.** [Conclusion]

To succeed in an action for fraud, a plaintiff must show all the following elements: **(1)** that a defendant made a false representation relating to, or concealed, a material fact and the defendant knew the representation was false or made it recklessly without any knowledge of its truth; **(2)** the defendant made the false representation with an intent to deceive the plaintiff; **(3)** the plaintiff reasonably relied and acted upon the representation; and, **(4)** the plaintiff suffered damages. <u>Myers v. Thomas G. Evans, Inc.</u>, 374 S.E.2d 385, 391 (N.C. 1988). [Broad discussion of Law]

Here, Larson might have reasonably relied upon the available information and suffered damage, but she cannot meet the first two elements of fraud. **First**, there was no misrepresentation or concealment of a material fact. **Second**, there is no indication that the Randalls knew about the graveyard, an essential element of an intent to deceive. [Order of Issues to be discussed]

Here is sample language for an overview of the analysis section. Looking at Larson's fraud claim, notice that there are two sections of this memo or two issues to discuss. The important fact is whether there was a purposeful misrepresentation of a material fact by the Randalls. The first part of the Discussion here is the Heading, which also serves as a conclusion statement. In this situation, 'Larson probably cannot recover for fraud since there is no indication that the Randalls knew about the graveyard in their backyard when they sold their home to Larson.' That is your conclusion, but also the subsection heading to organize the memo.

Then, begin writing the law that applies. Here is the general overview of the law: 'To succeed in an action for fraud a plaintiff must show all the following elements.' Then state the elements or legal requirements to satisfy an action for misrepresentation, including the citation so that people can find the souce of law you are quating where you. In memorandums, always be careful to cite appropriately because if the judge is reading the memo, they may want to read the case as well. If your partner or senior attorney is reading it, they might want to go look at the case. Memos are where you do the most citations as opposed to any other documents that you prepare.

c. CRAC — Key to Organizing subsections of a Memo

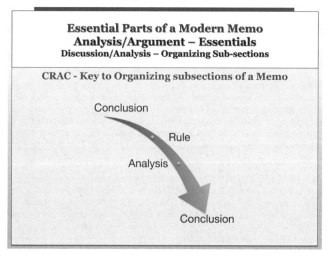

Your Analysis section has to be structured just like every other legal document according to CRAC or IRAC—Conclusion, Rule, Analysis, and restate Conclusion. Each subsection is also organized in the same way. Every element of writing that you do is organized in the same manner.

d. Organizing Subsections — CRAC applied to Memos

Analysis/Argument – Essentials
Discussion/Analysis – Organizing Sub-sections
CRAC applied to Memos

Conclusion	SHOULD deal only with the sub-issue SHOULD be only a single sentence USE headings to state the conclusion USE language from the corresponding legal rule USE facts that connect to the rule
Rule	STATE the legal element of the law at issue in the subsection PROVIDE a factual context for the legal element EXPLAIN the law's essential meaning GIVE appropriate weight to various sources of law CITE to supporting legal authority
Analysis	Organize each Paragraph by: 1) TOPIC SENTENCE stating the element or theme you are discussing 2) Then EXPLAIN CASE LAW or statutory authority 3) NEXT APPLY legal authority to facts
Conclusion (Re-stated)	BRIEFLY restate your conclusion No new facts or argument No more than one to three sentences

Let's examine how this CRAC writing structure applies to memos. When writing sub-sections, the Conclusion should always deal with only the sub-issue. Your conclusion in this section is about the one issue that you are talking about in that section. Use one sentence as the subheading to state the conclusion.

Again, the Rule is the statement of the law and elements to state a claim. Provide a factual context for the legal elements and explain the essential meaning of the law. Make sure to cite all the supporting legal authority when talking about the rule and give appropriate weight and citations to the various sources of law.

The Analysis section of CRAC explains how the law applies to the facts. Finally, the Conclusion, restates the ultimate result you reached based on the analysis. At this stage, do not give new facts or arguments.

e. Analysis/Argument — Sample Language

> **Essential Parts of a Modern Memo**
> **Analysis/Argument – Sample Language (1)**
>
> **A. Larson likely cannot succeed with a fraud claim because there was no misrepresentation of a material fact. [CONCLUSION]**
>
> Fraud requires a false representation of a material fact. <u>Myers v. Thomas G. Evans, Inc.</u>, 374 S.E.2d 385, 391 (N.C. 1988). A material fact is one that affects a purchaser's decision to buy property. <u>Powell v. Wold</u>, 362 S.E.2d 796, 798 (N.C. Ct. App. 1987). A representation "must be definite and specific." <u>Ragsdale v. Kennedy</u>, 209 S.E.2d 494, 500 (N.C. 1974). An "unspecific statement of opinion" is not a representation. <u>Carpenter v. Merrill Lynch Realty Operating P'ship</u>, 424 S.E.2d 178, 180 (N.C. Ct. App. 1993).... **[RULE]**
>
> **In this case**, Larson probably cannot show that the Randalls made a misrepresentation of a material fact. There is little question that the existence of the graveyard is a material fact. Had Larson known about the defect, she presumably would not have agreed to pay $27,000 more than the value of the house. See <u>Powell</u>, 362 S.E.2d at 798.
>
> However, the Randalls' statements to Larson about the backyard do not amount to representations. The Randalls told Larson that the backyard was tranquil and sent her a fax stating that if she bought the house she could relax outside. As in <u>Carpenter</u>, where the broker's statements were based on common sense and without authority, the Randalls' statements were opinions based on common sense and do not constitute representations. See <u>Carpenter</u>, 424 S.E.2d at 181. **[ANALYSIS – CASE/FACT COMPARISON]**
>
> **In sum, Larson likely cannot succeed with a fraud claim because there was no misrepresentation of a material fact. [CONCLUSION]**

Example. Section A. is sub-section 1 of the Analysis section. Using the CRAC writing structure, the subheading states the Conclusion. 'Larson likely cannot succeed with a fraud claim because there was no misrepresentation of a material fact.' Next, we are talking about the Rule or the law of fraud, which includes the elements of the claim. Notice that the appropriate citations to the case law follow. All of the law that applies to the first issue in the analysis section is discussed here.

The following sentence begins the Analysis of Issue 1. A useful phrase to signal that you are applying the law to the facts of the case is, 'In this case…' Then move on to discuss how the law in the case applies to the facts. For example, 'Lawson probably cannot show that the Randalls made a misrepresentation of a material fact.' The fact that there is a graveyard is a fact and had she known it, she probably would not have paid the amount she did. However, the facts do not show that the Randalls made any actual statements to Larson about the backyard not having a graveyard.

Last, restate the Conclusion. 'In sum, Larson likely cannot succeed with a fraud claim because there was no misrepresentation of a material fact.' In this section, you can see that there is CRAC. This is the analysis of the first issue in the memo.

Essential Parts of a Modern Memo
Analysis/Argument – Sample Language (2)

B. Larson likely cannot succeed with an action for fraud since there is no indication the Randalls acted with an intent to deceive. [CONCLUSION]

Fraud requires that a representation or concealment be made with an intent to deceive. Myers, 374 S.E.2d at 391. Intent may be inferred from a party's conduct throughout a transaction. Harbach v. Lain & Keonig, Inc., 326 S.E.2d 115, 119 (N.C. Ct. App. 1985). There is no intent to deceive unless a seller has knowledge of a material fact. Compare Myers, 374 S.E.2d at 392 (no intent to deceive when no evidence defendant knew representation false), with Johnson, 140 S.E.2d at 313 (intent to deceive where knowledge established). **[RULE]**

In this case, the Randalls did not act with an intent to deceive because there is no indication that they knew about the graveyard. As discussed previously, there is no indication that the Randalls read the newspaper article about gravestones or knew that the gravestones were located on their property. Although many of the Randalls' neighbors knew of other graveyards in the area, none knew that there was a graveyard in the Randalls' backyard. **[ANALYSIS – Case/Fact Comparison]** Thus, without any proof that the Randalls had knowledge of the graveyard, it is un*likely* that the Randalls intended to deceive Larson. See Myers, 374 S.E.2d at 391. **[CONCLUSION]**

Section B. of the memo is Issue 2 or the second sub-section, which discusses whether the Randalls intended to deceive Larson. Again, using the CRAC writing structure, first the Conclusion says that Larson cannot succeed because there is no evidence that the Randalls intended to deceive in buying the house. We have a statement of the rule about the fraud requirements and intent to deceive for a seller. Note that the law statements are found in case law, which is the common law. In common law, you are searching for legally and factually similar cases to your situation. This is where case law research becomes important in order to analyze the issues as opposed to only looking at statutes for the law statements.

The next paragraph begins the analysis of the sub-issue. In this case, there is no proof that the Randalls knew about the graveyard in the backyard or that they intended to deceive Larson because they did not know the graveyard existed. Finally, we have a restatement of the conclusion. 'Thus, without any proof that the Randalls had knowledge of the graveyard, it is unlikely'—using the non-absolute language—'that the Randalls intended to deceive Larson.'

f. Analysis/Argument — Present Counter Arguments

Essential Parts of a Modern Memo
Analysis/Argument –Present Counter Arguments

- Discuss any **negative or weak** points about the facts or law
- Don't **just restate** the opposing argument
- State the negative information from the **client's point of view**
- Start sentences with **"Although"**

  Sample Language:

  Although many of the Randalls' neighbors knew of other graveyards in the area, none knew that there was a graveyard in the Randalls' backyard.

- Use **parentheticals** to dismiss or distinguish negative case law

  Sample Language:

  There is no intent to deceive unless a seller has knowledge of a material fact. *Compare Myers, 374 S.E.2d at 392 (no intent to deceive when no evidence defendant knew representation false), with Johnson, 140 S.E.2d at 313 (intent to deceive where knowledge established).*

CRAC writing structure is important in terms of the internal logic of the document. It is always best to use headings and subheadings to make the document easy to read. The purpose of these memos is to be predictive in the legal analysis, not persuasive. Therefore, if you find negative or weak points in the law or facts of your situation, you should include those points in the memo as well. Otherwise, you are not giving full and accurate advice. That also means that you have to research the arguments against your case and the law that supports or goes against the opposing view.

In our example, we have a situation with the client who bought the house. We cannot prove fraud unless we can show that the seller knew about the graveyard. And, if we cannot prove that the seller knew about the graveyard, most likely we will lose the argument. That is the main point of the legal analysis after reviewing the case law. The typical language to introduce negative information is, "Although many of do Randalls' neighbors knew about other graveyards in the area, no one knew that there was a graveyard in the backyard." Begin the sentence with "Although," and then explain the situation or negative point. You could also say, "Unfortunately, analysis has shown..." That is typical language to use for negative information.

When discussing law that is negative to your position, you are either dismissing or distinguishing those negative cases. If you find cases that are against your point of view, one way to distinguish the case is by using parentheticals (), and explaining why the case law does not apply. For example, see the citation above that says, "Compare... [case], where there was no intent to deceive because there was no evidence the defendant knew the representation was false, with another case, Johnson, where there was an intent to deceive because there was knowledge established." Underline 'Compare' and then explain why the other cases do or do not apply.

If you find counterarguments or bad information that the other side does not seem to make, you should include them in the memo as well. You shoud not only include the arguments or the negotiation tactics that the other side is using. It should be part of the analysis because the other side might discover or make the argument later.

V. Conclusion

Essential Parts of a Modern Memo Conclusion Section	
✓ <u>Briefly</u> restate your conclusion ✓ No new facts or argument ✓ No more than one to three sentences If applicable: ✓ Give <u>Recommendations</u> ✓ Provide the <u>Next Steps</u> ✓ State the <u>Likely Outcome</u>	**Sample Language** <u>Based on the facts of this case</u>, Larson will <u>probably not be able</u> to succeed with an action for fraud. Since there is no indication that the Randalls knew of the graveyard, <u>it is unlikely</u> that Larson will be able to prove that there was a misrepresentation of a material fact. Further, as knowledge is a necessary prerequisite to an *intent to deceive*, <u>it is doubtful</u> that a fact-finder could find an intent to deceive by the Randalls.

At the end of the analysis section, you briefly restate the conclusion. The conclusion should be short with no new facts or arguments. Depending on the type of memo you are writing, you may give recommendations, provide next steps or state the likely outcome of the situation as part of the conclusion.

Suggested language to use in the Conclusion section is, 'Based on the facts of this case...' You always should make sure that you are articulating very clearly the basis of your opinions. In the example, 'Larson will probably not be able to succeed with the action.' Good conclusion language will not be too strong or absolute, such as 'it is unlikely' or 'it is doubtful.'

VI. Review of Memo Drafting Essentials – Lectures 1-3

> **Review of Memo Drafting Essentials
> Lectures 1-3**
>
> **Important Stylistic Points**
>
> ✓ <u>Plain English</u> (simple, direct, straightforward language)
>
> ✓ <u>Formal writing</u> (no contractions or slang)
>
> ✓ <u>Use an objective tone</u> (Predictive Writing)
>
> ✓ <u>Quotes only for key phrases</u> (otherwise paraphrase)
>
> ✓ <u>Short paragraphs</u> with only one topic per paragraph
>
> ✓ <u>Strong direct</u> thesis sentences
>
> ✓ <u>Make a definite decision</u> (Yes or No)

We will review the drafting essentials to write memos. Use plain English—simple, direct, and straightforward language when writing memos. Write formally, which means no contractions or slang. Use an objective tone when writing predictive memos, not persuasive ones.

If you quote from a statute or law, only do so when it is important. For example, quoting is appropriate when citing the elements of fraud from case law. Otherwise, simply paraphrase or summarize the information that you are quoting.

Your paragraphs should be short and only one topic per paragraph. Make strong topic sentences when writing headings or conclusions. Finally, come to a definite decision or give clear advice. Try to answer the question or issue by saying "yes" or "no."

第 2 部　企業内弁護士がやり取りをする文書の作成
——Drafting In-house Attorney Communications

Next, we will discuss drafting in-house attorney communications. In-house attorneys are in a unique position because they are in companies and mostly deal with non-lawyers. Whereas, law firm lawyers have daily interaction with other lawyers and the clients are actually outside the office. For law firm lawyers, the internal communications typically are not going to clients or non-lawyers. Rather, internal communications are being shared among other lawyers.

On the other hand, the in-house attorney is in a different situation because often the attorneys are working with other departments and negotiating deals or advising as part of a business team with non-lawyers. Most of the written communications are with non-lawyers, i.e., board of directors, CEO or CFO, Department Supervisors, or HR.

1. 企業内弁護士の立場で行う典型的な文書作成
Typical Drafting for In-house Attorneys

Typical Drafting for In-house Attorneys

- Most of your written communications will be with and for non-lawyers
- Drafting transactional documents re: company financing
- Negotiating and re-drafting contracts and NDAs for employees/outside counsel (Discussed in Lectures 5 & 6)
  - Ex: *Contracts and NDAs; Letters to employees, outside counsel or opposing attorneys discussing proposed terms of contracts or NDAs; Letters sending revised contracts or NDAs for review and approval; etc.*
- Collaborating with outside counsel to defend the company's rights in settlements, business transactions, etc.
  - Ex: *Letters and Memos to outside counsel: outlining issues requiring their assistance; providing information related to company IP, business transactions, terms of settlements; and give recommendations handling a legal matter*
- Preparing new corporate procedures and/or written reviews of articles of incorporation and bylaws

The types of drafting that most in-house lawyers are doing are communications for non-lawyers: day-to-day work, drafting transactional documents, negotiating and re-drafting contracts and nondisclosure statements for employees and outside counsel, letters to employees on employment issues, and dealing with outside counsel on various issues.

Other matters in-house counsel handles are collaborating with outside counsel to defend the company's rights in settlements or business transactions. The attorneys are essentially the liaison between the company and outside counsel. And, that creates specific issues in terms of drafting and the manner of communication. In-house attorneys also give recommendations and direct the outside counsel as to the authority they have to represent or act on behalf of the company. Finally, in-house counsel often prepares new corporate procedures or reviews of articles and bylaws.

2. 文書作成のためのヒント
Tips for Drafting

In-House Attorney Communications
Tips for Drafting

❏ **Always summarize the answer up front**
  - Your business partners do not want to read through many pages of text to get to the answer
  - Decide the main point of your email/memo and put it at the beginning, in summary form
  - If the answer is not clear, note that and set out the "most likely" answer/outcome. After setting out the "short answer," then you can write a detailed discussion of the facts and the analysis, if needed

❏ **Make it easy to read**
  - Break up blocks of text to make it easier to read and more interesting to look at
  - Use headings to transition to different sections or points
  - Use bullets to quickly set out information
  - use **boldface**, *italics*, or underline to distinguish or emphasize things

Your reader should be able to skim through the document and quickly get the idea of what you are saying

We will go through some tips for drafting in-house attorney communications. These tips apply to in-house attorneys, but also to those working in law firms or as solo practitioners.

The first drafting tip is to summarize your answer or response to some issue upfront. This will enable the reader to know immediately the point of your communication. Decide the main point of the e-mail or memo and put it at the beginning in summary form. If the answer is not clear, note that in the summary using language, such as "most likely [X] would be the outcome." After giving the short answer, write a detailed discussion of the facts. This writing style is similar to the structure of a memo but briefer.

The next tip is to make the document easy to read. You can do so by using paragraphs and headings rather than large blocks of text. Use bullets point to set out information, and boldface, etc. to distinguish and emphasize important points. Your reader should be able to read quickly through the document and to understand the main points.

In-House Attorney Communications
Tips for Drafting

❏ **Give a clear answer/options/recommendation**

<u>Never write</u>: "On one hand, the court might do X. On the other hand, the court might do Y."

<u>Write:</u> There are a number of factors that can impact how the court will decide the issue. <u>Based on what we know today, and in particular [Y], we think the court will most likely do [X]</u>."

❏ **Call to action/Next steps**

o Always be clear with your reader about the next steps, i.e<u>., what will happen or is needed next</u>
o If your email is urgent with action required, put that in the subject line or in the beginning sentences
  ➢ **EX: Subject: Urgent Action Required – Send Notices for Directors Meeting by 5pm today**
o Tell the reader what steps are needed next, even if nothing more is needed at this point
  ➢ *EX:* **The next draft of the contract is due on Thursday. We need to give direction to the negotiating team by Wednesday at noon. <u>We recommend to go with Option A. Please let us know if you agree or if you need additional information.</u>"**

Similar to memos, you need to give a clear answer, and options or recommendations. Never write: "On one hand, the court might do this. On the other hand, the court might do Y." This is not legal advice or why people are relying on you. Better or stronger language would be: 'There are a number of factors that can impact how the court will decide...; 'based on what we know today...; or 'we think the court will most likely do [X].' It is good to have a clear opinion about some issue.

In addition, make sure to have a call to action or next steps. Be clear about next steps and what will happen or what is needed. Sometimes there are no next steps, and if they need to wait, then explain. If there is an urgent matter or a certain action is required, put it in the subject line or in the beginning sentences. For instance, in an e-mail, you can put 'Urgent Action Required' in the subject line. This is very common language when trying to communicate that some action is necessary immediately.

Example. Tell the reader what steps are needed next even if nothing is needed at this point. 'The next draft of the contract is due on Thursday. We need to give direction to the negotiating team by Wednesday at noon. We recommend to go with Option A. Please let us know if you agree or if you need additional information.' This is an example of language that you would use to advise on the status of a matter and explain what is needed from them.

> **In-House Attorney Communications**
> **Tips for Drafting**
> ❏ **Watch for privilege issues/stay professional**
>
> o **Be careful** because in the U.S. <u>only legal advice is confidential NOT business advice</u>
>
> **Two things you need to do:**
>
> i) take all the necessary steps to establish and protect attorney client privilege, including **stating up front that you are "providing legal advice"** and
>
> ii) be sure you are actually giving legal advice
>
> ➢ If the document is "mixed," try to **separate the legal discussion from the business discussion** so the legal part can be easily redacted if necessary.
>
> [Note: Drafting Attorney Privileged Communications will be discussed in Lecture 6]
>
> ❖ **Always be professional with your in-house writing,** even casual emails. Everything you write on the job as in-house attorney is a business document
>
> ❖ **You never know who might be reading something you write** so be sure you *write smart* and keep it professional at all times

An important issue that often arises for in-house attorneys is privileged and confidential information that is communicated. You should watch for privilege issues when communicating internally with other staff or externally with outside counsel. You always have to be careful when dealing with issues of privilege because what is privileged under the law in Japan might not be the same as in the U.S. Generally, if dealing with a U.S. attorney, their idea of what is privileged information and your idea based on Japanese law about what is privileged information might not be the same. Therefore, you should articulate your understanding of the information that is considered privileged. Particularly in the U.S., only legal advice is confidential, not business advice. You must make sure that the advice you are giving is legal advice and identify it as such.

Make clear efforts to show that the information communicated in the writing is legal advice. You can say phrases in the beginning, "I am providing you legal advice on this issue." Some have a practice of stamping "Confidential Information" on the document.

I am sure all of you have on the bottom of your e-mails stating that the information that you are sending is privileged, attorney-client information and that if the e-mail is sent to the wrong person, they should ignore it, etc. E-mails will have this language to try to be as obvious as possible that the information may be privileged. In examining whether some communication is privileged, U.S. courts look for obvious attempts by the attorney to show that they are giving legal advice. And if such evidence does not exist, the courts will consider this to determine if the privilege applies.

In-house attorneys face a difficult situation because they tend to be more involved with the business teams in terms of deals. And when deals are being made, the advice is not always legal advice, rather it is "business advice." You need to separate the communication or information that might be considered business advice. For example, if you have a document discussing more than one issue and some information is legal advice and some is potentially business advice, then separate that document into two parts. The first part would say, "This is the legal discussion. I am providing you legal advice on these issues." In this section, only talk about the legal advice that you are giving. The second part would be business advice and you say, "This is the business discussion." In the end, if the document is questioned, at least you can show that what you consider to be legal advice in this document can be treated as privileged and the business advice is not privileged.

Some of the other matters that I want to emphasize here is that you should always be professional in your in-house writing, even in casual e-mails. Everything you write in your job as an in-house attorney is a business document. And what that means is at some point, if there is a question about the deal, if there is something later that comes up, you never know who is going to read something that you wrote. And, you never know when or why someone may read it. That is why it is important even in casual e-mails to be as professional as possible. Try not to be too casual because later on you may be embarrassed by some casual e-mail that you wrote, thinking that you were just writing it to someone that you work with.

3. やり取りの例
Examples of Communications

I. In House Attorney to Client

In-House Attorney Communications
Examples of Communications
In-House Attorney to Client

Sample Communications	Sample Expressions
Letters/E-mails/Memos that: - Provide **legal advice, opinions or recommendations** (See Lecture 3) - Provide **status updates** (will be discussed in this lecture) - Provide **documents for review** and/or signature - Provide **information or summaries** regarding meetings or negotiations **These communications are:** - Predictive (See Lecture 2) - Simple, direct, and easily understood	**Documents for Review or signature** ➢ **Please find attached** [list document(s)] **for your review and signature.** ➢ **Please note that** [list any specific information, instructions, or points you want to emphasize]. ➢ **If you have any questions, please let us know.** **Providing information or summaries** ➢ **We would like to provide you with a summary of the results of our meeting/discussion/ negotiation with** [other party] **regarding** [describe subject-matter] on [date]. ➢ **During the meeting, we discussed the following**... [List discussion points] ➢ **In the end, we agreed on the following...** ➢ **We were unable to resolve the following points...** ➢ **Next steps will be**...

When writing to the client, these communications with your client could be to provide legal advice, opinions or recommendations, which we talked about in Lecture 3. An important function of the attorney's communication with the client is to give status updates, provide documents for review, and give summaries regarding meetings or negotiations. These communications are the predictive writing type, as we covered in Lecture 2, and always should be done in a simple, direct and easily understood way.

We will go through some of these expressions to use depending on the type of document that you are writing. For example, if you are writing a document for the client to review, typical language to use is, 'Please find attached' listing the documents that are attached 'for your review and signature.'

If you need to emphasize some point or call their attention to some point in the documents that you sent them, say 'Please note that...' and then explain the special information. For example, "Please note that there are two agreements with respect to..."

When providing information or summaries, then the typical language or expressions that you would choose is, 'We would like to provide you with a summary of the results of our meeting/ discussion/negotiation with...' and then discuss the subject matter. For example, "We would like to provide you with the summary of the results of our meeting with NCC Corporation regarding the possible merger on May 17, 2017."

When talking about what happens during a meeting or negotiation and you want to list it, you can use the expression, "During the meeting, we discussed the following," and then list all of the things that you discussed.

If talking about some agreements made during a meeting or negotiation, then you would say, "In the end, we agreed on the following," and then list the matters that you agreed to. On the contrary, if you were unable to agree and you want to set forth the matters that are still outstanding, you can say, "We were unable to resolve the following points..." Finally, when talking about what will happen next, you would say, "The next steps will be..."

II. In House Attorney to Outside Counsel

In-House Attorney Communications
Examples of Communications
In-House Attorney to Outside Counsel

Sample Communications	Sample Expressions
Letters/E-mails/Memos that: • Outline issues requiring their assistance; • Set forth the terms of their representation (See Lecture 3 - Retainer Agreement) • Provide information related to company IP, specifics of business transactions, terms of settlements • Provide guidance and/or authority for how to proceed **These communications are:** • Predictive (See Lecture 2) • Drafted carefully even though they are confidential • Direct – no need to explain minor legal points. Can include limited legalese	**Outline Issues for representation** ➢ The matter we wish your assistance with involves... ➢ Please note that [list any specific information, instructions, or points you want to emphasize] **Providing information or summaries** ➢ Please find the following in response to your request for information on (add subject): [add bullet point list of what is being provided] ➢ We would like to provide you with a summary of the results of our meeting/discussion/ negotiation with [other party] regarding [describe subject-matter] on [date]. **Providing guidance or authority** ➢ You are hereby authorized/not authorized to... [list authorities] ➢ Our recommendation is that you proceed as follows...

Next, we will discuss communications with outside counsel. The typical situation is that you are in-house or general counsel and need to retain or hire an outside lawyer to handle some pending matter. The types of communications with outside counsel would be when you are outlining issues that require their assistance, setting forth the terms of their representation, which usually involves retainer agreements or engagement letters that we discussed in Lecture 3.

There was a question about whether these types of agreements are negotiated between counsel. The answer is "Yes." When you are an in-house counsel, just because the outside counsel sends you a retainer agreement, does not mean you have to automatically accept all terms. The retainer agreement is like any other contract. You can negotiate if there are points that you want to negotiate. If there are provisions that you want in that retainer agreement or the engagement letter, you can absolutely request that those provisions be included. Outline the issues requiring the outside counsel's assistance and define the terms of their representation.

In addition, if outside counsel represents your company in a negotiation or as part of a case, you will need to provide them with relevant information about the company relating to intellectual property or specifics of business transactions that would be relevant. As in-house counsel, you will be the one sending the information to the outside lawyers. The lawyers will always deal with each other.

And then, you will often provide guidance or authority for how to proceed in a legal matter. What this means is you will be the one telling the lawyer what they need to do and what they have the right to do and what they do not have the right to do as part of their representation of your client. This always has to be done very formally, because giving a lawyer authority or telling them they cannot do something is crucial in terms of the relationship. For instance, if outside counsel is negotiating a deal and you give them authority to settle or to make an agreement up to a certain amount of money, you cannot let them go beyond their authority.

For example, when I dealt with insurance companies and their lawyers, they would tell us, "We'll agree to settle this claim, but you can only settle it for up to $200,000 dollars and that's it. You can't go beyond 200,000." And so, as outside counsel, you get the authority from the "client." As an in-house counsel, you are the "client" and give the authority or guidance as to what you want the outside lawyer to do.

Again, these communications are predictive, meaning that you need to make sure that they are objective and that any relevant information is always included. The one point I wanted to make is even though technically they are outside counsel and represent your company, you still have to draft carefully the communications and documents that you send to them. Even though they are representing your company and there is privilege, you should still be very careful about how you articulate information when you send it to them, particularly information that is confidential. Even though there may be a privilege that applies, as the in-house counsel you should always be extremely careful about how you are sending and drafting this information. You do not know who may be privy to the communication or document, and therefore, you have to be careful when communicating with outside counsel.

One point about the way of writing or communicating with outside lawyers—because you are talking to attorneys as opposed to clients, you do not have to explain minor legal points, and you can use legalese or technical legal terms. If dealing with lawyers, it is acceptable to say, for instance, "material facts" instead of "bad information." You can use these types of legal terms with lawyers, of course, because they will understand them.

Here are a few sample expressions. Outlining issues for representation: 'The matter we wish your assistance with involves...' Use this phrase when stating what you want the outside lawyer to do or to explain the situation. Again, if you need to point something out specifically, say 'Please note that' and then you list any specific information or instructions or points that you want to emphasize.

Providing information or summaries: 'Please find the following in response to your request for information...' Again, always be clear in your correspondence. If providing information to outside counsel, it is good to list exactly what has been provided to them, such as contracts, articles of incorporation, etc. This communication then becomes the written record of what you gave to outside counsel.

Providing information or summaries: 'We would like to provide you with a summary of the results of our meeting.' If you are talking about meeting with the board of directors on the issue and you need to summarize for them what the board would like in a certain situation, 'We would like to provide you with a summary of the results of our meeting regarding.' This is similar to what you would do with clients.

Providing guidance and authority: 'You are hereby authorized' or 'You are hereby not authorized.' This is important because these will have legal effect later if your outside counsel does something that they were not authorized to do, you need to have a clear record of what you told them they had the right to do and did not to do.

If we are talking about giving recommendations on how to proceed, 'Our recommendation is that you proceed as follows.' This is where you are giving instructions to outside counsel. And, this protects your company because if outside counsel does something beyond what you recommended, you need to be able to show that this is what you told them that they should do. You need to have a very clear record and show that your communications are clear on those points.

III. In House Attorney to Opposing Counsel

In-House Attorney Communications
Examples of Communications
In-House Attorney to <u>Opposing Counsel</u>

Sample Communications	Sample Expressions
Letters and E-mails that: • <u>Outline your client's position</u> (Ex. Offer Letter; Negotiations; Response to Opposing Counsel Letter) • <u>Demand/Request certain actions</u> (Ex. Cease and Desist Letter; Demand Letter) • <u>Summarize discussions or agreements</u> • <u>Provide documents or information</u> related to business transactions or agreements • Transmit legal documents and pleadings related to litigation **These communications are:** • Persuasive (See Lecture 2) • <u>Drafted using formal language</u> • <u>Thorough in explaining legal issues and positions</u>, including using legal citations where necessary • Drafted with expectation that they may be closely examined in court at some future point	**Outline Client Position** ➢ <u>Our client's position on this matter is</u>... ➢ <u>In response to your assertion that...we are of the opinion that</u>... **Demand/Request Certain Actions** ➢ <u>We demand that your client immediately cease and desist from the following</u>...[describe actions] ➢ <u>We request that your client</u> [describe action] <u>by</u> [date]. **Summarize Discussions or Agreements** ➢ <u>Based on our discussions of...we understand the following</u>... ➢ <u>We would like to confirm our understanding of the agreement</u>... **Provide documents or information/ Transmit legal documents related to litigation** ➢ <u>Pursuant to your request for...please find attached the following</u>... ➢ <u>In response to your inquiry about...we can inform you that</u>...

Next, we will look at some examples of communications between in-house counsel and opposing counsel. Communications with opposing counsel are a different situation because we move from the predictive style of writing to persuasive writing.

Here are sample communications with opposing counsel. These types of communications serve a particular purpose. For instance, writing letters or e-mails that outline the client's position in an offer letter, or in response to opposing counsel's request. Another type of communication is a demand or request for the other side to take certain actions, such as in "Cease and Desist" letters or demand letters. A letter to cease and desist is when you want the opposing side to stop doing some action, such as demanding that they cease violating your client's intellectual property rights. Then, there are demand letters, which is when you are demanding some action from the opposing side.

The other types of communications are summarizing discussions or agreements, and providing documents of information relating to business transaction or agreements, such as sending drafts of contracts back and forth, or transmitting legal documents that are related to litigation. You have to draft the types of communications using formal language.

You should be thorough in explaining legal issues and positions using legal citations where necessary. Similar to memorandums, when dealing with opposing counsel, you have to be very formal. If making some assertion, you need to cite the law or case law that supports the assertion. Provide the legal authority for any important law that is favorable to your side or some important point that you need to make. Again, you draft these communications with the expectation that they might be closely examined in a court at some point.

Here are some sample expressions when outlining the client's position: 'Our client's position on this matter is...' and then explain. Another example is, 'In response to your assertion that...' If trying to respond to the other side you could say, 'In response to your assertion that our patent was invalid, we are of the opinion...'

For demands or requests for certain actions, such as cease and desist letters, you can use, 'We demand that your client immediately cease and desist from the following...,' then, state the requested action. Requests such as these have a legal effect, and therefore should be formal. For instance, 'We request that your client send us a draft contract by Wednesday, December 31st.' Later, you can use the communication to show that you have requested them to take some action.

If talking about summarizing discussions or agreements, the expressions to use are similar. For instance, 'Based on our discussions...we understand the following...' This is when summarizing a meeting. "Based on our discussions or negotiations of May 17th, we understand the following. Your client is willing to purchase our business for this certain amount of money" or whatever are the terms. 'Based on our discussions, we understand the following' and then list your understanding of the circumstance. You could also say, 'We would like to confirm our understanding of the agreement.' These phrases are useful if you have gone through some negotiations and you want to communicate with the other side before writing a letter of intent or a contract, and you want to summarize the points of the agreement.

Finally, if providing documents or transmitting documents relating to litigation, you can use the following phrases: 'Pursuant to your request for...' For instance, 'Pursuant to your request for...please find attached the following...' If the other side is inquiring about information, you can state, 'In response to your inquiry about...' For example, "In response to your inquiry about closing dates, we can inform you that...," then list the information. These are good expressions if responding to requests for information.

IV. Example to Client

> **In-House Attorney Communications**
> **Example <u>To Client</u>**
>
> **Subject: Case Update and Recommendations**
>
> Dear Ms. Larson,
>
> <u>We would like to update you</u> on our discussion with Mr. Smith, the real estate appraiser, whom we met on May 15, 2017.
>
> <u>Based on the information we provided him</u> on your purchase of the home from the Randalls, <u>and his research</u> on housing values in the area, Mr. Smith informed us that <u>in his opinion</u> the value of the property is $27,000 less than what you paid for it.
>
> As the Randalls purposely did not inform you about the graveyard in the backyard, <u>it is our recommendation</u> that we write a formal letter to the Randalls requesting that they refund $27,000 of the purchase price to you as a result of their actions.
>
> <u>Please let us know if you have any questions or concerns.</u>

Next, we will discuss an example of in-house attorney communications to a client giving a case update and recommendations. In this case, we are going back to the purchase of the house with the graveyard. We are going to give the client a case update and recommendation. 'We would like to update you on our discussion with Mr. Smith, the real estate appraiser, whom we met on May 15, 2017.' This is the situation where you want to find out the decrease in the value of the property. There is a graveyard so the property is not worth as much. You had a meeting with an appraiser who gave this opinion. You are communicating this opinion to your client. We are talking about case updates.

When talking about communicating information from other people, be sure to show the basis of their opinion. What did they rely on? What information did they look at? Here, 'Based on the information we provided him on your purchase of the home from the Randalls, and his research on the housing values in the area, Mr. Smith informed us that in his opinion the value of the property is $27,000 less than what you paid for it.' 'As the Randalls purposely did not inform you about the graveyard in your backyard, it is our recommendation that we write a formal letter to the Randalls' requesting that they refund $27,000 of the purchase price to you as a result of their actions.'

In the next example, we will look at this situation and the way of writing the letter to a client compared to opposing counsel. In the latter, you may use formal, technical legal words, such as "material facts." However, with clients, you should not use technical terms. Rather, explain and give the update in simple, easy to understand language. In this instance, you say, "They purposely did not inform you about the graveyard." That is very simple language. When talking to other lawyers, you would say, "They refused to conceal" or "They did not disclose a material fact," which is the technical legal definition of concealment. But, when talking to a client, you do not need to say terms like "material representations" and "material facts" because the client is less likely to understand the legal meaning or significance of the terms. Simple, direct language is always best when communicating with a client.

V. Example to Outside Counsel

**In-House Attorney Communications
Example To Outside Counsel**

Subject: Confirmation of Engagement (Larson – File XXX)

Dear Mrs. Jones,

This letter will <u>confirm our discussions</u> on May 25, 2017, where <u>we agreed that your firm would represent our client</u>, Susan Larson, in her fraud claim against Mr. and Mrs. Randall <u>arising out of</u> her purchase of their home on April 15, 2017...

<u>In this regard, please find enclosed</u> a signed engagement letter from our client dated May 30, 2017.

As we discussed, <u>your representation of Ms. Larson will be limited to</u> her fraud claim against the Randalls. <u>You are hereby authorized to enter into negotiations</u> with the Randalls attorney for the recovery of $27,000 from the purchase price... <u>No further actions are authorized at this time.</u>

<u>We look forward to receiving your recommendations for next steps.</u>

The next example is about writing to outside counsel. In this situation, we are writing to outside counsel and confirming that they are representing your client in a case. In the subject line, clearly state the subject matter of the communication. If there is some internal way of identifying the matter, usually by name or number, it is good to put that information in the subject line as well.

In this communication, we are confirming the discussion between in-house counsel and outside counsel. 'This letter will confirm our discussions on May 25 where we agreed that your firm would represent our client, Susan Larson, in her fraud claim arising out of her purchase of their home...' Again, when talking to outside counsel, using more technical legal terms is appropriate, such as 'arising out of her purchase,' because this is the definition under the law of fraud.

In the next section we are attaching the engagement letter or agreement and detailing the scope of the outside counsel's representation in the matter. 'As we discussed, your representation of Ms. Larson will be limited to her fraud claim against the Randalls.' To narrow the scope of the representation, use language such as, 'Your representation will be limited to...' and 'You are hereby authorized to enter into negotiations with the Randalls for their recovery of the $27,000 from the purchase price...No further actions are authorized at this time.' This is the language explaining what outside counsel may or may not do. Essentially, what you are saying is that counsel only has the authority to negotiate. Here is the language to limit their authority. 'No further actions are authorized at this time.'

Finally, 'We are looking forward to receiving your recommendations for next steps,' which is a typical way to close a letter.

VI. Example to Opposing Counsel

> **In-House Attorney Communications**
> **Example To Opposing Counsel**
>
> **Subject: Larson Fraud Claim against James Randall**
>
> Dear Mr. Johnson,
>
> We are writing with regard to our client, Susan Larson, and her purchase of a home from your client, James Randall, on April 15, 2017, for $127,000.
>
> Upon moving into the home, Ms. Larson promptly discovered that a graveyard existed in the backyard of the house, which your clients purposely failed to disclose to her despite repeated communications between them about the backyard. These communications took place orally on March 25, 2017, while Ms. Larson was doing a walkthrough of the property; and again in writing on March 27, 2017, when Mr. Randall wrote an e-mail to Ms. Larson....
>
> As a direct result of your client's fraudulent actions, Ms. Larson has suffered damages in the amount of $27,000, representing the decrease in value of the property due to the existence of a graveyard in the backyard. We have enclosed the report of our real estate appraiser reflecting the $27,000 decrease.
>
> We look forward to hearing how your client intends to resolve this matter.

The last example in this section will deal with a communication to opposing counsel. In the same example regarding the purchase of a house, we are writing to opposing counsel to request reimbursement of $27,000 dollars due to fraud. This type of letter is different because this is a persuasive letter meaning that this is argumentative. We are representing the client's position, not trying to give a balanced and a fair approach. When writing to opposing counsel, you are trying to persuade them that they owe something to your client or that they have done something inappropriate and owe damages. This is a much different style of writing.

The example language begins with 'We are writing with regard to...' and then explains the claim. The next paragraph gives the essential facts that will lead to your conclusion. For instance, 'Upon moving into the home, [she] promptly discovered that a graveyard existed in the backyard, which your clients purposely failed to disclose to her despite repeated communications between them about the backyard.' Why is this factual detail important? This information is important because we do not have conclusive facts about the situation. We still have to prove that the original homeowners knew about the graveyard but failed to disclose. When talking to opposing counsel, this information would be persuasive. The style of writing is persuasive and the language presents the facts in the best light for your client. Therefore, you are saying, we believe that your client purposely failed to disclose this information even though the parties spoke repeatedly about the home. This is a much more persuasive way of writing. You are not balancing what did the neighbors know—maybe they did not know this or that. You are just stating the claim to the opposing counsel in a way that is as persuasive as possible.

Next, set forth the facts that support your arguments. For instance, 'These communications took place orally on March 25th while they were doing a walkthrough of the property; and again in writing...' The following sentence begins with 'As a direct result of,' which is language to use when explaining that your client has suffered some problem or some damages. In this case, we say 'fraudulent actions,' but we can say, 'As a direct result of your client's actions, she has suffered damages in the amount of $27,000 dollars, representing the decrease in the value of the property.' Again, it is acceptable to use more technical legal terms with opposing counsel and write in a more formal manner.

A nice expression to use when trying to resolve the issue is to say, 'We look forward to hearing how your client intends to resolve this matter.' 'Intends to resolve' is the important language there.

It is important to note the differences in language when writing as an in-house attorney to a client, outside counsel, and opposing counsel. There are also occasions when to cite to legal authority supporting your argument, such as citing to a statute or case law. You can cite to legal authority in a letter or e-mail to opposing counsel.

第3部　進捗報告のためのメモランダムの作成準備 ——Preparing Case Status Memoranda

1. 進捗報告のためのメモとはどんなものか？ What is a Case Status Memo?

Case Status Memoranda

What is a Case Status Memo?

- A <u>Case Status Memo</u> informs the reader on the current state of <u>all or a portion</u> of a legal matter

- The Memo can be written for <u>internal purposes</u> (usually for a partner or supervising attorney) or <u>external purposes</u> (for a client)

- The <u>purpose of the memo will determine the length and depth</u> of the document

Note: See earlier Lecture on Client Communications vs writing for other lawyers

Finally, I want to talk about preparing case status memoranda. A case status memo informs the reader on the current state of either all or a portion of a legal matter or a deal or whatever it is that you are working on. It can be written for internal purposes, meaning for a partner in a law firm, your supervising attorney, or for a client. The purpose of the memo will determine the length and depth of the document. For instance, you are summarizing a meeting with a real estate appraiser or explaining the status of negotiations.

The length of a case status memo depends on the topic of your memo and the complexity of the issues involved. As a tip, always look at earlier client communications.

In terms of best practices in your case file management, it is important to have status memos because someone should always be able to open that file and know exactly what has been done, what still needs to be done, and what the issues are. The file should always be in a state where you can look at it quickly and understand where the case is or where the deal is or whatever it is that you are doing.

2. 参考例
Sample Format

Case Status Memoranda
Sample Format

Memorandum

To: [Recipient]
From: [Writer]
Date: May 25, 2017
Re: [Topic]

I. Introduction Statement

II. Background/Facts

III. Topic I

IV. Topic II

V. Topic III

VI. Recommendations/Next Steps

Here is the sample format for memorandums. Again, you have the recipient, the writer, and the topic. Then, you have an introduction statement, background facts, substantive topics or issues involved, followed by recommendations and next steps. We will go through each of these sections.

I. Heading

When talking about the heading here, you should give the basic but important information, such as the client name, the case type or description and any case file designation. For instance, here, if writing this memo to a senior partner, Sandra Smith, and this memo is from James Jones regarding 'Tokyo Drug Company Patent Infringement File Number.' This is the file number. Let's say your client is Tokyo Drug Company and there is a question about a patent infringement matter. As one of your handouts in this lecture, I have distributed the full case status memo. You can take a look at it to see how it all fits together as well.

Case Status Memoranda
Sample Format - Heading

Memorandum

To: [Recipient]
From: [Writer]
Date: May 25, 2017
Re: [Topic] – <u>Should state Client name, case type/description, and any File# designation</u>

Sample - Internal
Memorandum

To: **Sandra Smith, Senior Partner**
From: **James Jones, Associate**
Date: May 25, 2017
Re: **Tokyo Drug Company Patent Infringement, File # XXXXX**

II. Introduction Statement

> **Case Status Memoranda**
> **Sample Format – Introduction Statement**
>
> ❏ The <u>Introduction Statement should be a simple explanation</u> of the purpose of the memo
>
> **Typical Language:**
> - The purpose of this memo is to provide an update on the status of... (formal)
> - This memo will give an update on... (informal)
>
> ------
>
> **Sample - Internal**
>
> **I. Introduction Statement**
>
> The purpose of this memo is to provide an update on the status of the Tokyo Drug Company patent infringement claim against California Drug Company, and to make recommendations for next steps.

The introduction statement should be simple. You are explaining the type of document and the purpose of the writing. For instance, 'The purpose of this memo is to provide an update on the status of' and then list why you are writing. This language is more formal. Status memos can be a formal letter or, more commonly, e-mails. The level of formality depends on what it is that you are doing and who you are writing to. The informal way of making an introduction statement is, 'This memo will give an update on.' For instance, 'This memo will give an update on our discussion with the real estate appraiser on May 17th.' But, if more formal, 'The purpose of this memo is to provide an update on the status of negotiations for the sale of a company X to company Y.'

Here is some sample language. 'The purpose of this memo is to provide an update on the status of the Tokyo Drug Company patent infringement claim against California Drug Company, and to make recommendations for next steps.' This example is about a drug company that developed a drug, received a patent, and then some other company started selling a generic version of that drug. The introduction statement is simple.

III. Background Facts

Case Status Memoranda	
Sample Format – Background Facts	
❖ <u>Tell the background story</u> - who are the parties, what is their relationship, and what is the problem ❖ <u>Include all relevant facts</u> ❖ Draft the facts in context of the <u>legal issues</u> ❖ <u>Describe past</u> court proceedings or important meetings (if applicable) ❖ <u>Keep the story short</u>, but thoroughly discuss the factual issues ❖ Organize facts in a <u>logical manner</u>	Sample - Internal **II. Background/Facts** Tokyo Drug Company, through its New York subsidiary, developed the new cancer drug CANCEX, obtaining a ten year patent and FDA approval for exclusive sale of the drug in April 2016. In June 2016, Tokyo Drug Company began selling CANCEX to hospitals and pharmacies in all 50 states. In December 2016, it came to the attention of Tokyo Drug Company that California Drug Company had started selling generic CANCEX to hospital and pharmacies in California, in violation of Tokyo Drug Company's patent. After consultation with Tokyo Drug Company, it was determined that our firm should send a *Cease and Desist Let*ter to California Drug Company.

The next section is the background facts. These facts are similar to when writing any other office memo. You need to include certain basic information, such as the parties, their relationship, and any court proceedings. Include all of the relevant facts. Keep it short but thoroughly discuss the factual issues. And, organize the facts in a logical manner.

In this situation, the facts are the 'Tokyo Drug Company, through its New York subsidiary, developed a new cancer drug CANCEX, obtaining a ten year patent and FDA approval for exclusive sale of the drug in April 2016. In June 2016, Tokyo Drug Company began selling CANCEX to hospitals and pharmacies in all 50 states. In December 2016, it came to the attention of Tokyo Drug Company that California Drug Company had started selling generic CANCEX to hospital and pharmacies in California, in violation of Tokyo Drug Company's patent...' 'After consultation with Tokyo Drug Company, it was determined that our firm should send a Cease and Desist Letter to California Drug Company.'

After the background facts, you are writing about the topics or matters of the update. When doing so, state the facts up to the moment that you begin the status update. In the example, the background facts explain the facts up to the point where we sent a cease and desist letter. The update is about what happened after we sent the cease and desist letter. Therefore, the background facts should take the reader all the way up to the point when giving the update.

Case status memos are what we call "stand alone documents," which means that the reader should be able to read the document and understand the circumstances clearly without needing to read other documents. For example, after reading this document, I should be able to know that we are representing the drug company that developed a drug, and that someone is violating their patent. You need to make sure that if the reader only has time to read this one case status memo, they would be able to understand the context of the case and the update you are providing.

IV. Topics

Case Status Memoranda
Sample Format – Topics

❑ Each portion of the matter that you are updating should have a **separate Topic Heading** ❑ The Topic Heading should **clearly identify the matter** that is being updated ❑ Each Topic section should include **a full discussion** of the status of the matter being updated, including specific dates and document names.	**Sample – Topic - Internal** **III. The Cease and Desist Letter of December 24, 2016 and California Drug Company Response of May 10, 2017** Following the agreement made with our client during the meeting of December 15, 2016, a *Cease and Desist Letter*, dated December 24, 2016, was drafted and sent to California Drug Company at their headquarters in Los Angeles, California. The Letter was hand-delivered and signed for by the company's President on December 27, 2016. The Cease and Desist Letter demanded that California Drug Company stop selling generic CANCEX immediately, and to compensate Tokyo Drug Company... Several months of communications between the companies occurred, and on May 10, 2017, California Drug Company delivered a certified letter to our office, through their legal counsel, stating that they did not infringe on Tokyo Drug Company's patent for CANCEX because the patent was issued invalidly due to the fact that Tokyo Drug Company provided faulty data to support its patent application. Consequently, they have refused to comply with the *Cease and Desist Letter* of December 24, 2016.

In this example, we are updating on what happened after we sent the cease and desist letter. Each portion of the topic should have a separate heading which should clearly identify the matter that is being updated. In addition, each topic should include a full discussion of the status of the matter that is being updated, including relevant documents and dates.

In this situation, we are discussing 'The Cease and Desist Letter of December 24, 2016 and California Drug Company Response of May 10, 2017.' Here is good language to explain what happened after we sent the letter. 'Following the agreement made with our client during the meeting of December 15, a Cease and Desist Letter, dated December 24, 2016, was drafted and sent to California Drug Company.' In this situation, the update will include all of the relevant legal facts that are important. We will state that the letter was hand-delivered and signed for by the company's president. We discuss this factual detail because this proves that the letter was sent and received. The letter 'demanded that California Drug Company stop selling generic CAN-CEX immediately, and to compensate Tokyo Drug Company.' Therefore, you are including all of the relevant information from this moment that the letter was sent.

Then, you are stating that 'Several months of communications between the companies occurred' and discussing what happened after this point. 'On May 10, 2017, California Drug Company delivered a certified letter to our office, through their legal counsel, stating that they did not infringe on [our] patent… because the patent was issued invalidly due to the fact that Tokyo Drug Company provided faulty data to support its application,' and therefore, they refuse to comply. This sentence explains the topic and gives the information about what happened up to this moment in time. Now we are informing that the other side answered us saying that, number one, they did not infringe our patent; and, number two, they are refusing to comply with the cease and desist letter.

Writing the case status memo in this manner, the reader can immediately understand the important information and what happened next in the sequence of events. Everything that is important is stated in the document.

V. Recommendations/Next Steps

Case Status Memoranda
Sample Format – Recommendations/Next Steps

❏ Conclude with clear recommendations ❏ State any future issues/ problems and deadlines ❏ **Typical Language** • Our options are... • Our recommendation is/We recommend... • Next steps in this process would be...	**Sample – Recommendations/Next Steps** **IV. Recommendations/Next Steps** Given California Drug Company's refusal to comply with our *Cease and Desist* request, <u>our options at this point</u> are to either pursue some form of litigation or try to enter into some type of alternative dispute resolution. Due to the time and expense of litigation, <u>our recommendation is</u> to propose entering into some form of mediation with California Drug Company. The mediation could be binding or non-binding, with a benefit of binding mediation being that the parties can agree on a damages price range based on the California Drug Company sales data. <u>Next steps in this process would be to</u> discuss this recommendation with Tokyo Drug Company, and if acceptable to them, formally propose mediation to California Drug Company.

Finally, every case status memo should have a recommendations and next steps section. You always should conclude with clear recommendations and state any future issues or problems. Typical language in this situation: 'Our options are' and then list the options; 'Our recommendation is;' 'We recommend;' and 'Next steps in this process are.' These are all very useful expressions to use in this section.

In this example, we state, 'Given [that the drug company refused] to comply with our cease and desist, request, our options at this point are to either pursue some form of litigation or to try to enter into some type of alternative dispute resolution.' Next, you are recommending mediation in this matter and advising that the mediation could be binding or non-binding. 'Due to the time and expense of litigation, our recommendation is to propose entering into some form of mediation...' Finally, the expression, 'Next steps in this process would be to discuss the recommendation for mediation with Tokyo Drug Company...' These recommendations are clear and state what we should do in the future.

3. 検　討
Sample Language Review

Case Status Memoranda
Sample Language - Review

(Intro)
- We would like to update you on the status of (describe matter)

(Completed Tasks)
- Currently, we have finalized...
- We have completed...
- We have already...

(Uncompleted Tasks)
- We are still in the process of...
- At present, we have yet to complete...
- We have not...yet.
- We expect...to be completed by...

Let's review the useful expressions when writing case status memorandums. Good introduction language to use: 'We would like to update you on the status of...' and you describe the matter. For completed tasks: 'Currently, we have finalized' and list what you have completed. A less formal expression for completed tasks: 'We have completed' or 'We have already...' and make a list. These are different expressions with the first one being a little bit more formal and the other two being a little less formal.

For uncompleted tasks: 'We are still in the process...' or 'At present, we have yet to complete...' These two are formal expressions. Less formal expressions for uncompleted tasks: 'We have not finished yet' or 'We expect [insert task] to be completed by...' Those are the expressions that you can use when writing case status memos.

Presentation Addendum

1. Addendum 1: Sample Case Status Memoranda

Sample Case Status Memorandum

Memorandum

To: Sandra Smith, Senior Partner
From: James Jones, Associate
Date: June 9, 2017
Re: **Tokyo Drug Company Patent Infringement, File # XXXXX**

I. Introduction Statement

The purpose of this memo is to provide an update on the status of the Tokyo Drug Company patent infringement claim against California Drug Company, and to make recommendations for next steps.

II. Background/Facts

Tokyo Drug Company, through its New York subsidiary, developed the new cancer drug CANCEX, obtaining a ten year patent and FDA approval for exclusive sale of the drug in April 2016. In June 2016, Tokyo Drug Company began selling CANCEX to hospitals and pharmacies in all 50 states. In early December 2016, it came to the attention of Tokyo Drug Company that California Drug Company had started selling generic CANCEX to hospital and pharmacies in California, in violation of Tokyo Drug Company's patent. After consulting with Tokyo Drug Company, it was determined that our firm should send a Cease and Desist Letter to California Drug Company.

III. The Cease and Desist Letter of December 24, 2016 and California Drug Company Response of May 10, 2017

Following the agreement made with our client during the meeting of

December 15, 2016, a Cease and Desist Letter, dated December 24, 2016, was sent to California Drug Company at their headquarters in Los Angeles, California. The Letter was hand-delivered and signed for by the company's President on December 27, 2016. The Cease and Desist Letter demanded that California Drug Company stop selling generic CANCEX immediately, and compensate Tokyo Drug Company for any damages that their patent infringement caused.

Several months of communications between the companies occurred, and on May 10, 2017, California Drug Company delivered a certified letter to our office, through their legal counsel, stating that they did not infringe on Tokyo Drug Company's patent for CANCEX because the patent was issued invalidly due to Tokyo Drug Company providing faulty data to support its patent application. Consequently, they have refused to comply with the Cease and Desist Letter of December 24, 2016.

IV. Recommendations/Next Steps

Given California Drug Company's refusal to comply with our Cease and Desist request, our options at this point are to either pursue some form of litigation or try to enter into alternative dispute resolution.

Due to the time and expense of litigation, our recommendation is to propose entering into some form of mediation with California Drug Company. The mediation may be binding or non-binding, with a benefit of binding mediation being that the parties can agree on a damages price range based on the California Drug Company sales data.

Next steps in this process would be to discuss this recommendation with Tokyo Drug Company, and if acceptable to them, formally propose mediation to California Drug Company.

2. Addendum 2 - Sample Legal Memorandum

SAMPLE LEGAL MEMORANDUM

Memorandum [1]

To: Sandra Smith, Senior Partner
From: John Jones, Associate
Date: June 1, 2017
Re: Julie Larson; Real Estate Fraud; File No. 04-567

Does Larson have a claim for fraud against the Randalls when she purchased a house from the Randalls unaware that there was a graveyard in the backyard, if the Randalls deny that they knew about the graveyard?

Brief Answer

No, Larson probably does not have a claim for fraud against the Randalls. A fraud claim requires a false representation or concealment of a material fact. A defendant must know a representation is false or that a material fact is being concealed, and have an intent to deceive. Here, while Larson may have reasonably relied on the Randalls' representations and suffered damages, it does not appear that the Randalls made any false representations, concealed any material facts, or that they intended to deceive Larson.

---

[1] This Sample Memo is excepted from
http://www.law.duke.edu/curriculum/coursehomepages/Fall2004/160_02/writSamples/sample_e.pdf

Discussion/Analysis

I. Larson Probably Cannot Recover for Fraud since There is No Indication That the Randalls Knew about the Graveyard in Their Backyard When They Sold Their Home to Larson.

To succeed in an action for fraud, a plaintiff must show all the following elements: (1) that a defendant made a false representation relating to, or concealed, a material fact and the defendant knew the representation was false or made it recklessly without any knowledge of its truth; (2) the defendant made the false representation with an intent to deceive the plaintiff; (3) the plaintiff reasonably relied and acted upon the representation; and (4) the plaintiff suffered damages. Myers v. Thomas G. Evans, Inc., 374 S.E.2d 385, 391 (N.C. 1988).

Here, Larson might have reasonably relied upon the available information and suffered damage, but she cannot meet the first two elements of fraud. First, there was no misrepresentation or concealment of a material fact. Second, there is no indication that the Randalls knew about the graveyard, an essential element of an intent to deceive.

A. Larson likely cannot succeed with a fraud claim because there was no misrepresentation of a material fact.

Fraud requires a false representation of a material fact. Id. at 391. A material fact is one that affects a purchaser's decision to buy property. Powell v. Wold, 362 S.E.2d 796, 798 (N.C. Ct. App. 1987). Fraud also requires a false representation. Myers, 374 S.E.2d at 391. A representation "must be definite and specific." Ragsdale v. Kennedy, 209 S.E.2d 494, 500 (N.C. 1974). An "unspecific statement of opinion" is not a representation. Carpenter v. Merrill Lynch Realty Operating P'ship, 424 S.E.2d 178, 180 (N.C. Ct. App. 1993). For example, in Carpenter a broker told a buyer that a road-widening project would probably take place on the opposite side of the road from the buyer's house since there were already curbs and gutters on the buyer's side. Id. Because the statement was manifestly based on common sense, not knowledge, it was considered an unspecific opinion, not a representation. Id.

In this case, Larson will probably not be able to show that the Randalls made a misrepresentation of a material fact. There is little question that the existence of the graveyard is a material fact. Had Larson known about the defect, she presumably would not have agreed to pay $27,000 more than the value of the house. See Powell, 362 S.E.2d at 798.

However, the Randalls' statements to Larson about the backyard do not amount to representations. The Randalls told Larson that the backyard was tranquil and sent her a fax stating that if she bought the house she could relax out back with a cup of tea. As in Carpenter, where the broker's statements were based on common sense and without authority, the Randalls' statements were opinions based on common sense and do not constitute representations. See Carpenter, 424 S.E.2d at 181.

In sum, Larson likely cannot succeed with a fraud claim because there was no misrepresentation of a material fact.

B. Larson likely cannot succeed with an action for fraud since there is no indication the Randalls acted with an intent to deceive.

Fraud requires that a representation or concealment be made with an intent to deceive. Myers, 374 S.E.2d at 391. Intent may be inferred from a party's conduct throughout a transaction. Harbach v. Lain & Keonig, Inc., 326 S.E.2d 115, 119 (N.C. Ct. App. 1985). Intent is closely tied to the element of knowledge; it exists when a seller knows that a representation would be relied on by a buyer. Calloway v. Wyatt, 97 S.E.2d 881, 885 (N.C. 1957). There is no intent to deceive unless a seller has knowledge of a material fact. Compare Myers, 374 S.E.2d at 392 (no intent to deceive when no evidence defendant knew representation false), with Johnson, 140 S.E.2d at 313 (intent to deceive where knowledge established).

In this case, the Randalls did not act with an intent to deceive because there is no indication that they knew about the graveyard. As discussed previously, there is no indication that the Randalls read the newspaper article about gravestones or knew that the gravestones were located outside toward the back of their lot. Although many of the Randalls' neighbors knew of other graveyards in the area, none knew that there was a graveyard in the Randalls' backyard. Thus, without any proof that the Randalls had knowledge of the graveyard, it is likely that it cannot be established that the Randalls intended to deceive Larson. See Myers, 374 S.E.2d at 391.

Conclusion

Based on the facts of this case, Larson will probably not be able to succeed with an action for fraud. Since there is no indication that the Randalls knew of the graveyard, it is unlikely that Larson will be able to prove that there was a misrepresentation of a material fact. Further, as knowledge is a necessary prerequisite to an intent to deceive, it is doubtful that a fact-finder could find an intent to deceive on the part of the Randalls.

Lecture 5

国際法務における交渉及びこれに伴う契約文書作成の基礎と応用

◆

Negotiating and Contracting Drafting in International Law Practice

> 国際法務における交渉の留意点やこれに伴う契約文書作成スキルを習得することを目的として，基礎から応用までを例を挙げながら具体的に解説します。

Welcome to our fifth lecture in our six-part series. Tonight, we will discuss negotiating and contract drafting in international law practice. Specifically, we will discuss: 1) professional lawyering skills for negotiating contracts in international settings; 2) legal practices for drafting letters of intent; 3) the writing process for contract drafting, analysis and review; and 4) negotiating and drafting non-disclosure agreements.

Lecture Five: Negotiating and Contract Drafting in International Law Practice

---

Agenda:
- ❑ Professional Lawyering Skills for Negotiating Contracts in International Settings
- ❑ Legal Practices for Drafting Letters of Intent
- ❑ The Writing Process for Contract Drafting, Analysis and Review
- ❑ Negotiating and Drafting Non-Disclosure Agreements

Marc Lassman
Adjunct Professor of Law
Temple University School of Law, Japan Campus
June 19, 2017
18:00 – 20:00

Lecture 5 Negotiating and Contracting Drafting in International Law Practice

The focus tonight will not be on providing general advice about negotiation and contract drafting. We will discuss the language to use or expect to see as part of contracts or as part of the negotiation process. Also, we will talk about the way in which common law attorneys think and approach negotiating and contract drafting.

With regard to drafting of letters of intent, we will discuss when to use letters of intent and the important provisions that are generally found in letters of intent, specifically binding versus non-binding provisions which are important aspects. In discussing the negotiation and drafting of non-disclosure agreements, we will focus on when to use non-disclosure agreements, the important provisions that you should expect to see, and negotiating non-disclosure agreements. We will look at whether the non-disclosure agreement is mutual or non-mutual, the duration of such agreements, and defining confidential information. Those will be the main points for tonight's lecture.

第1部 国際法務における契約交渉を行う弁護士のための専門スキル ——Professional Lawyering Skills for Negotiating Contracts in International Settings

First, we will talk about professional lawyering skills for negotiating contracts in international settings.

1. 交渉に成功するためのヒント
Tips for Successful Negotiations

I. Key Goals to Remember

> **Tips for Successful Negotiations**
> **Key Goals to Remember**
>
> **Prioritize: focus on getting key business points into the contract**
> - The other side will be tough on the points that it really cares about
> - Often flexible/reasonable on less important points
> - To do this effectively, ***must understand (in advance) your own key objectives and deal points for the transaction***
> - <u>Know when to push & when to compromise</u>
>
> **Take a practical approach to the contract**
> - If sophisticated – the other side will try to obtain rights that it can actually enforce without too much delay or expense
> - <u>Where is the money in the transaction</u>: in case of a dispute – what's the fastest, surest, cheapest way to get access to that money
> - <u>Maximize leverage if there is a dispute</u>: this analysis may be the highest value-add of an experienced business person or legal counsel

In general, when negotiating with common law attorneys, these are the main goals that they will have in mind. The priority is to make sure that the key business points are in the contract. The other side that you are negotiating with will be tough on the points that they really care about, and then often they will be flexible on less important points. To be effective in this situation, you should understand in advance the key objectives for the negotiation and the deal points for the transaction.

An additional point to consider is when it is acceptable to be tough on an issue or when it is best to compromise. A common law attorney is going to take a practical approach to a contract. And what that means is, they are going to focus on the basic issues and try to obtain rights that they can actually enforce without too much delay or expense. Generally, a common law lawyer will look forward in a deal and try to understand the potential issues that might occur in the future. As part of the negotiation, the lawyer will try to eliminate the potential problems or create options and remedies to deal with those problems in the most favorable manner to their side.

When negotiating the deal, lawyers look for where the money is in the transaction. For instance, if the deal is a sale of property, the property itself is the money or the value in the deal. The focus is on the value in the deal. In case of a potential dispute, the question or issue to look for is the fastest and easiest way to get access to that value, whether it is property, rights, or liquidated money.

Another key point to think about is the best way to maximize leverage in case there is a dispute. What that means is you have to make sure that your client is always in the best position should something go wrong in the deal. When negotiating, always try to think ahead and identify any potential problem. If there is a problem, how can you make sure within the contract that the client is safe or can be protected.

II. Establish Opening, Target, and Bottom Line Offers

Tips for Successful Negotiations Establish Opening, Target, and Bottom Line Offers	
Type of Offer	**Negotiation Points**
Opening Offer	- Your starting point in the negotiation - **Should be credible but always leave yourself negotiating room** - Your opening offer **should not be too close to your target or bottom line offer**
Target Offer	- The point or amount you believe is **most reasonable based on your information** - **This is the agreement you are hoping to work towards**
Bottom Line Offer	- The point **below which you will never agree** and would be willing to walk away from the deal - Never go below your bottom line **unless you become convinced that you seriously misanalysed the problem**

Before beginning the negotiation, it is important to think about and establish your opening offer, target offer, and bottom line offer. Your opening offer is the starting point in the negotiation. When creating the opening offer, whether it is for buying a company, property, any sort of deal, make sure that the offer is credible but always leave some space to negotiate. I can guarantee you that your common law colleague is always going to think in this way. Their opening offer will be calculated to ensure that they have room to negotiate but that the offer is at least credible.

You should always make sure that the opening offer is not too close to the target or bottom line offer. The target offer is what you think the deal should be based on your research and information. The target is what you think is fair and what you think you should be working towards. Whereas, the bottom line offer is the point below which you will not agree to the deal. You should be aware and communicate with your client to make sure that you know their bottom line offer.

The advice that I always got when I was practicing in the U.S. is you should always figure out in any deal what it is that you need and what it is that you want, which are two different ideas. What you need is the necessary points that you must have in that deal—it is your bottom line. Next, think about the areas that you would like to see happen but are potentially open to compromise. The idea is to get everything that you need and as much as you want as possible.

Furthermore, the initial thinking about negotiation is to define the parties' interests in the deal. There are essentially three types of interests. First, there is a shared interest, which means an interest that both parties have in doing the deal. Second, there is an independent interest, which means an interest that your party or client might have that the other party to the deal might not share. An example of an independent interest would be if your client wants to have a confidentiality portion of the contract but this detail does not matter to the other side or hurts their position. Third, there are conflicting interests, which means an interest that would be good for one side but bad for the other side.

The advice is that when starting negotiations, identify the shared interests and independent interests. Those are the most negotiable points. You do not want immediately to negotiate the conflicting interests because the negotiation can quickly become difficult. If possible, deal with the conflicting interests at some point later in the negotiation.

III. Language of Negotiations

Tips for Successful Negotiations
Language of Negotiations (1)

Making Proposals
- We'd like to propose that ...
- We propose / suggest ...
- Regarding your proposal, our position is
- How do you feel about ...

Responding to Suggestions
- Maybe it would be better to ...
- Perhaps a better idea would be ...
- May we offer an alternative? We propose that
- From where we stand, a better solution might be ...

Agreeing to Proposals
- I think we can both agree that...
- I agree with you on that point.
- I think that would be acceptable.

Objecting to Proposals
- That's not exactly how I look at it.
- If you look at it from my point of view...
- I have some reservations about that...
- From my perspective...
- I'm afraid we couldn't agree to that...

Giving a Reason
- The reason for that is ...
- This is because ...

Prioritizing Interests
- The most important issue for us is ...
- Our intention is ...
- Our main priority is ...
- We might like to ...

The next point we will discuss is the language of negotiating. These are the common phrases that you can use or that you will hear as part of the negotiation process.

The first set of phrases relates to making proposals. The common examples you will hear are, 'We'd like to propose that...' For instance, 'We'd like to propose that you sell us the property for...' A more formal version of this phase is, "we propose or suggest." If you receive a proposal from the other side and you want to communicate your response, a good phrase to use is, 'Regarding your proposal, our position is...' and then state your position. An informal expression would be, 'How do you feel about...' For instance, 'How do you feel about increasing the price?' Those are expressions for making proposals.

The next would be responding to suggestions. This is the situation where the other side has made a proposal to you or a suggestion and you want to respond. These phrases are good to express your own ideas. If you want to disagree in a polite manner and give an alternative suggestion, you can say, 'Maybe it would be better to do' or 'Perhaps a better idea would be...' You can also be more formal by stating, 'We propose that...' To make a counter proposal, the language that you can use is, 'Maybe we can offer an alternative' or 'from where we stand, a better solution might be...' These are good ways to respond to suggestions.

Now, how do you agree to a proposal? You would say something like, 'I think we both can agree that...' For instance, "I think we both can agree that it is in our interests to finish this agreement before June 30th." Phrases to agree are, 'I agree with you on that point' or 'I think that would be acceptable,' which are common ways of showing agreement.

The more difficult situation is when objecting to proposals. Here are some expressions that you can use. 'That's not exactly how I look at it.' This phrase means that you do not agree with what someone is saying. Another phrase is, 'If you look at it from my point of view...' For instance, "if you look at it from my point of view, doing this agreement in such a short time would make it very difficult for us to be able to deliver the product on time." As a way of disagreeing and expressing concern, you can also say, 'I have some reservations about' or 'From my perspective' or 'I am afraid we couldn't agree to that...' These phrases are perfectly fine ways to object to proposals in a polite way and reflect that you have a counter proposal or another idea.

When giving proposals it is important to explain the reasons for the proposal. Expressions you can use to show a reason for your proposal, 'The reason for that is...' or 'This is because,' and then explain your reasons.

Finally, prioritizing interests, which is when you are trying to express the client's most important points. For example, you can say, 'The most important issue for us is,' and then state the issue. 'Our intention is' or 'our main priority is' or 'we might like to,' which is more informal. These are ways to state your client's most important aspect of the deal or negotiation.

Tips for Successful Negotiations
Language of Negotiations (2)

Clarifying a Point	*Accepting a Proposal*
o If I understood you correctly ...	o This agreement is acceptable to us.
o Are you suggesting that ...	o I think we have reached an agreement here.
o Do you mean ...	
o What do you mean by ...?	o That sounds reasonable.
o I'm not sure I fully understand your point.	o I think we have a deal.
o Could you clarify one point for me?	o I believe we have an agreement.
o Could you be more specific?	o I can agree to that.
Compromising	*Concluding a Negotiation*
o If you were prepared to ..., we might be able to...	
o We are ready to accept your offer; however, there would be one condition.	o Let's just summarize our agreement?
	o I think you've covered everything.
o Would you be willing to accept a compromise?	o Let's just confirm the details, then.
o In return for this, would you be willing to ...?	o Have I left anything out?

While negotiating, it is always important to make sure you completely understand the position of the other side. If clarifying a point, these are expressions you can use. 'If I understood you correctly,' and then you summarize the other side's point. 'Are you suggesting that,' or 'Do you mean...' These are ways to summarize the other side's position.

To make sure that you completely understand what someone is saying, you can use, 'What do you mean by...,' or 'I'm not sure I fully understand your point.' These are important is because, for example, we are in a negotiation and the other side says we must finish quickly. You do not know what quickly means—it could be next week or next month. The expressions that you use in this situation would be, 'what do you mean by' quickly?

Another example is when the other side says, "we should take a whole new approach to this idea," which seems vague. You are unsure about the meaning of "a whole new approach." Expressions you would use would be, 'I'm not sure I fully understand your point,' or 'could you be more specific,' 'what does a whole new approach mean?' I want to emphasize these phrases because as part of negotiating people often try to speak in a very quick and general way or try to move past uncomfortable points. You need to know exactly what they mean or what some contract term means.

The next set of phrases are expressions for compromising. If you want to offer an agreement or a compromise, but you want to set a condition or clarify a matter, good expressions are, 'If you were prepared to...we might be willing to...' or 'We are ready to accept your offer; however, there would be one condition.' Another way of talking about compromising in return for something is, 'Would you be willing to accept a compromise?' For example, in return for lowering the price, would you be willing to buy more product?

Phrases to use for accepting proposals are: "This agreement is acceptable to us, 'I think we have reached an agreement here; That sounds reasonable; I think we have a deal; I believe we have an agreement; and I can agree to that." These sorts of expressions are perfectly fine to reflect that you are accepting a proposal.

Finally, these are phrases to conclude the negotiation. At the end of the negotiation, summarize the agreement and check that you fully understand what you have agreed to. The expression you use is, 'Let's just summarize our agreement,' and then state the agreed upon terms. You can also say, 'We have agreed to...' For instance, we have agreed to this many units or we have agreed to this date and time, and then summarize the exact agreement.

Another phrase you can use is, 'I think you've covered everything,' which means that you have agreed on the important issues. 'Let's just confirm the details then' is another way of saying let's summarize our agreement. The last phrase is 'Have I left anything out,' which means you think the points have been summarized but you want to make sure that nothing was missed. That is the language you will hear commonly and need to use as part of negotiation when dealing with common law attorneys or working in common law countries.

2. 典型的な契約条項に関する交渉のためのヒント
Tips for Negotiating Typical Contract Provisions
I. Governing Law

Tips for Negotiating Typical Contract Provisions
Governing Law

❖ The law selected to govern the contract can have a significant impact on your legal rights under the contract ❖ Under the laws of certain countries, some of the key rights and remedies in your contract: 　o **May not be enforceable** 　o May need to be structured in a special way in order to be enforceable [Note: These issues can arise frequently in Asian countries with evolving legal systems and structures like China or Vietnam]	As a general rule, it is advisable to choose a legal system that: 　o **has a good reputation** in the international business community for providing contractual and regulatory fairness and certainty; 　o **is commonly used as the governing law** in international commercial contracts in general and in the relevant industry in particular; and 　o **provides easy access to sufficient numbers of high quality experienced commercial lawyers** (this factor will become important in the event of a dispute under the contract) Tip: Widely used systems of law include: French, German, and Swiss in Europe; New York in the U.S.; Japanese, Hong Kong and Singaporean law in Asia

I want to talk about tips for negotiating certain provisions of international agreements. These are going to be cross border agreements and one of the most important provisions will be the governing law. We are talking about the law that will govern the contract should there be a disagreement or need to interpret the terms of the contract. When negotiating, you will need to think about the fact that under the laws of certain countries, some of the key rights or remedies in the contract might not actually be enforceable, or the contract may need to be structured in a special way to be enforceable.

For example, from my own experience, when I was working in eastern Europe, we were helping to revise the law in a country that had no mechanism in the law to obtain money from someone's bank account if a company owed money or if there was judgment against that company. Often in contracts, in the event of a breach, the remedy is to recover money and then the first step is to go to the company's bank account to obtain the money; however, in some countries, that remedy may not be available. Always keep in mind that when choosing a governing law to make sure that the rights and remedies that you are trying to write into the contract are potentially available in that country.

One of the main concerns to think about is when agreeing to the governing law. It is always advisable to choose a legal system that has a good reputation for international business, providing contractual and regulatory fairness, and is often commonly used as the governing law in international contracts.

The leagal system, also shold provide easy access to sufficient numbers of high quality commercial lawyers because you do not want to go and be subject to the law in a country where you cannot hire outside counsel in that country or there are very few outside counsel in that country that you can trust. The tip that people would give is that the widely used systems of law for international contracts are France, Germany, and Switzerland. In the U.S., people most commonly use New York as the governing law. In Asia, good countries are Japan, Hong Kong, and Singapore. Those are the countries that people commonly use for international contracts as the governing law.

II. Dispute Resolution

Tips for Negotiating Typical Contract Provisions Dispute Resolution	
Dispute resolution – litigation or arbitration?<ul><li>When determining the governing law, the parties also need to agree the "forum" for resolving any future disputes. **"Forum" refers to the dispute resolution process and the country where such process takes place.**</li><li>If the parties wish to use litigation to resolve any disputes, **they commonly agree to litigation in the country of the governing law of the contract**</li><li>**A party who has agreed to litigation in the counterparty's country will often be at a disadvantage** because the counterparty will be more familiar with the court's processes and language and have easier access to local litigation experts</li></ul>	Arbitration largely resolves common dispute resolution problems<ul><li>The parties can **choose to conduct the arbitration in a country which is not the country of the governing law of the contract** (EX: arbitration in Hong Kong regarding an English law governed contract)</li><li>The parties can **choose the language and particular procedures** for use in the arbitration.</li><li>Awards rendered in arbitrations seated in a New York Convention state may, in principle, be enforced in any of the other current 143 signatory states</li><li>**Selection of the forum is equally important as governing law** in terms of maximizing the likelihood of a successful resolution of disputes</li></ul>Tip: If faced with the choice of compromising on either governing law or forum, **there may be merit in agreeing to the governing law proposed by the counterparty provided they agree to your choice of forum**

The next topic that is a very important aspect when negotiating is dispute resolution. When determining the governing law, you also agree on a forum for where the dispute resolution will take place. Forum means the place where the dispute resolution will be held, such as New York state court. If both parties wish use litigation, which means both parties decide that they want to go to court and not use arbitration or mediation, they will commonly choose the country of the governing law of the contract.

In addition, it is important to be strategic about the choice of forum because, if for instance, you have a contract with a company in China and you agree to have the law of China be the governing law of the contract, remember that the Chinese company will be more familiar with court processes, know the language of the court, and have easier access to litigation experts; therefore, your client will be at somewhat of a disadvantage if you agree to have the forum in the country where the other company is located.

Commonly, in international commercial law and dispute resolution, the parties will agree to arbitration. The reason why is because parties can choose to conduct arbitration in a country which is not the actual country of the governing law. Even if you have a contract with a Chinese company and the governing law is Chinese law, as part of your dispute resolution you can agree to arbitration in Hong Kong or Singapore, for example. You can agree on the language that will apply in the arbitration, and you can choose the procedures will be applicable.

These matters are important because of the New York Convention, which is an agreement that arbitration awards are enforceable in countries that have signed the agreement. Currently, 143 countries have signed the New York Convention. Thus, if you have arbitration in a country that has signed that agreement, and the company that you are dealing with is from a country that has signed that agreement, you have some protection to enforce the judgment that comes out of the arbitration. Therefore, the selection of forum where disputes will be settled is equally as important as choosing the governing law.

In terms of negotiating these contract provisions, if faced with a choice of compromising on either the governing law or the forum of where disputes will be resolved, there may be merit in agreeing to the governing law being of one country as long as the other party agrees to your choice of forum. For example, that means if the other company insists that a specific country's law should apply, it is advisable to agree to that if the forum for disputes will be arbitration in Singapore and the language of the arbitration will be English. You can separate those issues.

III. Remedies – Contract Enforcement

> **Tips for Negotiating Typical Contract Provisions**
> **Remedies – Contract Enforcement**
>
> ❖ Common examples of remedies in a contract include **indemnification, termination rights, expense reimbursement, payment of specified damages**
> ❖ **Better to include specific remedies in the contract language, instead of relying solely on your rights under applicable law in case of breach**
> ❖ Your rights under law may be subject to important conditions and limitations, and may be hard for you to enforce as a practical matter
>
> **Tips**
> ✓ Create remedies that work well for you and your deal
> ✓ Anticipate potential futures damages that could occur to your client under the deal and address them in the remedies provisions (i.e. identifying and mitigating your client's risks under the agreement)
> ✓ Be sure to limit where possible your clients financial liabilities under the contract
> ✓ Consider the applicable international treaties that allow for enforcement of judgments

Finally, we will discuss negotiating remedies into a contract. Common examples of remedies in contracts are indemnification, termination rights, the right to terminate the agreement, expense reimbursement, and payment of specified damages where if something goes wrong the parties agree to a certain amount. A main strategy for common law lawyers is that it is better to include specific remedies in the contract language, rather than relying solely on rights under the law in case of the breach. What I mean by that is you want to put into the contract all the specific things that you or your client will be able to do in case there is a problem later with the contract. They will not merely rely on what is written in the law or allow for a generalized statement within the contract that would govern if there is a problem. The strategy will be to put as much detail into the contract as possible to define what will happen in case there is a breach of the contract or a problem with the contract.

The tips I can suggest are always to create remedies that work well for you and your deal. Every situation is different, but think about your situation and how to best create a remedy for your situation. For example, are you buying a large piece of property to build a shopping mall? If so, then think about will happen to that property and what is the best way to protect your interests if something goes wrong with the property. If it is money, what is the best way to access the money or to be indemnified should a problem arise. The specific agreement or deal should contain the remedies that work well for your deal. And, I have said this before, but try to anticipate potential future damages that could occur under the deal and address them in the remedies provisions.

Be sure to limit where possible your client's financial liabilities under the contract. If there is a provision for damages, try to limit what could happen should something go wrong with the contract; and consider the applicable international treaties that allow for enforcement of judgments.

For instance, the company that you are dealing with is from Switzerland and you have an arbitration in London. You obtain a judgment from a London court and take that court judgment from London to Switzerland to have a remedy in Switzerland. Always consider the applicable international treaties that will allow for such situations. There is a Hague convention on the enforcement of judgments, but not so many countries are signatories. I choose Switzerland as an example because one of my experiences as a practicing attorney is that we had a case against a bike manufacturer who was from Switzerland with their assets and bank accounts being there. In my experiences, I unfortunately learned that it is nearly impossible to take a foreign court judgment, a judgment from the United States and go to Switzerland with that court judgment and have a remedy in Switzerland. Therefore, be sure that you can enforce that judgment. Otherwise, the judgment is useless. For this reason, many people and businesses use the arbitration method because the New York Convention gives more assurance that the judgment is enforceable.

第2部 レターオブインテント（LOIs）作成の法律実務
——Legal Practices for Drafting Letters of Intent

Now we will move to drafting letters of intent and talk in general about the strategic uses of letters of intent and when use them.

1. レターオブインテント（LOIs）の戦略的な利用
Strategic Uses of Letters of Intent (LOIs)

> **Strategic Uses of Letters of Intent (LOIs)**
>
> ❖ A Letter of Intent (LOI) is a document that sets forth the key terms agreed upon by the parties during negotiations prior to reaching a final, definitive agreement
>
> ❖ Commonly used for a manufacturing agreement, share purchase agreement, services agreement, development agreement, supply agreement, commercial lease agreement, among others
>
> **Use a Letter of Intent if:**
>
> ❖ You are ready to enter serious negotiations for the sale or purchase of a whole or part of a company or corporation and you **would like to define your intentions formally in writing**
>
> ❖ You are negotiating the purchase of a company or interest in a company and want to **exclude the seller from negotiating with another party**
>
> ❖ You are negotiating the **purchase real estate and want to minimize misunderstanding and document progress towards a sale**. It's also a great way for a **buyer to help secure financing.**
>
> *Note:* **Memorandums of Understanding** are also used in research (EX. R&D Development in Pharmaceuticals)

A letter of intent is a document that sets forth the key terms agreed upon by the parties during negotiations. The parties have agreed on the essentials of the deal, and the letter of intent sets forth the agreement up to the point prior to finalizing the contract. Why use a letter of intent? A letter of intent is advisable if negotiating for the sale or purchase of a company or a corporation and you want to define your intentions formally in writing.

Another example of when a letter of intent might be useful is if trying to purchase real estate and you want to make sure that the there is no misunderstanding of the terms, of the purchase or a lease, or if leasing a property. The letter is a good way for a property buyer to secure financing. For instance, if you have a letter of intent showing the agreement of both sides, then the buyer can take it to a bank and use it as a basis to secure a loan.

A typical situation may be if you have a preliminary agreement for a company to do construction and they need to purchase the materials for the project. If a letter of intent is in place, it can bind the parties so that the company doing the construction will feel confident to begin purchasing the materials even though the formal agreement is not yet finalized.

These are example situations where letters of intent can be very useful. Please note that there are times when memorandums of understandings or MOUs are used. A good example is in the R & D phase in pharmaceuticals when companies agree to do clinical testing, they will execute a memorandum of understanding, which has the same effect as a letter of intent, or in some instances can be the final agreement.

2. レターオブインテント作成上の留意点
Letter of Intent — Drafting Considerations

Letter of Intent
Drafting Considerations

- ❖ When drafting LOIs carefully question the client whether the LOI is intended to be an **outline for the negotiation and later execution of a final contract or are certain terms intended to be binding**
- ❖ A poorly drafted letter of intent creates a **risk that a term or clause a party intends to be non-binding will be construed by a court as binding or ambiguous**
    - ○ Generally, **whether a term in a LOI is binding or non-binding is a question of fact for the fact finder. However, if the terms of the LOI have a definite and certain meaning, then the question becomes one of law to be decided by the court**
    - ○ **A party's actions and conduct can be used as evidence that they intended that their LOI bind them**. In the alternative, a party's reliance on a portion of a LOI that they do not intend to be binding can be used to establish their intent to be bound by the entire agreement

Tip: It is normally advised that the **purchase price, confidentiality and third party negotiation provisions be binding**. Parties may also bind themselves regarding other key terms while leaving less important terms for further negotiation.

Drafting considerations for letters of intent. The main drafting consideration to keep in mind is whether the letter of intent is just an outline for the negotiation and the later execution of a final agreement, or do you only want certain terms of this letter of intent to be binding. In terms of drafting, you must be careful about poorly drafted letters of intent because they can create a risk that a term or clause not intended to be binding could later be construed as binding. When writing letters of intent, be clear about your intentions, particularly when defining non-binding or binding terms.

Generally, whether a term in a letter of intent is binding or non-binding is a question of fact, which is a matter that a U.S. court will decide. If the terms of a letter of intent are definite and certain, then the enforceability of the LOI becomes a question of law. Another point to consider is the way the parties behave according to the letter of intent, which might also become a basis for a U.S. court to decide whether a term is binding. If the parties behave as if the LOI is a binding agreement, then a court might later determine it to be binding even though that was not what you intended.

A tip when negotiating and drafting such letters is to consider making the purchase price, confidentiality provisions and third-party negotiation provisions binding. Often parties will bind themselves to other key terms if agreeable to them or if there are less important terms they want to negotiate later.

I. Binding vs. Non-binding

> **Letter of Intent**
> **Drafting Considerations**
> Binding vs. Non-Binding
>
> ❖ **If no part of the letter of intent is meant to be binding,** you can either use headings at the top of the Letter of Intent which are in bold and all capitalized such as:
>
> "NON-BINDING LETTER OF INTENT" or "NON-BINDING MEMORANDUM OF ANTICIPATED TRANSACTION"
>
> ❖ Another option is to **include a separate paragraph, at the end of the LOI, directly stating the non-binding nature**
>
> **Sample Language**
>
> It is **expressly understood and agreed** by [Party A] and [Party B] that this **Letter of Intent is not a binding contract between the parties, rather it outlines the terms and conditions for discussions regarding a possible** [describe deal here – ex. sale of property located at 28 West Ave. New York, New York, by Party A to Party B].

We will further discuss binding and non-binding terms. If no part of the letter of intent is meant to be binding, meaning that it is just an offer, or you are simply summarizing an agreement, but the parties do not want to be bound, use clear language and terms in the LOI that it is non-binding. Literally, in bold type at the top of the letter write, "non-binding letter of intent" or "non-binding memorandum of anticipated transaction." Another option is to include a separate paragraph at the end of the letter of intent, stating directly that it is not binding. Here is sample language: 'It is expressly understood and agreed by Party A and Party B that this Letter of Intent is not a binding contract between the parties, rather it outlines the terms and conditions for discussions regarding a possible....,' and then you describe the deal.

Lecture 5 Negotiating and Contracting Drafting in International Law Practice

<table>
<tr><td colspan="2" align="center">**Letter of Intent**
Drafting Considerations
Binding vs. Non-Binding</td></tr>
<tr><td colspan="2">❖ If **certain terms and conditions are intended to be binding, and others non-binding**, then you can **divide the terms and conditions into separate sections with headings (similar to the above) that state the binding and non-binding paragraphs**</td></tr>
<tr><td>**Option 1 - Example Format**
Binding Terms
The following terms and conditions are <u>intended to be binding</u> on the parties:
1. Purchase Price...(set out provision)
2. Confidentiality... (set out provision)
3. Third-Party Negotiations...(set out provision)
Non-Binding Terms
The following terms and conditions are <u>not intended to be binding</u> on the parties:
4. Tenant Improvements... (set out provision)
5. Term of the Agreement...(set out provision)</td><td>**Option 2 – Single Paragraph at End**
18. <u>**Not a Binding Agreement**</u>: This Letter of Intent does <u>**not create a binding contract and will not be enforceable, except in respect of the obligations set out in paragraphs 10, 13, 15, 16 and 17**</u>. Only the Formal Agreement, duly executed and delivered by the Vendors and Purchaser, will be enforceable, and it will supersede the provisions of this Letter of Intent and all other agreements and understandings between the Parties with respect to the subject matter of this Letter of Intent.</td></tr>
</table>

The typical situation is when certain portions of the letter of intent are binding but other portions are not. In that situation, there are two options to separate these terms within a letter of intent. The first option is to divide the letter of intent into two subsections with the headings—binding and non-binding. Then, list the matters that are in the two categories. For instance, confidentiality and third-party negotiations would be in the binding subsection, and non-fixed terms would be in the non-binding subsection.

The more common option is that you have a single paragraph at the end of the agreement that states that this is not a binding agreement or that this letter of intent does not create a binding a contract and will not be enforceable, except in respect of the obligations set out in paragraphs 10, 13, 15, and 17, which contain the specific binding terms. This is good language, which is part of the handout.

II. Remedies, Confidentiality, Third-party Negotiations

Letter of Intent
Drafting Considerations
Remedies, Confidentiality, and Third Party Negotiations

- For binding provisions, be sure to provide a **means of enforcement** (specific performance, damages, jurisdiction, venue, attorneys fees, etc.)
- **Confidentiality provisions and third party negotiation provisions are designed to prohibit the parties from "shopping" the transaction pending the negotiation and execution of a definitive contract**

  Sample Language:
  Confidentiality: All negotiations regarding the Target and the Shares will be confidential and will not be disclosed to anyone other than respective advisors and internal staff of the parties and necessary third parties, such as lenders approached for financing. No press or other publicity release will be issued to the general public concerning the proposed transaction without mutual consent unless required by law, and then only upon prior written notice to the other party.
  Exclusive Opportunity: Following the execution of this Letter of Intent, the Vendors will not negotiate or enter into discussions with any other party or offer the Shares or any interest therein for sale to any other party until the time herein provided for settlement of the Formal Agreement has expired.
- Lesser details and terms too complicated or labor intensive to be realistically agreed upon at the letter of intent stage, are often omitted to be negotiated at a later date

  Sample Language: Future negotiations may cover additional points [including...]
- Be careful to make sure that certain vague provisions (like promises to use best efforts) are not included in LOIs

---

Other important matters to consider when drafting these letters of intent, for the provisions that are intended to be binding, it is like any other contract, which means that you should make sure that the terms are enforceable in case some problems arise. To protect your interests, one binding provision should be the remedy provision. You would treat that like any other contract. The handout to this lecture has a letter of intent with sample language for remedies.

I also provided sample language related to confidentiality agreements and third-party negotiation provisions because a main purpose of the letter of intent is to protect your client from the other party shopping the deal to third parties. Here is language for confidentiality: 'All negotiations regarding the Target and the Shares will be confidential and will not be disclosed to anyone other than the advisors and internal staff...' That is the important language to create confidentiality. The exclusive opportunity provision deals with third-party negotiations. Exclusive opportunity is the common expression to use to limit the other party from shopping the deal to others. Here is the sample language: 'Following the execution of this letter of intent, the vendors will not negotiate or enter into the discussions with any other party to offer Shares or any interest therein for the sale until the time herein provided for the settlement of the Formal Agreement has expired.'

Letters of intent do not need to cover every small detail of the deal. You can add language as in the example above to state that 'Future negotiations may cover additional points including...,' and then list the broad topics that the parties may negotiate later.

A final point to remember is that a letter of intent is not like a regular contract. You do not need to include vague or general provisions such as promises to use best efforts. That language is better to put directly into the final contract.

3. 検討：レターオブインテント作成上の主な考慮事由
Review — Main Considerations for Letters of Intent

> ### Review
> ### *Main Considerations for Letters of Intent*
>
> In summary, the most important provisions in a letter of intent are as follows:
>
> 1. Whether the letter of intent is intended to be binding or non-binding;
> 2. Which provisions of the letter of intent are intended to be binding or non-binding;
> 3. Enforcement provisions related to binding provisions; and
> 4. Effective Termination Date of the LOI.
>
> #### Sample Termination Provision
>
> This *Letter of Intent* **shall expire without any action by the parties** in the event that a Definitive Purchase Agreement is not signed by the parties **within fifteen (15) days of the Closing Date**. **Neither party shall be liable to the other party for alleged losses or liabilities of any kind whatsoever**, including claims of lost profit, lost business opportunity, punitive damages, speculative damages, or incidental damages, arising from or based upon the failure of the parties to sign the Definitive Purchase Agreement or the expiration of this *Letter of Intent* without the signing of a Definitive Purchase Agreement.

To summarize, the important matters to consider in a letter of intent are 1) whether the letter is intended to be binding or non-binding; 2) if portions are binding indicating clearly which provisions are binding and which ones are not binding; 3) for the provisions that are binding make sure that you have provisions or remedies to enforce those should there be some violation of the agreement; and 4) make sure that there is an effective termination date of the letter of intent.

The termination date is the period or duration for which the letter of intent is valid. After that period if there is no agreement, then the letter of intent is no longer valid. Because if you never come to an agreement, an open-ended LOI with no expiry date can remain valid, which could pose serious problems in the future.

Here is sample language: 'This Letter of Intent shall expire without any action of the parties in the event that a Definitive Purchase Agreement is not signed by the parties within 15 days of the Closing Date. Neither party shall be liable to the other party for alleged losses or liabilities of any kind whatsoever... [for] failure of the parties to sign...'

第3部　契約文書の作成プロセス，分析，検討
——The Writing Process for Contract Drafting, Analysis and Review

Now, I will move on to the writing process for contract drafting, analysis and review. We will talk about general principles and provisions applicable to contract drafting from an international viewpoint.

1. 契約文書にも使えるライティングの基本
General Writing Principles Applicable to Contract Drafting

General Writing Principles Applicable to Contract Drafting	
❖ Be clear about what **parts** the contract must include and what **situations** the contract must cover ❖ Know what the parties want ❖ Try **outlining** the contract to make sure that all the needed pieces are included and are organized logically ❖ **Think through the life of the contract** under various future potential outcomes/events ❖ Clearly and consistently **set forth the parties' rights and obligations** ❖ Use **recitals and definitions** to reflect the parties' specific transaction	**Every contract should clearly answer six questions:** 1) who is obligated to perform; 2) what is the obligation; 3) by when must the obligation be performed; 4) where will the performance take place; 5) how is the obligation to be performed; and 6) if performance involves money or goods, how much?

The main areas to consider when dealing with an international contract is to know the necessary parts of the contract, the situations that the contract must cover, the parties' intent, and the nature of the deal.

When drafting, a good practice is to try outlining the various contract provisions to ensure that all the necessary parts are included. Outlining the agreement means to list the potential provisions that will become part of the contract and the issues that may arise. For instance, in a real estate acquisition, you can make short outline notes of the deal provisions reflecting the basic agreement or understanding between the parties, such as stating the deal, the purchase amount, remedies, and any other conditions under the agreement. Starting with a draft outline makes the contract drafting writing process smoother.

As you draft, think about the life of the contract under various future potential outcomes and events. International attorneys strategize and identify all the possible issues that could go wrong under the contract. They will try to put as much language as possible in the contract to protect their client in case of a problem. You will notice that international attorneys tend to be more aggressive when negotiating and their drafts are usually more detailed than what you might expect, because in their mind they are protecting the client. Therefore, you might receive a draft contract from a common law attorney that is excessively detailed, restating matters that are already in the law.

Recitals are the portions of the contract at the beginning that are not technically enforceable terms. These paragraphs usually begin with "whereas" to define the agreements between the parties. Even though they are not technically portions of the contract that are enforceable, you always want to make sure that these recitals state clearly the purpose of the contract. Additionally, the definitions in a contract also help to make the parties' intent in entering into the contract clear.

In drafting contracts, every contract should clearly answer six questions: 1) Who is obligated to perform or who are the parties; 2) what is the obligation; 3) what is the deal; 4) when must the obligation be performed; 5) where will the performance take place; and 6) how the obligation is to supposed to be performed. These are some basic ideas that common law attorneys are looking at in a contract.

2. 国際取引における契約書の作成スタイル
Contract Drafting Styles in International Context

> **Contract Drafting Styles in International Context**
>
> - **Expect the other side to provide you with an aggressive – or even unreasonable – first draft of an English language contract**
>   - To see what they can get away with — especially if other party expects the first draft to be "reasonable"
>   - <u>This is a negotiation tactic</u>, seeking to sway results even after oral agreement
> - **English language contracts often have a lot of detail**
>   - <u>Rights and obligations are written into the contract</u> — instead of relying on rights under law, or on personal relationships between the parties
>   - <u>"If not in writing, then it doesn't exist"</u>
> - **Parties try to cover major potential issues in the relationship that may arise after signing – including points where the parties are likely to have different interests**
> - **The contract is often the most important resource if the parties' relationship breaks down so rigorous attention is used in drafting**

Your common law colleagues or the other party's attorney may have a very different style or approach to drafting contracts. The first draft contract that you receive from the other side might not exactly reflect what you negotiated and agreed to. The attorney will use the draft contract as a part of a negotiation strategy. For example, they will likely give you an aggressively drafted contract that is completely in favor of their client simply to get your reaction. In this context, contract drafting is part of the negotiation. The strategy is to protect their client as much as possible.

I talked about this earlier, but English language contracts usually have a lot more detail. A legal expression that American lawyers often say is if it is not in writing it does not exist. That means if something is not directly written into the contract, then it is not applicable. The international contract will try to cover the major issues in the parties' relationship that may arise after the signing including points where the parties are likely to have differing interests. If there is a problem, you will see provisions that protect the other party even if it is not good for your client. And, at least in common law countries, the contract is often the most important resource if the parties' relationship breaks down, meaning if there is a problem with the agreement, courts will look at what is written in the contract. That is why common law lawyers are very detail-oriented about what is in the contract.

3. 契約書を作成する際のヒント
Language of Contracts — Drafting Tips

Language of Contracts Drafting Tips

❖ **State requirements positively**	❖ **Repeat key terms**
○ Use single negatives as little as possible. **Never use double negatives**. This can lead to misunderstandings. ▪ <u>Better</u>: can... only if ▪ <u>Worse</u>: cannot.... unless ▪ <u>Better</u>: must be X or more/ must be at least X ▪ <u>Worse</u>: must be no less than X ▪ <u>Better</u>: This includes... ▪ <u>Worse</u>: This does not exclude...	○ In the case of a novel, it can be boring for the reader to see the same word repeated many times. In the case of a legal document, **using the same word with the same meaning is vital to avoid misunderstanding** ○ However, <u>avoid the opposite problem – do not use one term in several ways</u>, especially legal terminology with more than one meaning (e.g., *sanction, agreement*)

In drafting contracts, write the requirements using positive language rather than negative language. Use single negatives as little as possible and never use double negatives. For example, 'I cannot <u>not</u> do something.' Double negatives can lead to misunderstandings. I make this point because in Japanese, negatives are more common than in English. When literally translating Japanese into English there are a lot more negatives in sentences because that is Japanese language structure.

In the example above, a better sentence structure is, "must be X or more, or must be at least X." The negative way of expressing this idea is "must be no less than fifty."

The second drafting tip is repeat key terms. Often if you are writing novels or poetry, people say do not keep repeating the same word over and over again. However, when writing contracts it is easier to repeat the terms in the contract so that the words have the same meaning every time to avoid misunderstandings.

In the Sample provided, we have the term 'Agreement' and that refers to the actual contract. 'Under this Agreement each party will do this or that.' There is also the verb 'agreement' or to agree, which means that the parties have a common understanding of something. You can talk about agreeing to something versus the Agreement itself. Be careful because you do not want to use the same word if they may have two different meanings.

For example, if in your definitions section of the contract you have Agreement meaning, 'the Agreement in this contract is the sale of property from this person to that person;' do not to use the word agreement again in as in its common usage. 'The agreement should last for five months.' This creates a vague definition and usage of the term in the contract.

Another aspect is, do not refer to the same parties differently. For instance, you represent Tokyo Incorporated ('Tokyo Inc.'). They are the buyer in the sale of property agreement. In the contract, do not sometimes refer to the party as Tokyo Inc. and then other times refer to the same party as 'the Buyer.' Always refer to the party by one name, either using Tokyo Inc. throughout the contract or defining 'the Buyer' in the contract as Tokyo Inc. and using 'the Buyer' throughout the contract. Try to be careful because a lot of times people will make this mistake where they alternate.

Language of Contracts Drafting Tips (2)	
Sentences: keep subjects and verbs together: The following: <u>The courts generally</u>, when a taxpayer hands over all books and records and otherwise makes a full and complete disclosure of all of the facts to a third party to whom the task has been given of preparing the taxpayer's annual tax return, <u>**will not find fraudulent intent**</u>. *looks better as:* <u>**The courts generally will not find fraudulent intent**</u> when a taxpayer hands over all books and records and otherwise makes a full and complete disclosure of all of the facts to a third party to whom the task has been given of preparing the taxpayer's annual tax return.	**Sentences: keep compound verbs together** The Director **may**, in accordance with the procedures set forth in part 104 of this chapter, **take** action against counsel for improper conduct in the course of an investigation. *This should read:* The Director **may take** action against counsel for improper conduct in the course of an investigation. Procedures are in part 104 of this chapter.

An additional drafting tip is to keep subjects and verbs together. Here is an example. 'The *court* generally, when a taxpayer hands over all books and records otherwise makes a full and complete disclosure of all facts to a third party to whom the task has been given or preparing the taxpayer's annual return, *will not find* fraudulent intent.' The subject is the 'courts' and the verb is 'will not find,' but, often when people draft they split the subject and verb in the contract, which is confusing. Correct writing and better grammar is to keep the subject and verb as close together as possible. For example, you can re-write the same sentence as 'the courts generally will not find fraudulent intent when...,' and then explain.

Common grammar mistakes we often see in contracts are when compound verbs are split. For example, 'The director may, in accordance with procedures set forth in part 104 of this chapter, *take* action against counsel for improper conduct or in the course of investigation.' The compound verb is 'may take,' but people split it as part of the sentence. A better sentence is 'The director *may take* action...' Therefore, do not split verbs because this makes the contract more difficult to understand.

I. Describe Obligation, Rights, Prohibition and Permission

Language of Contracts
Describe obligation, rights, prohibition and permission

To express	Use	Example
Obligation (an order)	Must (preferred contract term) vs. Shall (unclear language but commonly used)	X **must** deliver the goods by… X **shall** provide all notices in writing…
Authorization (option)	May	X **may** terminate at any time…
Prohibition (a ban)	Must not/May not	X **must not** disclose to a third party…
Preference (a Recommendation)	Should	X **should** provide guidance before…
Intention (promise imposing no requirement)	Will	X **will** make best efforts to…
No obligation	Need not (softer language)	X **need not** provide advance payment for…

Next, we will discuss describing obligations, rights, prohibitions and permissions in contracts. This is an important point because a mistake in using the wrong verb can absolutely change the meaning of the agreement. When drafting, especially if drafting in a different language, you have to be very careful to describe accurately the obligation or whatever the situation you want it to be; therefore, here are examples to express certain types of obligations or rights as part of a contract.

An obligation or an order is something that under the agreement the party must do. In that situation, the best term is 'must.' For example, 'X must deliver the goods by…' is the clearest way to reflect obligation. You will often see that people use the word 'shall' in this situation, but shall is a bit unclear because sometimes shall can mean 'should' or a 'recommendation' as opposed to an obligation.

An authorization means an option to do something. The best word to use to express this idea is 'may.' For example, 'X may terminate at any time.' May is good to use in that situation.

A prohibition means that you do not want someone to do something. When trying to prohibit or ban someone from doing something, good terms to use are 'must not' or 'may not.' For example, 'X must not disclose to a third party.' Must not is the clearest and strongest term to ban.

A preference is similar to a recommendation. The term to use is 'should.' For example, 'X should provide guidance before delivery is accepted.' In expressing a recommendation or suggestion, the best verb to use is 'should.'

Intention is a promise that does not impose a requirement. For example, we are talking about best efforts and the expression is 'X will make best efforts…' Often in contracts you will see 'the parties' intent to make best efforts to resolve any disputes.'

If trying to express that either party has no obligation to do something, you would use softer language, such as 'need not.' For example, 'X need not provide advance payment.'

4. 標準的な英文契約書の条項
Standard English Language Contract Provisions

> **Standard English Language Contract Provisions**
>
> ❖ English language contracts typically contain the following types of provisions:
> - Definitions
> - Deal provisions
> - Deliveries/mechanics
> - Representations
> - Covenants
> - Conditions
> - Remedies
> - Governing law
> - Dispute resolution
> - General

I know that people here do a lot of different types of work and when talking about contract provisions, all of those are going to be very much dependent on the type of work that you do. But, we can generally discuss the types of provisions that you would see in different types of contracts. I will talk separately talk about each type of provision and then suggest the type of language you would expect to either see or the type of language that you should use.

Typically, in contracts, we see sections related to definitions, deal provisions that describe the actual agreement between the parties, deliveries and mechanics of the deal, representations, covenants and conditions, remedies, governing law, dispute resolution and general provisions.

I. Definitions

Standard English Language Contract Provisions *Defined Terms*	
❖ ***Use defined terms when*** you will **refer to the same concept more than once in a contract** and it takes more than a few words to explain the concept ❖ **Definitions section can be at the beginning or end of a contract**	❖ The definitions section will either define the term or cross-reference the section of the contract where the term is defined **Ex: This License Agreement, as defined in section 2.1...** ❖ Defined terms can also be defined within the body of the contract where they are first used
Defined Terms	**Sample Language**
• List only appears once to create a well-organized contract • Allows you to make changes only once as the terms of the transaction are negotiated and modified over time • Helps prevent a maze of cross-references	**Definitions** 1. **Licensor** when used in this agreement refers to Tokyo Technology Inc. 2. **Licensee** when used in this agreement refers to CA Solutions, Ltd. 3. **License Agreements** when used in this agreement mean collectively, the Trademark License and the Technology License; and **License Agreement** means either of them. 4. **Collateral** has the meaning set forth in Section 2.1....

First, I want to talk about definitions. At the beginning of the agreement, the definitions section defines and refers to the same idea or concept in the contract. The main purpose of defining terms is to list only once, the terms in the contract, and then later on you can just refer to it.

For example, let's say we are doing a sale of property. You want to define the property, including the property address and the buildings that are the subject of the agreement. Under the agreement, you can refer to 'the Property' in quotes. Once the term is defined in one place, then you can refer to that term throughout the agreement.

For instance, maybe you have experience when doing deals in which the actual deal changes, or the terms of the agreement change. If you put specific descriptions of certain terms in different places in the agreement rather than defining the term and using it consistently throughout, then you will need to keep revising the agreement to reflect the changes. This saves a lot of problems in drafting the agreement and also helps to prevent a maze of cross references.

In the example, the definition section defines the 'Licensor' when used in the agreement as Tokyo Technology. 'Licensee' when used in the agreement refers to 'CA Solutions.' 'License Agreements' means collectively 'The Trademark License and the Technology License...' Finally, the term 'Collateral' is defined in a later section 2.1. If the first time 'Collateral' is defined in a later section of the contract, then the term will have that meaning going forward in the contract.

II. Deal Provisions

> **Standard English Language Contract Provisions**
> ***Deal Provisions***
>
> ❑ These provisions capture **the core business deal** – for example, license of IP, sale of assets, grant of distribution rights
> ❑ Include pricing and other key economic terms
> ❑ These provisions need to "work" from a legal perspective. The provisions need to validly create the legal rights and duties that the parties want to have
> ❑ The core deal provisions are often located at or near the beginning of the contract
>
> <u>Examples</u>
>
> - The Assignor does hereby **unconditionally, absolutely and irrevocably grant, bargain, sell, transfer, assign, convey, set over and deliver** unto the Assignee all of the Transferred Assets.
> - **Sale of Business. Seller agrees to sell and Buyer agrees to purchase, free from all liabilities and encumbrances,** the above-described business, **including the lease to such premises, the goodwill of the business as a going concern, all of Seller's rights under its contracts, licenses, and agreements, and all assets and property owned and used by Seller in such business as specified in Exhibit A,** other than property specifically excluded. This **sale does not include the cash on hand or in banks at the date of closing or such other property as is listed in Exhibit B.**

The next general contract provision we will discuss is the deal provisions section. Deal provisions are the core business deal. For example, if doing a licensing of IP or sale of assets or granting distribution rights, the deal section is what describes the actual deal. These provisions are located at the beginning of the contract. Make sure that your drafting is clear and precise as to the exact deal provisions reflecting the agreement between the parties.

Those of you doing this kind of work know that it is easy to find the model provisions if working on certain types of contracts. You can go in and find specific provisions that apply to the types of contracts that you are dealing with whether it is a sale of business, etc. The above example shows the deal provision for the sale of a business. 'Seller agrees to sell and Buyer agrees to purchase, free from all liabilities and encumbrances...' If granting some assets to the other party, you can use the language, 'the Assignor does hereby unconditionally, absolutely and irrevocably grant, bargain, sell, transfer, assign, convey, set over and deliver unto the Assignee all of the Transferred Assets.' Check the language in this example as well as the handout.

III. Delivery/Mechanics

Standard English Language Contract Provisions
Deliveries/Mechanics

❖ These provisions show the **physical deliveries and other actions that must be completed to close the deal**, or to put the business or commercial relationship into effect
- **Ex:** wiring of funds, delivery of share certificates, delivery of design drawings for key technology

❖ Can serve as a good "checklist" for items and actions that are needed to close the deal

Example

At the Closing, Buyer shall deliver to Seller: (i) the Purchase Price, by **wire transfer of immediately available funds to an account of Seller designated in writing by Seller to Buyer no later than two Business Days prior to the Closing Date**; (ii) ...

The delivery and mechanics section of a contract deals with the schedule for the parties to take some action, whether it is delivering products, performing some service, or actions that must happen to close the deal or perform under the contract. For instance, wiring funds, delivery of share certificates, or delivery of design drawings for key technology. These provisions define what must happen under the agreement.

Here is an example. 'At the Closing, Buyer shall deliver to Seller: (i) the Purchase Price, by wire transfer of immediately available funds to an account of Seller designated in writing by Seller...' The point is to make sure the delivery and mechanics contract provisions clearly set forth the exact obligations to perform under the deal.

IV. Representations

Standard English Language Contract Provisions *Representations*	
❖ **Statements by parties that confirm key facts about the transaction** 　▪ Ex: ownership and quality of transferred assets ❖ **Representations allocate risk between the parties** 　▪ Ex: which party should be responsible for unknown, pre-closing risks (litigation, payment obligations) that are not discovered until after the closing? ❖ **Potential consequences for breaches of representations can include:** 　▪ Claim against the breaching party for damages 　▪ "Walk-away" right – ability not to close the transaction 　▪ Terminate a commercial arrangement	**Sample Language** ❖ Except as set forth in Section XX of the Disclosure Schedules, **the Company has complied, and is now complying, with all Laws applicable to it or its business, properties or assets.** ❖ **Representations of Seller.** Seller **represents and warrants that**: (a) He is duly qualified under the laws of the State of _____ to carry on the business as now owned and operated.' (b) He is the owner of **and has good and marketable title to the property involved in this sale, free of all restrictions on transfer or assignment and all encumbrances except** for those disclosed in Exhibit C.

The representations section confirms the key facts about the transaction. For example, if someone is selling property, they must represent that they own it lawfully. Representations also allocate risk between the parties, such as which party will be responsible for potential future litigation or the consequences for breaches of the agreement.

In the sample language, the representation is the company complying with all laws applicable for its business properties or assets. This would be language for representations if talking about the sale of a business. As part of the handouts, another example would be 'the Seller represents and Warrants that He is the owner and has good marketable title to the property involved in the sale, free of all restrictions on transfer or assignment and encumbrances...'

V. Covenants

Standard English Language Contract Provisions *Covenants*	
<u>Commitment by you or the other side to do something, or to not do something</u> - Types of covenants can include **payment, performance, financial, "negative" covenant (commitment not to do something)** <u>Covenants can help address specific risks in a business relationship</u> - Ex: a **borrower agrees not to create liens on the lender's collateral; to provide regular financial reports to the lender** - These covenants help the lender to reduce or manage its risk in the loan relationship	<u>Sample Language</u> ❖ The Company <u>shall not, directly or indirectly, incur, assume, guarantee or otherwise become liable or responsible for any Indebtedness</u>. ❖ **Covenant Not to Compete.** <u>Seller shall not engage</u> in a business similar to that involved in this transaction in any capacity, directly or indirectly, within _____ for a period of _____ years from the date of closing or so long as Buyer or his successors carry on a like business, whichever first occurs

Covenants are commitments by the parties to do or not to do something. Covenants address specific risks in the business relationship. For example, if lending money, you want to make sure that the borrower of the money does not agree to create any liens on the collateral.

An example here is, a company 'shall not directly or indirectly incur, assume, guarantee, or otherwise become liable or responsible for any Indebtedness.' This is a covenant not to do something. Common covenants that we see in contracts are covenants not to compete, which mean the, 'Seller shall not engage in a business similar to that involved in the transaction.' This covenant prevents the company you are purchasing from making a competing business.

VI. Conditions

Standard English Language Contract Provisions
Conditions

❖ Qualifies a party's obligation to perform a covenant – <u>if the condition is not met, then the party doesn't have to perform</u> ❖ Common conditions to the closing of a deal include <u>receipt of required regulatory approvals, no important legal challenges to the deal, the accuracy of a party's representations contained in the contract</u> ❖ Conditions can create great uncertainty that performance will actually happen 　▪ Ex: "I'll pay you if the bank lends me the money on acceptable terms" ❖ <u>Watch out for conditions that are controlled by the other side</u>. In this case: instead of a true commitment, *the other side has an option to perform or not perform*	<u>**Sample Language**</u> Purchaser's **obligations** to consummate the Closing **shall be subject to the fulfillment of each of the following conditions**: (i) Seller shall have obtained each of the third party consents identified in Schedule 1.

The next typical contract provision is the conditions section. Conditions qualify a party's obligation to perform a covenant such that if the condition is not met then the party does not have to perform. A common condition to close a deal might include receipt of the required regulatory approvals, or that there are no important legal challenges to the deal. The parties must give accurate representations. Thus, a common condition would be that the sale of property is conditioned on receiving approval from a homeowner's association.

Sample language in this situation is, 'Purchaser's obligations... [are] subject to the fulfillment of each of the following conditions; (i) Seller shall have obtained each of the third party consents identified in Schedule 1.'

What you should be careful about are conditions that create uncertainty that the performance will happen. For example, I will pay you if the bank lends me money on acceptable terms. The problem here is that we do not know the meaning of 'acceptable terms,' which means that it is up to me to decide whether I am happy about the bank loan or not. If you create a condition that makes it uncertain whether the contract will happen, this can become a problem for the client, especially if it is a condition that is controlled by the other side. You always want to be careful about the other side putting conditions in the contract that your side cannot control.

VII. Remedies

Standard English Language Contract Provisions *Remedies*	
❖ Common examples of remedies in a contract include: • **indemnification, termination rights, expense reimbursement, payment of specified damages** ❖ Better to include specific remedies in the contract language, instead of relying solely on your rights under applicable law in case of breach	**Sample Language** Seller **shall indemnify and hold Purchaser harmless** from and against all **losses, liabilities, costs and expenses arising from or relating to any breach by Seller of any of its representations, warranties, covenants or obligations** contained in this Agreement.

Again, we will talk about the language of remedies. Usually the common provisions will be indemnification provisions or termination of rights, expense reimbursement, and payment of specified damages. Your common law colleagues will want to include these specific remedies in the contract instead of relying on what might be available to them under the law.

Here is common language, which you also can find in the handout. 'Seller shall indemnify and hold harmless from and against all losses, liabilities, costs and expenses arising from or relating to any breach by Seller of any of its representations, warranties, covenants or obligations...' This is very standard language that you can find in model contract language on the internet or other legal sources. There will always be specific provisions that should apply to your contract.

VIII. Governing Law

Standard English Language Contract Provisions *Governing law*	
❖ The **Governing Law** clause specifies that the laws of a mutually agreed jurisdiction will govern the interpretation and enforcement of the contract ❖ Controlling the governing law is an important objective for the parties because differences in local laws may control the outcome of a dispute ❖ **The chosen jurisdiction need not be the same as the venue or choice of forum.** The parties can even choose different jurisdictions depending on the type of dispute. In general, courts will respect the parties' selection	<u>Sample Language</u> **Governing Law and Consent to Jurisdiction and Venue** **Governing Law.** This agreement, and any dispute arising out of the [SUBJECT MATTER OF THE AGREEMENT], shall be governed by laws of the State of [GOVERNING LAW STATE]. **Consent to Jurisdiction.** Each party hereby irrevocably consents to the [exclusive, non-exclusive] jurisdiction and venue of any [describe court type] court located within [VENUE COUNTY] County, State of [VENUE STATE] in connection with any matter arising out of this [agreement / plan] or the transactions contemplated under this [agreement / plan].

We talked about governing law previously, but here is language that you can use related to disputes arising out of the subject matter. 'This agreement... shall be governed by laws of...' and then state the law. 'Each party hereby irrevocably consents to the exclusive jurisdiction and venue...' and then state the forum jurisdiction. This is the important language that is drafted in a simple and direct manner.

IX. Dispute Resolution

**Standard English Language Contract Provisions
Dispute Resolution**

❖ **Often ignored** by business team but if not specified in the contract it can be unclear what happens if there is a dispute • If your deal is in China with a Chinese company, does this mean litigation in Chinese courts? ❖ Usually you will want to **avoid** litigation in countries without well-developed and efficient court systems ❖ **Key factors** for dispute resolution in a cross-border deal include: cost, timing, convenience, overall fairness of process ❖ **Arbitration in a neutral city** (ex. Singapore) under well-accepted commercial arbitration rules is common for cross-border deals	**Sample Language** NEGOTIATIONS The Parties **will attempt in good faith to resolve any dispute or claim arising out of or in relation to this Agreement** through negotiations between a director of each of the Parties with authority to settle the **relevant dispute**. **If the dispute cannot be settled amicably** within ___ days from the date on which either Party has served written notice on the other of the dispute then the remaining provisions of this Clause [ ] shall apply. ARBITRATION **In the event of a dispute between the parties concerning the interpretation of any provision of this agreement** or the performance of any of the terms of this Agreement, such matter or matters in dispute shall be finally settled: a. under [the Rules of Conciliation and Arbitration of _____]; b. by three arbitrators, one appointed by each Party, and the third, who shall be the chairman, selected by the two appointed arbitrators and failing agreement by the [Chairman of the (name of Forum)] c. **the language of the arbitration shall be** ___; and d. **the place of the arbitration shall be** ___.

I want to make a point about dispute resolution that we did not discuss earlier. Often the resolution of disputes is not something that the business team consider during the deal negotiation. Your job as counsel is to ensure that such provisions are covered in the contract because the business deal people are understandably interested in getting the deal done. They are worrying so much about what happens if there is a problem later.

Dispute resolution provisions are within the attorney's area of expertise. For example, if the deal is in China, does this mean that any dispute resolution, such as litigation must be held in Chinese courts? Your job is to know the answer and make sure that the correct language regarding dispute resolution makes it into the contract.

The handout contains sample language that you can use. 'The Parties will attempt in good faith to resolve any dispute or claim arising out of or in relation to this Agreement...' and then list the forum jurisdiction. Here is sample language for an arbitration. 'In the event of a dispute between the parties concerning the interpretation of any provision this agreement...' then state where the arbitration will be held.

X. General Provisions

Standard English Language Contract Provisions
General Provisions

Examples of General Provisions:
- Entire agreement
- No assignment
- No third party beneficiaries

Sample Language

- **This Agreement constitutes the entire agreement of the parties relating to the subject matter addressed in this Agreement**. This Agreement **supersedes all prior communications, contracts, or agreements between the parties** with respect to the subject matter addressed in this Agreement, whether oral or written. (**Entire Agreement**)

- Except as provided in this Agreement, **no Party may assign or delegate any rights or obligations hereunder without first obtaining the written consent of the other Party**; provided, however, that the Company may assign this Agreement to any successor (whether direct or indirect, by purchase, merger, consolidation or otherwise) to all or substantially all of the business or assets of the Company. (**No assignment**)

- Except as provided in Section XX, this Agreement is for the **sole benefit of the parties hereto** and their respective successors and permitted assigns and **nothing herein**, express or implied, is **intended to or shall confer upon any other Person or entity** any legal or equitable right, benefit or remedy of any nature whatsoever under or by reason of this Agreement. (**Third Party Beneficiaries**)

Finally, I want to talk about general provisions. There is something called the entire agreement, which means you want to make sure that the contract contains only those matters that are binding on the parties. I gave you sample language and again it is in the handout. 'This agreement constitutes the entire agreement between the parties.' That is the most important and basic language to use. 'No assignment' meaning 'no Party may assign or delegate any rights or obligations hereunder without first obtaining the written consent of the other Party...' which means that no one may assign rights to a third party without informing you first.

第4部　秘密保持契約に関する交渉と契約書作成 —Negotiating and Drafting Non-Disclosure Agreements

Finally let's talk about negotiating and drafting non-disclosure agreements or NDAs.

1. 秘密保持契約書はどのように用いられるか
When to Use an NDA

When to Use a NDA

When Does a Non-Disclosure Agreement Make Sense?

- When you need to protect business data, personal data, and/or proprietary information
- When you wish to convey something valuable about your business or idea and need to ensure the information is not stolen or used without your approval

Typical situations where you may want to use a NDA are:

- ☐ <u>Presenting an invention or business idea to a potential partner</u>, investor, or distributor
- ☐ <u>Sharing financial, marketing, and other information</u> with a prospective buyer of your business
- ☐ <u>Showing a new product or technology</u> to a prospective buyer or licensee
- ☐ <u>Receiving services from a company or individual who may have access to some sensitive information</u> in providing those services
- ☐ <u>Allowing employees access to confidential and proprietary information of your business</u> during the course of their job

---

NDAs are used to protect business data as part of the deal, such as personal data or proprietary information as part of the agreement, or if you want to convey something about your business or idea to another party. Other examples are if you are exploring working together and you want to make sure that no ideas are stolen or used for other purposes. These are the most common uses for non-disclosure agreements.

Typical situations when to use an NDA would be presenting an invention or a business idea to a potential partner and you are sharing financial, marketing or other information with a perspective buyer of your business. You are receiving services from a company or an individual who may have access to some sensitive information, such as someone working on the computers and having access to data, or employees have access to confidential and proprietary information as part of your business. I am sure all of you have NDAs regarding your work with your law firms. Those are the common uses for NDAs.

2. 秘密保持契約における留意事項
Key Elements of NDAs

> **Key Elements of NDAs**
>
> ✓ Identification of the parties
> ✓ Definition of what is deemed to be confidential
> ✓ The scope of the confidentiality obligation by the receiving party
> ✓ The exclusions from confidential treatment
> ✓ The term of the agreement
>
> **TIP: NDAs don't have to be long and complicated. In fact, good ones are usually no more than a few pages long.**

The key elements of an NDA are identifying the parties, defining what is deemed to be confidential, and the scope of the confidential obligation. In addition, the exclusions, if there are any, from confidential treatment, and the term of the agreement. The one tip that I want to convey is that NDAs do not need to be long and complicated. In fact, the best ones are only a few pages long, so you do not need to think that an NDA agreement should be ten pages long. A normal NDA agreement can be two or three pages long and still be effective.

3. 典型的な秘密保持契約書の条項
Typical NDA Provisions

Typical NDA Provisions (1)	
Define Nature of the Obligation ❖ Requires language prohibiting one party from wrongfully using or disclosing certain information received from the other ❖ Agreement should require the recipient to use a **reasonable degree of care** to protect the confidential information **Mutual v. Unilateral** ❖ Lawyers should inquire what types of information will be disclosed by each party **Tip: In most cases both parties will disclose some sensitive information so it makes sense to include mutual confidentiality obligations**	**Protected Material** ❖ To define ***Confidential Information*** NDAs often gives examples, such as **"technical, financial and business information"** and state that it may be in **oral, written, physical or electronic form** ❖ **Other typical language**: "anything that should be reasonably be deemed confidential" or may grant protection "only if the information is **marked as confidential**" **Carved-Out Exceptions** Excludes certain types of sensitive information such as: • Information available to the general public, or previously known • Independently developed • Rightfully received by the recipient, through legal means

A typical NDA provision that you will see is to define the nature of the obligation. The language prohibits one party from using or disclosing certain information and that the party who is receiving the information is using a reasonable degree of care to protect it.

The main portion of concern is whether the non-disclosure agreement is mutual or unilateral. Mutual means both sides have the obligation, whereas unilateral means one side has the obligation of non-disclosure. In most cases, both parties are exchanging information, and therefore, have mutual confidentiality agreements.

The next section covers the protected material. In this section, you are defining the confidential material and stating the exact material that is confidential. Typical language that you will see is technical financial and business information and can be oral written, physical or electronics. In drafting this provision, define the confidential material in broad terms to ensure a wide net of protection. Other typical language is anything that might be reasonably deemed confidential, which is a general statement or may grant protection only if the information is marked as confidential.

If you are on the other side of a non-disclosure agreement, which means you are receiving the information, you do not want the NDA to be general or broad. When negotiating and drafting the NDA, you may want to require the other side to be specific about the categories of protected information. This will reduce the likelihood of breaching the NDA. An additional requirement would be to mark any material as confidential so that it is open and obvious about the nature of the material that is being disclosed.

There are exceptions that are usually 'carved out' (separated) in agreements. Information that is generally available to the public or information that you might have received independently or rightfully received through other legal means is not subject to an NDA. Again if you are on the side of receiving the non-disclosure agreement where you are supposed to keep information confidential, there might be situations where you obtained that information in a manner that does not imply an obligation on your side to keep it confidential, and you want to make sure the agreement has that kind of language.

Typical NDA Provisions (2)

Permitted Use
- NDA must state that Confidential Information may be used only for a particular purpose
    Ex. exploring the possibility of a business relationship between the parties

Permitted Disclosure
- NDAs typically contain an exception **permitting disclosure by the recipient to its attorneys, accountants or employees who have a legitimate need to know; in response to a court order, legal regulation, etc.**
- **Ensure the legitimate "need to know" requirement is directly stated**

Duration of Obligation
- State two time periods in the NDA: (1) the **term for the entire NDA, and (2) the time period for the confidentiality obligation.**

Typical Language: "For the Term of this Agreement and __ years thereafter."

No Warranties/*As-Is*
- NDA should state that "**all information is disclosed "As Is" and without warranties.**"
- Such language can give some protection against unmerited claims though not fraud or concealment

Remedy for Breach
- The NDA should state that "**in the event of a breach monetary damages would not be sufficient and the parties agree injunctive relief is proper.**"

Other provisions that you will see are permitted use, which defines how each party can use the information; for instance, exploring the possibility of a business relationship between the parties. You want to define specifically the way in which the other party can use the information. Depending on the type of agreement or situation, you might have a circumstance where one party actually is required by law to disclose that information.

Here's a good example. If you are a pharmaceutical company and having a company do clinical trials to test the product, there may be requirements under the law that the company provides certain information to the government agency (e.g. U.S. Food and Drug Administration) that does approvals for the drugs. Technically, those results might be considered confidential information, but the law requires the company to disclose that information. Draft the NDA to account for such situations where certain disclosures are required.

The duration of the obligation defines how long the non-disclosure agreement will be in effect. The drafting strategy depends on whether you are giving the information or receiving the information. If giving the information, you want the period to last as long as possible; whereas, if receiving the information, you want to make sure that there is a specified period because you do not want to receive this information and have, to keep it confidential for fifty years. Typical language that you will see is 'For the Term of this Agreement and [X] years thereafter.' For example, the confidential information must be maintained for the term of this agreement and five years thereafter.

Some NDAs contain warranty language depending on the type of confidential information to protect you later from future unmerited damages. The sample language is that 'all information is disclosed As Is and without warranties.'

Remedies for Breach. If the other side has an obligation to keep the information confidential but they fail to do so, include language in the agreement to recover for damages. The usual mechanism for breach is to include the right to seek injunctive relief by court order. This court remedy is not money damages, although you should include such a remedy in the agreement as well. Rather, an injunction prevents the other side from further harming your client's interests by continuing improperly to disclose that information. Therefore, write into the non-disclosure that you have the right to injunctive relief in the event of a breach.

4. 検 討
NDA Provisions

I. Mutual vs. Non-Mutual NDAs

> **NDA Provisions**
> ***Mutual vs. Non-Mutual NDAs***
>
> NDAs come in two basic formats:
>
> 1) a **mutual agreement**; or
>
> 2) a **one-sided agreement**
>
> ❖ The **one-sided agreement** is when you are contemplating that only one side will be sharing confidential information with the other side
>
> ❖ The **mutual NDA form** is for situations where each side may potentially share confidential information
>
> - Although there is always some appeal to using a mutual form of NDA, some lawyers try to avoid the mutual form if their client is not planning to receive confidential information from the other side
>
> - One way to decide this early on is to let the other side know that you don't want to receive any of their confidential information so you don't see the need for a mutual form if they ask for one

Non-disclosure agreements usually are either mutual or non-mutual, which means that the obligation to keep the information confidential is one-sided or by both sides. One-sided agreements can be useful to protect your client from receiving and maintaining confidential information. Sometimes you do not want the confidential information. If this is the case, make it clear to the other side that you do not want to receive confidential information as part of the agreement, which would be a one-sided NDA. This strategy relieves your client from such obligations.

II. Parties to NDA and What is Deemed Confidential

NDA Provisions
Parties to NDA & What is Deemed Confidential

The Parties to the Agreement	What Is Deemed Confidential?

❖ If it's an agreement where only one side is providing confidential information, then the <u>*disclosing party*</u> <u>can be referred to as the disclosing party</u> and the <u>recipient of the information can simply be referred to as the recipient</u>
 	
❖ <u>Third Parties</u> - If any other people or companies will get access to the Confidential Information, the NDA should be careful to cover these third parties as well
	❖ You must define <u>what confidential information means</u> (ex. is it any information? Is it information that is only marked in writing as "confidential"?)
	   ▪ The *disclosing party* wants this <u>definition of confidential information to be as broad as possible</u> to make sure the other side doesn't find a loophole and start using its valuable secrets
	   ▪ If you are the recipient of the information, you should ensure that the information you are supposed to keep secret is <u>clearly identified</u> so that you know what you can and can't use
	❖ **Must consider oral information as well**
	Tip: Usually oral information can be deemed confidential information, but the disclosing party should confirm the confidential nature of the information to the other side in writing shortly after it is disclosed

The important non-disclosure provisions define the parties subject to the agreement. Sometimes there will be third parties involved, such as consultants receiving financial or proprietary information. Include language in the NDA that covers any potential third parties that may receive the confidential information.

There is also the issue of covering both written and oral confidential information. Oral communications are the most common problem when dealing with NDAs. For example, you have a non-disclosure agreement in place and give the other side confidential materials; however, during a telephone conversation you give additional confidential information to them orally. This poses a serious problem, and to cure this potential issue, the agreement should have language that refers to oral information. If the type of information includes oral communications, put in language saying that information communicated orally can be deemed confidential as long as the party confirms the confidential nature of the information to the other side in writing shortly thereafter. People often give confidential information in writing, and then as part of a meeting or phone call, confidential information is improperly disclosed.

III. Terms of the Agreement

> **NDA Provisions**
> **Term of the Agreement**
>
> ❖ If you are the recipient of confidential information, you should insist on a <u>**definite term for when the agreement ends**</u>
>   - <u>**Avoid costly "forever" obligations**</u>
>
> **What is a reasonable term for the agreement**
>
> ❖ Depends on the industry you are in and the type of information conveyed.
>   - *Ex:* a few years may be acceptable in some industries because the technology changes so fast that the information quickly becomes worthless.
>   - Most agreements have a <u>**time limit of two to five years**</u>
>
> **Tip: NDA should always state: "even if the term is ended, the disclosing party isn't giving up any other rights that it may have under copyright, patent, or other intellectual property laws."**

The term of the agreement depends on which side of the agreement you are on. If giving the information, you want to make the term of the agreement as long as possible. If receiving the information, you want to make sure that you are not being obligated to keep information confidential for the next fifty to one hundred years. Avoid costly 'forever obligations.' Look at the agreement in terms of making sure that the terms are reasonable. In the U.S., most non-disclosure agreements are from two to five years. Although you can make it for as long as you would like, the term often depends on the industry. For instance, if working in the technology industry, information is usually only good for two years. After three or four years it is not that useful any more. Therefore, you do not need to worry about the information remaining confidential after two or three years.

IV. Exclusions From Confidentiality Treatment

> ### NDA Provisions
> ### *Exclusions from Confidentiality Treatment*
>
> **Exclusions from Confidentiality Treatment**
> - ❖ Every NDA has certain exclusions from the obligations of the receiving party. These exclusions are intended to address situations where it would be unfair or too burdensome for the other side to keep the information confidential.
>
> **The common exclusions include information that is:**
> - <u>**Already known to the recipient**</u>
> - <u>**Already publicly known**</u> (as long as the recipient didn't wrongfully release it to the public)
> - <u>**Independently developed by the recipient**</u> without reference to or use of the confidential information of the disclosing party
> - <u>**Disclosed to the recipient by some other party who has no duty of the confidentiality**</u> to the disclosing party
> - The NDA can also deal with the situation in which the recipient of the information is <u>**forced to disclose the information through a legal process**</u>. The recipient should be allowed to do that if forced by court order or applicable law without breaching the NDA as long as the recipient has warned the disclosing party in advance of the legal proceeding.

We discussed this topic earlier. Therefore, please see addendum 3 for the non-disclosure agreement language related to exclusions from confidentiality treatment.

Presentation Addendum

1. Addendum 1: Sample Letter of Intent

Sample Letter of Intent [1]

June 19, 2017

To: Airwaves Sound Design Ltd.
Second Floor, 25 East Second Avenue
New York, New York

RE: Purchase of all of the issued and outstanding shares (the "Shares") of Airwaves Sound Design Ltd. and Airwaves Digital Group Ltd.

The following sets out the basic terms upon which we would be prepared to purchase the Shares. The terms are not comprehensive and we expect that additional terms, including reasonable warranties and representations, will be incorporated into a formal agreement (the "Formal Agreement") to be negotiated. The basic terms are as follows:

1. Purchaser: InternetStudios.com, Inc. (the "Purchaser")

2. Target: Airwaves Sound Design Ltd. and Airwaves Digital Group Ltd. (collectively, the "Target")

3. Principal Shareholders: Alex Downie and any other shareholders of the Target (the "Vendors")

4. Shares: The Purchaser agrees to purchase from the Vendors and the Vendors agree to sell, assign and transfer and to cause all holders of the Shares to sell, assign and transfer to the Purchaser, the Shares free and clear of all

---

[1] Sample Excerpt taken from:
http://contracts.onecle.com/marchex/pine.lease.2004.02.11.shtml

liens, charges and encumbrances.

5. Transaction: The Purchaser, the Target and the Vendors will enter into a business combination (the "Combination") whereby the Purchaser will acquire all of the issued and outstanding securities of the Target from all the Vendors in exchange for 500,000 shares in the capital of the Purchaser and options to purchase 1,500,000 shares in the capital of the Purchaser at an exercise price per share equal to the price per share paid by the institutional investors in the Financing (as defined herein), which options will vest as is mutually agreed to among the Purchaser and the Vendors (the "Acquisition").

6. Structure: In order to facilitate the Acquisition, the Purchaser, the Target and the Vendors agree that each will use their best efforts to formulate a structure for the Combination which is acceptable to each of the parties and which is formulated to:

- comply with all necessary legal and regulatory requirements;
- minimize or eliminate any adverse tax consequences; and
- be as cost effective as possible.

7. Financing: The Vendors have advised the Purchaser that it will arrange for the private placement of shares in the capital of the Purchaser for a minimum of $2 million, which investment will close on or before the Closing (as defined herein) and will be on the same terms as the investment to be made by institutional investors being arranged by the Purchaser's advisors, WestLB Securities (the "Financing"). A portion of the proceeds raised in connection with this transaction contemplated by this Letter of Intent, shall be allocated toward the purchase of a company involved in post-production video services on terms acceptable to the Purchaser.

8. Access to Information: Immediately upon execution of this Letter of Intent, the Purchaser and its advisors will have full access during normal business hours to, or the Target and the Vendors will deliver to the Purchaser, copies of all documents (the "Materials") pertaining to the operations of the Target.

9. <u>Condition(s) Precedent</u>: The obligation of the Purchaser to purchase the Shares will be subject to satisfaction or written waiver by the Purchaser of the following condition(s) (the "Conditions Precedent") within 10 days after execution and delivery of the Formal Agreement:

- review and approval of all materials in the possession and control of the Target and the Vendors which are germane to the decision to purchase the Shares;
- the Purchaser and its solicitors having had a reasonable opportunity to perform the searches and other due diligence reasonable or customary in a transaction of a similar nature to that contemplated herein and that both the solicitors and the Purchaser are satisfied with the results of such due diligence;
- the Purchaser and its accountant having had a reasonable opportunity to review the audited financial statements (including corporate tax returns, general ledger listings, adjusting entries and opening trial balances) of the Target, prepared in accordance with generally accepted accounting principles and that both the Purchaser and its accountant are satisfied with the content of such financial statements;
- satisfactory arrangements being made to hire hourly and salaried staff necessary to operate the business of the Target including the Target entering into an executive management contract with Alex Downie;
- the Purchaser obtaining the consent from any parties from whom consent to the transfer of the Shares is required;
- the Purchaser obtaining confirmation that any names used in the business of the Target is available for use by the Purchaser and can be registered as a trade mark of the Purchaser;
- no material adverse change having occurred in connection with the business of the Target or the Shares;
- all representations and warranties of the Target and the Vendors being true and all covenants of the Target and the Vendors having been performed in all material respects as of the Closing;
- no legal proceedings pending or threatened to enjoin, restrict or pro-

hibit the transactions contemplated in this Letter of Intent;
- a satisfactory legal opinion being available from Vendors' counsel;
- completion of satisfactory physical inspection of the assets of the Target;
- satisfactory review of title to the assets of the Target; and
- approval of the Board of Directors of the Purchaser being obtained.
- it would be the expectation of the Purchaser that many of the Conditions Precedent will be narrowed or eliminated altogether as the Purchaser completes its due diligence and the Formal Agreement and schedules thereto are finalized.

10. Return of Materials: The Materials will be returned to the Target and/or the Vendors, as applicable, or destroyed if the Formal Agreement is not executed within the time provided.

11. Closing: The closing (the "Closing") of the transactions contemplated by this Letter of Intent will occur not later than 10 days following the satisfaction or written waiver by the Purchaser of the Conditions Precedent. At the Closing, the Vendors will transfer the Shares to the Purchaser free from any outstanding liens, charges, claims or encumbrances and execute all such documents as the Purchaser's solicitors may require in order to effect such transfer including a restrictive covenant agreement that the Vendors will not compete anywhere in Canada with the Purchaser in connection with the business of the Target. The Closing may take place by exchange of the appropriate solicitor's undertakings, which will involve each party's solicitors delivering to his or her counterpart all required cash and documentation, to be held in trust and not released until all such cash and documentation has been executed and delivered to the Purchaser.

12. Costs: The Purchaser and the Vendors will each bear their own expenses in connection with this Letter of Intent and the purchase and sale of the Shares.

13. Confidentiality: All negotiations regarding the Target and the Shares will be confidential and will not be disclosed to anyone other than respective advisors and internal staff of the parties and necessary third parties, such as

lenders approached for financing. No press or other publicity release will be issued to the general public concerning the proposed transaction without mutual consent unless required by law, and then only upon prior written notice to the other party.

14. Purchase and Sale Agreement: Upon execution of this Letter of Intent, the Purchaser will prepare a draft of the Formal Agreement for the Vendors' review.

15. Good Faith Negotiations: Each of the Purchaser and the Vendors will act honestly, diligently and in good faith in their respective endeavors to negotiate, settle and execute the Formal Agreement within 90 days following the execution of this Letter of Intent.

16. Exclusive Opportunity: Following the execution of this Letter of Intent, the Vendors will not negotiate or enter into discussions with any other party or offer the Shares or any interest therein for sale to any other party until the time herein provided for settlement of the Formal Agreement has expired.

17. Standstill Agreement: Following the execution of this Letter of Intent and until the Closing, the Vendors will not, directly or indirectly, purchase or sell any securities of the Purchaser.

18. Not a Binding Agreement: This Letter of Intent does not create a binding contract and will not be enforceable, except in respect of the obligations set out in paragraphs 10, 13, 15, 16 and 17. Only the Formal Agreement, duly executed and delivered by the Vendors and Purchaser, will be enforceable, and it will supersede the provisions of this Letter of Intent and all other agreements and understandings between the Purchaser and the Vendors with respect to the subject matter of this Letter of Intent.

19. Currency: All references to "$" in this Letter of Intent shall refer to currency of the United States of America.

20. Proper Law: This Letter of Intent will be governed by and construed in accordance with the law of the Province of British Columbia and the parties hereby submit to the jurisdiction of the Courts of competent jurisdiction of

the Province of British Columbia in any proceeding hereunder.

21. <u>Counterparts and Electronic Means</u>: This Letter of Intent may be executed in several counterparts, each of which will be deemed to be an original and all of which will together constitute one and the same instrument. Delivery to us of an executed copy of this Letter of Intent by electronic facsimile transmission or other means of electronic communication capable of producing a printed copy will be deemed to be execution and delivery to us of this Letter of Intent as of the date of successful transmission to us.

22. <u>Acceptance</u>: If you are agreeable to the foregoing terms, please sign and return a duplicate copy of this Letter of Intent by no later than by 5:00 p.m. on June 19, 2017. Facsimile is acceptable.

Yours truly,

INTERNETSTUDIOS.COM, INC.

/s/ Robert MacLean
Name: Robert MacLean
Title: President

The above terms are accepted this 19th day of June, 2017.

AIRWAVES SOUND DESIGN LTD.

/s/ Alex Downie
Name: Alex Downie_____
Title: President_____

AIRWAVES DIGITAL GROUP LTD.

/s/ Alex Downie
Name: Alex Downie_____
Title: President_____

2. Addendum 2: Sample Agreement for Sale of Business

Sample Agreement for Sale of Business [2]

Sole Proprietorship

AGREEMENT MADE ON _____, between

SELLER _____

Address _____

City/County/State/Zip _____

BUYER _____

Address _____

City/County/State/Zip _____

The parties recite and declare:
1. Seller now owns and conducts a business known as _____ at _____, City of _____, County of _____, State of _____.

2. Seller desires to sell and Buyer desires to buy such business for the price and on the terms and conditions hereinafter set forth.

FOR THE REASONS set forth above, and in consideration of the mutual covenants and promises of the parties hereto, Seller and Buyer covenant and agree:

---

2 Sample excerpted from:
https://freelegalforms.uslegal.com/sale-of-business/agreement-for-sale-of-business/

1. **Sale of Business.** Seller agrees to sell and Buyer agrees to purchase, free from all liabilities and encumbrances, the abovedescribed business, including the lease to such premises, the goodwill of the business as a going concern, all of Seller's rights under its contracts, licenses, and agreements, and all assets and property owned and used by Seller in such business as specified in Exhibit A, other than property specifically excluded. This sale does not include the cash on hand or in banks at the date of closing or such other property as is listed in Exhibit B.

2. **Consideration.** In consideration for the transfer of the above described business from Seller to Buyer, Buyer must pay to Seller the sum of _____ dollars, which Seller must accept from Buyer in full payment therefore, subject to the terms and conditions herein contained.

3. **Terms of payment.** The purchase price must be paid by Buyer to Seller as follows:

The sum of $_____ on the signing of this contract, to be held by Seller's attorney as escrow agent until the closing of this sale, and to be paid by the escrow agent to Seller at the closing; the balance of $_____, in cash or by certified check, shall be paid to Seller at the time of closing.

4. **Adjustments at Closing.** Adjustments shall be made at the time of closing for all operating expenses including, but not limited to, rent, insurance premiums, utility charges, payroll, and payroll taxes.

5. **Time of Closing.** The closing will take place at the office of Seller's attorney, on _____, at _____ o'clock . Upon payment of the portion of the purchase price then due to Seller, Seller will deliver to Buyer such instruments of transfer as are necessary to transfer to Buyer the business and property referred to herein. Such instruments of transfer will effectively transfer to Buyer full title to the business and property free of all liens and encumbrances.

6. **Covenant Not to Compete.** Seller must not engage in a business similar to that involved in this transaction in any capacity, directly or indirect-

ly, within _____ for a period of _____ years from the date of closing or so long as Buyer or his successors carry on a like business, whichever first occurs. For purposes of this Agreement, "business similar to that involved in this transaction" includes within its scope _____ _____.

7. **Representations of Seller.** Seller represents and warrants that:

(a) He is duly qualified under the laws of the State of _____ to carry on the business as now owned and operated.

(b) He is the owner of and has good and marketable title to the property involved in this sale, free of all restrictions on transfer or assignment and all encumbrances except for those disclosed in Exhibit C.

(c) No proceedings, judgments, or liens are now pending or threatened against him or against the business.

(d) Seller has complied with, and is not in violation of, all applicable federal, state, and local statutes, laws, and regulations affecting Seller's properties or the operation of Seller's business.

(e) He will, up to the date of closing, operate his business in the usual and ordinary manner and will not enter into any contract except as may be required in the regular course of business.

8. **Risk of Loss by Fire.** Seller assumes all risk of destruction, loss, or damage by fire prior to the closing of this transaction. If any such destruction, loss, or damage amounts to more than $ _____, Buyer may at his option terminate this Agreement. In such an event, the escrow agent will pay to Buyer the purchase money held by him, and the escrow agent will be discharged from all liability therefore.

9. **Assumption of Liabilities.** Buyer agrees to assume those contracts listed in the attached schedule of property, Exhibit A, and those liabilities that arise in the ordinary course of Seller's business after the signing of this Agreement but before closing. Buyer will not be liable for any of the obligations or liabilities of Seller of any kind and nature other than those specifically mentioned herein. Buyer will indemnify Seller against any and all

liability under the contracts and obligations assumed hereunder, provided that Seller is not in default under any of such contracts or obligations at the date of closing.

10. **Modification.** No alteration or other modification of this Agreement will be effective unless such modification must be in writing and signed by the parties.

11. **Binding Effect.** This Agreement is binding upon and will inure to the benefit of the parties and their successors and assigns.

IN WITNESS WHEREOF, the parties have executed this Agreement on _____.

_____
Seller

_____
Buyer

3. Addendum 3: Sample Non-Disclosure Agreement

Sample Non-Disclosure Agreement [3]

It is understood and agreed to that the Discloser and the Recipient would like to exchange certain information that may be considered confidential. To ensure the protection of such information and in consideration of the agreement to exchange said information, the parties agree as follows:

1. The confidential information to be disclosed by Discloser under this Agreement ("Confidential Information") can be described as and includes:

Technical and business information relating to Discloser's proprietary ideas, patentable ideas copyrights and/or trade secrets, existing and/or contemplated products and services, software, schematics, research and de-

---

3 Sample excerpt taken from:

http://www.ipwatchdog.com/tradesecret/standard-confidentiality-agreement/

velopment, production, costs, profit and margin information, finances and financial projections, customers, clients, marketing, and current or future business plans and models, regardless of whether such information is designated as "Confidential Information" at the time of its disclosure.

In addition to the above, Confidential Information must also include, and the Recipient has a duty to protect, other confidential and/or sensitive information which is (a) disclosed by Discloser in writing and marked as confidential (or with other similar designation) at the time of disclosure; and/or (b) disclosed by Discloser in any other manner and identified as confidential at the time of disclosure and is also summarized and designated as confidential in a written memorandum delivered to Recipient within thirty (30) days of the disclosure.

2. Recipient must use the Confidential Information only for the purpose of evaluating potential business and investment relationships with Discloser.

3. Recipient must limit disclosure of Confidential Information within its own organization to its directors, officers, partners, members and/or employees having a need to know and shall not disclose Confidential Information to any third party (whether an individual, corporation, or other entity) without the prior written consent of Discloser. Recipient must satisfy its obligations under this paragraph if it takes affirmative measures to ensure compliance with these confidentiality obligations by its employees, agents, consultants and others who are permitted access to or use of the Confidential Information.

4. This Agreement imposes no obligation upon Recipient with respect to any Confidential Information (a) that was in Recipient's possession before receipt from Discloser; (b) is or becomes a matter of public knowledge through no fault of Recipient; (c) is rightfully received by Recipient from a third party not owing a duty of confidentiality to the Discloser; (d) is disclosed without a duty of confidentiality to a third party by, or with the authorization of, Discloser; or (e) is independently developed by Recipient.

5. Discloser warrants that he/she has the right to make the disclosures under this Agreement.

6. This Agreement is not to be construed as creating, conveying, transferring, granting or conferring upon the Recipient any rights, license or authority in or to the information exchanged, except the limited right to use Confidential Information specified in paragraph 2. Furthermore and specifically, no license or conveyance of any intellectual property rights is granted or implied by this Agreement.

7. Neither party has an obligation under this Agreement to purchase any service, goods, or intangibles from the other party. Discloser may, at its sole discretion, using its own information, offer such products and/or services for sale and modify them or discontinue sale at any time. Furthermore, both parties acknowledge and agree that the exchange of information under this Agreement will not commit or bind either party to any present or future contractual relationship (except as specifically stated herein), nor will the exchange of information be construed as an inducement to act or not to act in any given manner.

8. Neither party is liable to the other in any manner whatsoever for any decisions, obligations, costs or expenses incurred, changes in business practices, plans, organization, products, services, or otherwise, based on either party's decision to use or rely on any information exchanged under this Agreement.

9. If there is a breach or threatened breach of any provision of this Agreement, it is agreed and understood that Discloser will have no adequate remedy in money or other damages and accordingly will be entitled to injunctive relief; provided however, no specification in this Agreement of any particular remedy is to be construed as a waiver or prohibition of any other remedies in the event of a breach or threatened breach of this Agreement.

10. This Agreement states the entire agreement between the parties concerning the disclosure of Confidential Information and supersedes any prior agreements, understandings, or representations with respect thereto. Any addition or modification to this Agreement must be made in writing and signed by authorized representatives of both parties. This Agreement is made under and construed according to the laws of the State of

_____, U.S.A. In the event that this agreement is breached, any and all disputes must be settled in a court of competent jurisdiction in the State of _____, U.S.A.

11. If any of the provisions of this Agreement are found to be unenforceable, the remainder will be enforced as fully as possible and the unenforceable provision(s) will be deemed modified to the limited extent required to permit enforcement of the Agreement as a whole.

WHEREFORE, the parties acknowledge that they have read and understand this Agreement and voluntarily accept the duties and obligations set forth herein.

Recipient of Confidential Information:

Name (Print or Type):

Company:

Title:

Address:

City, State & Zip:

Signature:

Date:

Discloser of Confidential Information:

Name (Print or Type):

Company:

Title:

Address:

City, State & Zip:

Signature:

Date:

Lecture **6**

米国民事裁判手続の基礎と
裁判前の法務文書作成
の留意点

◆

Practical Legal Writing
for U.S. Civil Litigation in the
Pre-Trial Phase

> 米国民事裁判手続の基礎と裁判前の法務文書作成の留意点などについて，例を挙げながら具体的に解説します。

Welcome to the sixth and final lecture in our lecture series, Legal Writing and Professional Lawyering Skills in Common Law Practice. Thank you for all of your participation and attention during the lectures.

We have covered many important topics during the course of this lecture series. We've covered a lot of fundamental principles relating to common law legal research and analysis, important principles in legal writing, writing case briefs, memorandums, client interviews, writing opinion letters, negotiating and drafting contracts and non-disclosure statements.

Today, we will discuss practical legal writing for U.S. civil litigation in the pre-trial phase.

Lecture Six: Practical Legal Writing for U.S. Civil Litigation in the Pre-Trial Phase

Agenda:
- ❑ Pre-Trial Strategies for Lawyers Handling U.S. Civil Litigation Cases
- ❑ Preparing Written Communications for Attorney/Client and Privileged Information
- ❑ Law Practices for Confidential Information in U.S. Civil Litigation Cases
- ❑ Negotiating and Drafting Settlement Agreements

Marc Lassman
Adjunct Professor of Law
Temple University School of Law, Japan Campus
July 7, 2017
18:00 – 20:00

What this means is a conduct of the discovery portion of litigation when gathering information in anticipation of a claim or prior to trial. In some ways, this is some of the most important discussions we will have related to litigation because it is in this discovery process, the process of gathering information. We will have a very practical discussion to give you examples from the perspective of how to deal with pre-trial litigation, whether dealing with outside counsel, in-house counsel, working in a law firm or with co-counsel outside of the country, or if you are having direct contact with opposing counsel.

We will talk about requests for production of documents because that is more likely the issue you will see; litigation holds, which are requests to preserve documents during the course of the pre-trial phase, which you will likely see either from your outside counsel or from opposing counsel on how to assert and protect the attorney/client privilege during this process and protective orders.

Finally, we will discuss negotiating and drafting settlement agreements, and closing cases.

第1部　米国の民事裁判手続に関わる弁護士のための訴訟前の戦略 ——Pre-Trials Strategies for Lawyers Handling U.S. Civil Litigation Cases

Our first topic is "Pre-trial Strategies for Lawyers Handling US Civil Litigation Cases." We will not cover court procedures today. Rather, the pre-trial issues are discussing what happens outside of court.

1. アメリカ司法システムにおけるディスカバリー制度
Discovery in the U.S. Legal System

> ### Discovery in the U.S. Legal System
>
> - **Discovery** is a pre-trial procedure where each party can **obtain evidence from the other party (ies) by means of specified discovery methods**, which primarily consist of:
>   - **request for production of documents**
>   - **interrogatories**
>   - **request for admissions**
>   - **depositions**
> - Civil discovery is wide-ranging and can involve any <u>**non-privileged matter**</u> that is <u>**relevant**</u> to any party's claim or defense and <u>**proportional**</u> to the needs of the case...
> - Certain types of information are generally **protected from discovery**, including:
>   - information that is **privileged and/or the work product** of the opposing party;
>   - juvenile criminal records;
>   - peer review findings by hospitals in medical negligence cases; and
>   - other types of evidence for reasons of **privacy, difficulty and/or expense in complying with the request**
> - <u>**Electronic discovery**</u> or "*e-discovery*" refers to discovery of information stored in electronic format (often referred to as *Electronically Stored Information or ESI*)

In the U.S. litigation system, discovery is a pre-trial procedure where each party can obtain information from the other party by specific methods generally consisting of requests for documents. In addition, parties may seek information through Interrogatories, which simply are questions to the other side. Another discovery tool is a request for admissions, which asks the other side to admit or deny certain facts so that you do not have to prove those facts at trial. Finally, as part of discovery, the parties may take depositions, which are essentially sworn statements of either parties or witnesses.

Pre-trial discovery is wide ranging and can involve any non-privileged matter that is relevant to a party's claim or defense and proportional to the needs of the case. The amount of information that parties likely will request will be broader than you probably are used to because the main limits on discovery are privilege and connecting the requested information to the claims. That is a wide scope of information. It is important always to limit the amount of discovery to ensure that the requested information is not too burdensome because discovery can be very costly and time-consuming if the requests are too broad.

The rules of civil procedure require that the requests be proportional to the needs of the case. For example, if the case is small, the other party cannot make requests for tens of thousands of documents. When the court is deciding if the request is appropriate, it will look at how big is the case and the claims, and examine if the requests fit the claim. If the claim is small and the requests are really large that may be a reason to ask the court to limit the discovery in the case. That is what I mean by proportional.

Another aspect of discovery is that certain types of information are generally protected from discovery, which means the information does not need to be disclosed to the other side or the disclosed information is very limited. Usually, that information is categorized as privileged or attorney work product, which we will discuss in tonight's lecture. Other categories of protected discovery are juvenile criminal records, peer review findings by hospitals in negligence cases, information protected by privacy, or requests that are too burdensome or expensive to comply.

A big trending topic and type of discovery is electronic discovery or e-discovery. This is discovery of information stored in any kind of electronic format (ESI), including information on databases, networks, on-drives, mobile phones, social media, e-mails, etc. In the last 10 years or so, this has become one of the largest areas of discovery. As in-house counsel or if working for a law firm, managing ESI is one of the biggest challenges facing the legal and business industries. Potentially, and depending on the size of the litigation, there could be hundreds of thousands of ESI subject to discovery. We will discuss discovery requests in this context as well.

I. Difference between Japanese system and U.S. system

Discovery Differences between Japanese System and U.S. System	
Japan	**U.S.**
1) Evidence collection <u>primarily starts after in-court proceedings commence</u>	1) Evidence collection <u>begins and ends prior to trial</u>
2) Most evidence collection <u>directed by the Judge/Court</u> during in-court proceedings	2) Evidence collection <u>primarily directed by attorneys</u>, with limited court involvement (i.e. only if disputes arise) <u>outside of court</u>
3) <u>Courts are taking parties/witness testimony</u> during discovery process	3) <u>Attorneys take parties/witness testimony</u> during discovery process through depositions
4) Only after all evidence has been examined will a judge make a determination if the facts have been substantiated. <u>Parties preparing for trial are not subject to the strict burden-of-proof standard</u> placed on parties by U.S. law	4) <u>Parties are subject to strict burden of proof standards prior to and during trial</u>, which could lead to case dismissals (ex. Summary Judgment)

Next, we will cover the differences between the Japanese system and the U.S. system regarding discovery. I want to point out the major areas where will see differences. This is important, because when dealing with U.S. common law attorneys, their obligations in the litigation and discovery process are different.

The main differences are, for instance, in Japan, evidence collection primarily starts after in-court proceedings commence, which means that the court has a huge influence over the information that is given between the parties through witness statements and documents. The court facilitates the document requests and questioning of witnesses.

In the U.S., evidence collection all happens outside of court. The parties facilitate their own discovery requests for information. Discovery happens at the beginning of the court proceeding immediately after the initial filing of the case. The vast majority of work in preparing for cases and your involvement will be in the beginning stages of the litigation. Most of the time will involve gathering information to provide to your co-counsel or outside counsel who will submit it to the other side directly. The court will not be involved in the exchanging of information between the parties.

Evidence collection in Japan is directed by the judge or the court during in court proceedings. In the U.S., evidence collection is primarily directed by the attorneys with very limited court involvement. The court only becomes involved in scheduling discovery deadlines and if there is a dispute about the discovery.

In Japan, courts take the party and witness statements during the discovery process; whereas, in the U.S., the parties through their lawyers take the testimony during the discovery process using depositions. A deposition is a sworn statement of a party or a witness having information relevant to the case. Depositions usually occur at one of lawyer's offices or at a neutral office location, not at the court or by a judge. The sworn witness statement could be used later at trial.

The next main difference is that in Japan, only after all the evidence has been examined will a judge make a determination, if the facts have been proven. What this means is, parties preparing for trial are not subject to strict burdens of proof, because the evidence will be developed by the judge during the course of the proceedings. This is very different in the U.S. system, because parties are subject to strict burdens of proof prior to and during trial. If plaintiff does not have enough evidence to support the claim, the case may be dismissed at the beginning. This puts a lot of pressure on the parties to make sure that they gather as much evidence as possible in the pre-trial phase, because there are strict evidence criteria that they have to meet.

Discovery Differences between Japanese System and U.S. System (2)	
Japan	U.S.
5) <u>Early dismissals for lack of evidence to support allegations are rare.</u> There is therefore little pressure on parties prior to trial to "discover" evidence that could later be procured at trial.	5) <u>Early dismissals for lack of evidence are more common</u> and parties have a strong interest to discover all relevant evidence prior to trial (ex. 12(b)(6) motions and motions to dismiss)
6) <u>Appellate courts in Japan can conduct fact finding</u> in the same way as courts of first instance. The first instance trial often serves as a form of pretrial discovery for the appeal (Note: Extensive discovery prior to the first trial can appear time-consuming and redundant)	6) <u>Appellate courts can only consider issues of law</u> and can not review facts or engage in fact-finding. Pressure to present all facts in first instance trial
7) <u>Experts are designated by judges</u> instead of the parties, and are only summoned when a judge deems their testimony or special knowledge necessary	7) <u>Experts are designated and summoned by the parties.</u> Providing/Obtaining expert testimony directed by attorneys during discovery process (e.g. through deposition or provision of expert reports)

In Japan, early dismissals of claims for lack of evidence are not as common. Generally, there is not as much pressure on the parties prior to trial to discover all of the evidence that they need. The court will do that on a slow and steady basis; whereas, early dismissals for lack of evidence are very common in the U.S. The parties have a strong incentive to discover all of the relevant evidence before trial.

The U.S. rules of civil procedure for court proceedings have something called 12(b)(6) motions, which are motions to dismiss the case. The party opposing the claim can file a motion with the court saying that the other side does not have sufficient evidence to support their claim so that the judge should dismiss the case prior to trial. There is a much higher burden and you can lose the claim quickly in the U.S. system if you do not develop enough evidence fast enough.

One of the other main differences between the Japan and U.S. litigation process is that appellate courts in Japan can conduct additional fact finding and gathering of evidence beyond the evidence obtained during the trial court proceedings. On the other hand, in the U.S., appellate courts can only consider errors in law by the lower court. They cannot engage in fact-finding or gathering evidence. That means that if you do not present evidence to the trial level court during the case, you lose the right to present new or additional evidence to the appellate court.

The last difference has to do with expert witnesses. In Japan, experts can be designated by the judges instead of the parties. The judge has the ability to decide if experts are needed in the case. In the U.S., experts are designated by the parties. The lawyer chooses the experts, collects expert reports, and conducts the depositions.

II. U.S. Federal vs. State Court

\multicolumn{3}{c|}{Discovery U.S. Federal vs State Court}		
Issue	**Federal Court**	**State Court**
Case Management	Case management is governed by FED. R. CIV. P. 16 and 26, with requirement of Initial Disclosures pursuant to FED. R. CIV. P. 26(a)(1)	The courts generally do not apply a "hands on" management style. Parties are responsible for moving the case along, and in some jurisdictions, a failure to take any action on a case for a long period of time could result in dismissal of the case.
Written Discovery	Parties are limited to 25 interrogatories, including subparts, unless the Court grants its permission to exceed that amount. FED. R. CIV. P. 33(a) Note: In both federal and state court, parties may send unlimited document requests	There is usually no limit on the number of interrogatories that one party may send to another (some exceptions exist like CA)

Discovery in the U.S. federal courts is different than doing the discovery process in the state courts. The main difference is that discovery the in federal courts tends to have stricter rules. It is governed by the Federal Rules of Civil Procedure, which sets forth the rules for conducting discovery. For instance, the rules explain the number of written questions the parties may ask or the number of depositions the parties may take. In federal court, the statutory rules dictate the information the parties must disclose to the other side. State courts generally do not have a hands-on approach to managing the case discovery. The rules tend to be more relaxed. The parties usually are allowed to conduct wider discovery, such as making more requests for information or allowing for more depositions. Each state will have different rules regarding the discovery process. Then, the federal court will have different rules than the state courts. Therefore, it is important to know the specific procedural rules that will apply to your case depending on the court.

III. U.S.-Japan Bilateral Treaty

Discovery
U.S.- Japan Bilateral Treaty

❖ United States and Japan have signed a bilateral treaty that allows for evidence to be taken directly in Japan by a U.S. representative following the Federal Rules of Civil Procedure or by a Japanese court conducting evidence gathering. *Consular Convention, Mar. 22, 1963, U.S.-Japan, 518 U.N.T.S. 179.*

❖ Evidence may only be directly taken by a U.S. attorney or recognized official representative **when it is offered voluntarily**. U.S. courts have no power to compel production of evidence or compliance with U.S. discovery rules.

❖ A U.S. party wishing to have a particular document examined or witness deposed may apply through a U.S. court to request a Japanese court conduct the examination.

❖ In practice such discovery has proven to be **extremely expensive and time-consuming**.

There is a bilateral treaty between the U.S. and Japan governing the ability to do litigation discovery in each country. The treaty indicates that evidence can be taken directly by a U.S. attorney or recognized official representative in Japan only when it is offered voluntarily, which means that a U.S. attorney could come to Japan and question a witness only if the witness volunteers to be questioned. The U.S. attorney also can make a request for documents to the other side, but they would have to voluntarily give the documents. In essence, this treaty is not used in practice because there is no real way to enforce it. The treaty provisions are not used that often in litigation.

2. 相手方弁護士からの要望への対処法
Receiving and Responding to Requests from Opposing Counsel

I. Requests for Documents

> **Receiving and responding to requests from opposing counsel**
> **Requests for Documents**
>
> ❖ **Duties**. The responding party has a **duty to provide a response to any part of a document request that is not objectionable. Failure to respond may result in sanctions** and a court order to respond. (See Handout of Sample Discovery Request for Documents)
> ❖ **Answer in full**. The responding party must **answer each document request separately, fully, and in writing. Answers must be responsive, complete, and not evasive.**
>   o The responding party has a **duty to furnish all of the information available to it at the time of the answer**
>   o **If only partial information is available,** the answering party should:
>   • respond with the information that it has;
>   • indicate that it is *"still gathering responsive information,"* and
>   • **supplement the response in a timely manner** with the additional and complete information
>   o A party has a duty to furnish all the information available to it, **but not a duty to search out new information in response to the document request**
>   • Generally, the **party answers in part** and **objects** on the ground of *"gathering additional information would constitute an undue burden or excessive expense"*

If you are involved in a litigation case in the U.S., the most common form of discovery will be a request for documents. As part of your lecture handout, there is a sample request for documents. You can look at the language and format, if you have to make such request.

Regarding the duties of the parties, if you receive a request for documents, you have the duty to provide or respond to any part of a document request that is not objectionable. If they are requesting documents that are not objectionable, you have the obligation to respond to that request and provide the documents and information. Failure to respond could result in sanctions from the court.

The parties, through their attorneys, must answer the requests in full, which means that if you receive 10 requests for documents, you have to make a written response to each request and provide complete documents. The answers must be responsive, complete and not evasive.

You have a duty to furnish all of the information available to you regarding the request. However, if you only have partial information, that means, they request documents and you only have some of those documents, but you may need to investigate and find some of the other documents that they are requesting, you have to supplement the answer in a timely manner. The handout contains the good sample language.

A crucial point is that a party has a duty to furnish all of the information that is responsive to the request and available to them. However, parties do not have a duty to create information that is not in their possession. If the other side ask, for documents in your possession, then you have to give them. But, there is no obligation to create new documents that did not exist before.

II. Responding to Document Requests – Sample E-mail/Letter

> **Receiving and responding to requests from opposing counsel**
> **Responding to Document Requests – Sample E-mail/Letter**
>
> Re: <u>Request for (*add description of documents requested here*) from Opposing Counsel</u>
>
> Dear Mr. Jones,
>
> In response to your letter dated July 6, 2017, <u>in which you requested copies of all documents pertaining to</u> (*add description of documents requested here*), <u>we are hereby attaching the following documents:</u>
>
> - (*add bullet point list of all documents attached* – *including any summary list of documents being provided, etc.*)
>
> Regarding the request for (*add document description here*), we were **unfortunately unable to find any responsive documents in our files.**
>
> Please let us know if you need anything further from us in this regard.
>
> **Other Useful Phrases**
> o Could you please clarify what you meant when you referred to…
> o We are unable to produce the documents you requested as they are subject to the [Attorney/Client] privilege. (For Opposing Counsel)
> o We are unable to produce the documents you requested as the effort to produce them would cause our client undue burden and expense. (For Opposing Counsel)
> o We are unable to produce the documents you requested as they are not the subject of proper discovery. (For Opposing Counsel)

Here is a sample response to a request for documents. In the subject line, list exactly the documents being requested. Requests for…add description of the documents from opposing counsel or co-counsel.

When responding to a request, specifically state the document or e-mail or whatever communication. For instance, 'In response to your letter dated July 6th, 2017…,' Then describe again the types of documents being requested. 'We are hereby attaching the following documents…,' then add a bullet point list of the documents. List the documents by category or titles to keep the documents organized and to make a detailed record of what was provided. The list is useful evidence in case the other side or a judge handling a discovery dispute needs to see a record of the documents.

For instance, regarding the request for documents, we are 'unfortunately unable to find responsive documents in our files.' Let's say they ask you for documents that you do not have. The language that you can use is: 'Unfortunately we are unable to find any responsive documents in our files.' The important legal term is, 'responsive documents' because you are required to produce all documents to the other side; rather, only those documents that are relevant and responsive to the request.

Sometimes the opposing side may ask for information and you are not sure what they want. In this situation, useful a phrase would be: 'Could you please clarify what you meant when you refer to...?'

In the situation where you refuse to produce documents due to attorney/client or work-product or other privilege, the language would be: 'We are unable to produce these documents because...,' then insert the type of privilege. For instance, 'We are unable to produce the documents you requested, as they are subject to the attorney/client privilege.'

The next example is a situation where the request is too burdensome. The other side is asking you to produce documents that would cause undue burden and expense. Example language: 'We are unable to produce the documents you requested, as the effort to produce them would cause our client undue burden and expense.' 'Undue burden and expense' are the important buzz words to have in your response.

The general denial language to use if the request is not the appropriate subject of discovery would be: 'We are unable to produce the documents you requested as they are not the proper subject of discovery,' which means these are documents that the other side does not have the right to receive under discovery. These are good sample expressions in language that you can use in these situations.

3. ディスカバリー制度を利用する場合の企業内弁護士の役割
In-house Counsel during Discovery

> **In-house Counsel during Discovery**
> **Questions for Outside Counsel re: E-Discovery**
>
> ❖ The volume of electronic data and the costs involved in collecting, sorting and reviewing ESI are critical considerations in any case
> ❖ To maximize the value of the e-discovery process, corporate counsel should ask how outside counsel plans to efficiently analyze ESI and reduce the expenses associated with e-discovery
>
> **Some specific questions to consider:**
> ❖ **Proportionality:** Are the costs associated with e-discovery proportionate to the size of the case and the amount in dispute?
> ❖ **Scope:** Are you negotiating the use of custodians, search terms and a date range to limit the amount of data subjected to the e-discovery process?
>   o ***Overly broad discovery requests can trigger the obligation to preserve, collect, process and review large volumes of data***, which can be very costly and time-consuming to manage
>   o The scope of ESI can be narrowed by **identifying records custodians and applying search terms and a date range designed to target responsive ESI**
>   <u>Ex: Tokyo Inc. Purchase (search term); April 1, 2011-December 31, 2016 (date range)</u>

I. Questions for outside counsel re: E-Discovery

If representing a client during discovery, these are questions that you want to be clear about with either your outside counsel or co-counsel regarding e-discovery. Again, e-discovery and the amount of documents a company may have to produce can be numerous. It is important to have a clear understanding of the process at the beginning to reduce the burden on the company.

Often, during discovery, the most time and money is actually spent on dealing with e-discovery. To maximize the value of the process, controlling the type and amount of documents to produce will enable you to reduce expenses as much as possible. Specific questions to consider are here in the slide.

Proportionality. Are the costs associated with this discovery proportionate to the size of the case and the amount of dispute? That means, if the case is not that large, is the amount of money that you are spending to produce or review all of these e-documents worth it? If you are spending hundreds of thousands of dollars to review documents, however, the case might only be worth $50,000 or $75,000. Perhaps, doing extensive discovery is not worth the expense.

Scope. Another point is to consider negotiating with the other side are matters such as, search terms or date ranges to narrow the scope of the documents to review. For example, the opposing side is asking for documents. Try to make sure that the date range of the request is relevant. They may ask for documents for the past 50 years even though the deal only started two years ago. The scope of the request is too broad and not relevant to the claim.

Here is an example of narrowing the document search terms. Let's say you are representing Tokyo Inc. in a purchase. You receive a request for all documents related to Tokyo Inc. You would negotiate to do a search in your databases for 'Tokyo Inc. Purchase.' That is your search term. Then the date range would be April, 1, 2011 to December 31, 2016. You would negotiate with the other side exactly what to search and the relevant date ranges to limit the amount of documents produced as part of the search.

In-house Counsel during Discovery
Questions for Outside Counsel re: E-Discovery (2)

1) **Preservation: What ESI do we really need to preserve, and how do we do that?**
   - The time and costs of preserving potentially relevant information should be weighed against the information's possible value and uniqueness. Agreeing on a clear preservation plan with opposing counsel early in the case can limit the volume of data you need to preserve.

2) **Cost-shifting: Are you shifting some e-discovery costs to the other party?**
   - Where e-discovery costs are high, outside counsel can ask the court to shift the costs of producing ESI to the requesting party, especially where the evidence sought is marginally relevant and not proportional to the case

3) **Project management: Can you prepare a budget for the ESI portion of the case?**
   - To manage e-discovery, corporate counsel should request a budget for the ESI portion that includes a financial estimate, priorities, strategy, and project staffing

Another important issue to discuss with outside counsel relates to preserving documents in anticipation of litigation. Ask the outside counsel questions, such as what documents need to be preserved and the best practices for doing so. The main point is to make sure that documents are not destroyed that may later be relevant to the case.

Also, think about requesting to shift some of the discovery costs to the other side. Initially, the burden is on the producing party to pay for the expenses related to discovery. However, if the costs are too high or not proportional to the damages requested in the case, you can negotiate with the other side or ask the court to require the requesting party to pay a portion of the costs.

An important matter to discuss with outside counsel is to set a specific budget for e-discovery. Outside counsel can estimate the amount of time and expense for the discovery based on the number of documents and information to search and produce to the other side. As corporate counsel, you need to make sure that you are managing this aspect of the claim, because this likely will be the most costly aspect of the litigation. Can you imagine if outside counsel has an associate attorney billing $200 per hour to review 200,000 documents? That will be very costly. Often, there are discovery management companies that you can hire to control costs, because they hire legal professionals at a lower rate to do the work rather than having a senior partner attorney performing this basic task. As corporate counsel trying to manage costs, it is a best practice to have a specific agreement with outside counsel as to how many people will work on the discovery requests, billing rates, and the estimated number of hours to complete the document review.

> **In-house Counsel during Discovery**
> **Questions for Outside Counsel re: E-Discovery (3)**
>
> 4) **Third-party ESI experts:** Do we need an e-discovery vendor or digital forensics expert for the ESI preservation and collection, or can our in-house staff do that?
> 5) **Process efficiency:** Should we use predictive coding or other document analytic tools on this project?
>   - One method to reduce e-discovery costs is the use of **predictive coding**, also called **technology-assisted review**. Outside counsel should conduct a cost-benefit analysis of using predictive coding, considering the volume of documents, the amount in controversy and the price of using a vendor's analytic tools.
> 6) **How is the discovery review project being staffed, and what is our role in the selection process?**

An option to better manage large scale e-discovery is to use the services of a third party vendor to collect documents and do searches. Typically, outside counsel recommends the vendor and works closely with the vendor to manage e-discovery.

There are also data analytic tools that do predictive coding or technology assisted review, which conducts the documents searches more quickly. This is a way to run a smoother and more efficient process of e-discovery to reduce costs.

Finally, consider asking outside counsel to give a detailed breakdown of each staff member that will work on the e-discovery, including their job title, responsibility, and billing rate. You should request to make the final decision or give final approval of who will work on the matter.

> # In-house Counsel during Discovery
> ## Questions for Outside Counsel re: E-Discovery (4)
>
> **7) Which corporate reps do you need to consult, and how often will you need to contact them?**
>
> - Dedicate at least one subject matter expert from your company to every claim area so a knowledgeable resource is available to outside counsel
>
> - Many project teams streamline communication by funneling questions through a single reviewer, who then submits them at the end of the day to your designated reps
>
>   - This helps eliminate redundancy, solidify ownership, and ensures timely responses

The last question to discuss with outside counsel is the need to designate corporate representatives within your company as experts on certain matters and as contact persons to obtain information. As in-house counsel, you control the level of access outside counsel has to the company executives and employees. Therefore, it is good practice to establish boundaries with the type and level of contact outside counsel will have with company employees. Often, companies choose one expert per subject matter as the contact person for communications with outside counsel. The usual situation is that outside counsel may need to know the location of documents or where to find certain information. The expert is the best person to respond to those requests and handle the communications.

In this regard, the company executives and employees are not receiving too many questions directly from outside counsel. Otherwise, handling the litigation case can be very difficult and burdensome. You should make an agreement with your outside counsel or co-counsel in the beginning to establish a good communication relationship.

II. Common Outside/Opposing Counsel Requests to In-house Counsel

a. Litigation Holds and Preserving Documents

> **Common Requests to In-house Counsel**
> **Litigation Holds and Preserving Documents**
>
> ❖ A *litigation hold* is a written directive advising custodians of certain documents and ESI **to preserve potentially relevant evidence in anticipation of future litigation.**
>
> ❖ Also called **"preservation letters"** or **"stop destruction requests"**
>
> ❖ These communications **trigger the duty to preserve relevant evidence**
>
> ❖ The same terms are used to describe the written notice lawyers send their clients advising them to suspend routine document retention/destruction policies and implement a legal hold on all evidence which may be relevant to future litigation

Next we will discuss litigation holds or preserving documents. A litigation hold is a written directive advising people who hold documents that they need to preserve potentially relevant information in anticipation of a future claim. Sometimes they are also called preservation letters or stop the destruction of documents. It means that you have been alerted that there is a potential claim, and you need to make sure that either your client or your company does not destroy, or get rid of documents. This letter is called the litigation hold.

Litigation hold letters trigger a party's duty to preserve relevant information. For example, if you receive a request for information or documents, and later it is revealed that some of the documents were destroyed, or deleted or modified, this can become a serious problem. Courts can impose sanctions, and in some cases, the responsible attorney could be disciplined.

Once you receive a notice of a potential claim, there is a duty that is created to preserve all of the relevant documents to that claim. Outside counsel will inform you to preserve certain documents, and then you immediately have to take all steps possible to make sure that those documents are kept in a safe place and not deleted or destroyed. Either you receive such letters from outside counsel or opposing counsel, or as in-house counsel you must write and distribute the letter to the relevant company employees.

> **Common Requests to In-house Counsel**
> **Litigation Holds and Preserving Documents**
>
> ❏ **Watch for Triggers**: Events that trigger a duty to preserve documents **can be obvious** (Ex: a letter threatening litigation) or **more subtle** (Ex: a group of supervisors talking about reported complaints)
> ❏ **Don't Wait**: Delaying action can cause destruction of relevant evidence
> ❏ **Put Your Client's Hold Notice in Writing, and Be Specific**: A good Litigation Hold Notice should **clearly identify the reason for the hold**, **prohibit the destruction of relevant documents**, and **identify relevant information**
> ❏ **Consider all your client's sources of data**: Look beyond just e-mail, calendar entries, contacts and task lists (Ex: employee cell phones, Text messages, Voice-mail messages, Backup tapes, Hard drives, Thumb drives, Office lap tops, Social networking sites, Home computers that access the office network)
> ❏ **Follow Up to Ensure Compliance with Litigation Holds**

There are certain events that can trigger or cause a duty to preserve documents. For example, a letter from outside counsel or opposing counsel saying to preserve documents because of potential litigation is an obvious trigger. Sometimes, they are more subtle. For example, if supervisors within the company have been talking or e-mailing about reported complaints from a customer or reported complaints from an employee, once you become potentially aware that there might be a claim, then that may trigger a duty to preserve documents. You may not always receive some formal notice. At that point, you should begin taking steps to start preserving documents.

Litigation hold notices always should be in writing and give specific details stating the reasons for the hold and what needs to be retained. Clearly state that the purpose of the letter is to prevent the destruction of relevant documents, and then identify the relevant information. State the scope of the documents to be retained and that they should not be deleted or modified.

One matter to be aware of is if the client is the source of the data. What I mean by that is not just e-mail or calendar entries, contacts or task lists, things like that, but also text messages or voice-mail messages might be relevant. In addition, people have USB drives or other hard drives and use social network platforms that may contain relevant information.

After sending out the litigation hold notice, the next step is to follow up with the relevant individuals to make sure that they are complying with the litigation hold. The obligation to maintain relevant documents is through the entire litigation process.

b. Tips for Drafting Litigation Hold Letters

Common Requests to In-house Counsel
Tips for Drafting Litigation Hold Letters

- ❏ **Introduction - Why Necessary: Explain why you are instituting a litigation hold** so recipients can identify relevant information. The explanation need not describe the lawsuit or subpoena in detail. A general description will usually suffice. **Example:**

  The Company was recently sued by XYZ Corporation for breach of contract involving the sale of widgets. We are in the process of identifying all paper and electronic documents that may be relevant to the matter . . . You have been identified as a person who has had involvement with the XYZ contract, or may possess relevant documents or communications. We request your attention and assistance in preserving this relevant information for our attorney's use in the litigation matter as appropriate.

- ❏ **What is to be Preserved:** The legal hold notice **becomes a checklist for what kind of records should be preserved**, including a time period and description of the relevant categories of information. **Example:**

  As part of this process, you must preserve all documents or communications that may be relevant for the time period of [date range]. This notice applies to all paper and electronic documents and communications . . . . If you are unsure about whether certain paper or electronic documents are relevant, you should preserve them . . .

Next, we will look at the language for drafting litigation hold letters. You can see an example in the lecture handouts. First, introduce and explain why you are instituting the litigation hold. The opening sentence explains the nature of the claim or litigation. Then, explain why you are writing to that specific individual. In the letter, indicate what needs to be preserved by describing the category of documents. It is important to note that the litigation hold applies to all paper and electronic documents and communications. Finally, make sure that the legal staff looks at all of the preserved data, not just documents.

> **Common Outside/Opposing Counsel requests to In-house Counsel Tips for Drafting Litigation Hold Letters (2)**
>
> ☐ **Instruction for Retention: Deliver the notice to key employees who control the ability to suspend normal deletion policies.** Recipients should be informed that potentially relevant evidence may be found in their paper files or on computers, external media, cloud-based service, personal devices, or mobile devices. Example:
>
> *To comply with our legal obligations, the Company must make all reasonable effects to preserve, or suspend from deletion, overwriting, modification, or other destruction of all relevant paper or electronic data in your possession, custody, or control that is relevant to this litigation matter.*
>
> ☐ **Defining the Scope:** Clearly **identify the scope of what is considered a relevant "document"** that must be preserved. Example:
>
> *As used in this Notice, the terms "document", "data", and "information" are used in the broadest sense and apply not only to paper documents but also electronic documents or communications . . . . In short, all documents and information, in whatever form, that is relevant to this matter must be retained and preserved.*

Two additional tips are to deliver the notice to all key employees that control the information that might be subject to the hold. And, define the scope of what is considered relevant information so that everyone knows what they are to preserve.

> **Common Outside/Opposing Counsel requests to In-house Counsel**
> **Tips for Drafting Litigation Hold Letters (3)**
>
> ❑ **Mandatory Preservation:** Emphasize that preservation is mandatory, and that failure to comply may diminish the company's ability to prosecute its claims or defend itself in the lawsuit. **Example:**
>
> > *Preservation is mandatory. Electronically stored information is an important and potentially irreplaceable source of discovery in this matter. Failure to retain these documents or communications, whether intentionally or accidentally or to ignore this notice may result in the Company's inability to prosecute its claims or defend itself in this matter. You must take every reasonable step to preserve this information until further written notice.*
>
> ❑ **Confidentiality:** Stress the confidential nature of the lawsuit and the company's expectation that employees will not discuss it with each other or outside the company unless approved by company counsel. **Example:**
>
> > *The company considers this litigation matter to be confidential and, unless otherwise permitted, you should not discuss, publish or disclose any information relating to this matter without permission from company counsel.*

Make clear that the obligation to preserve the information is mandatory. The language should state in bold type that 'Preservation is mandatory.'

Regarding confidentiality, it is important to stress the confidential nature of the lawsuit so that individuals are not openly discussing the litigation. That language should be part of the letter, and here is sample language that you can use in that situation.

Common Outside/Opposing Counsel requests to In-house Counsel
Tips for Drafting Litigation Hold Letters (4)

☐ **Request for Assistance:** Request the names of **any additional individuals that the recipients believe may have relevant information.** Example:

If you are aware of any individuals or service providers not listed on this notice that you believe may have additional and relevant information, such as those who may be under your supervision, direction, or control, please notify company counsel. Additionally, if you know of any other former employees who may have relevant materials, please forward the names to company counsel.

☐ **Duration of the Litigation Hold:** The notice should state that **individuals are required to preserve until they are notified that the litigation hold has been released.** Example:

You must continue to preserve all paper and electronic documents or communications until you have received written notice that the litigation hold has been released.

In many cases, you do not always know the departments or individuals who may have relevant documents or information. Therefore, in the litigation hold letter, you can ask the recipients of the letter to notify in-house counsel of anyone possessing such documents or information. Here is language you can use in that situation.

The litigation hold letter should state the duration of the hold. It is best to make a general statement that the hold letter is in place until recipients are notified of the release rather than giving a specific date.

> **Common Outside/Opposing Counsel requests to In-house Counsel**
> **Tips for Drafting Litigation Hold Letters (5)**
>
> ❑ **Prompt for Questions:** The notice should provide the name and contact information for company counsel or other person designated to provide assistance. **Example:**
>
> > *If you have any questions about this notice or your responsibilities to comply with this notice, please contact company counsel at extension 1234. We may also be following up with you directly regarding the preservation or collection of your data in response to this litigation hold notice.*
>
> ❑ **Receipt and Acknowledgment:** Require recipients to respond in writing that they have read the notice and will comply with its requirements. Follow up with any recipients who fail to respond. **Example:**
>
> > *Please reply to acknowledge that you have read and understood the preservation obligation stated in this litigation hold notice. Your attention and assistance with this Notice is greatly appreciated.*

The final two points about litigation hold letters are to provide contact information in case the recipients have questions and to make sure that the recipients acknowledge in writing that they received and read the hold letter.

第2部　文書によるやり取りと秘匿特権付き情報 —Preparing Written Communications for Attorney/ Client and Privileged Information

Now, I want to move on to preparing written communications for attorney/client and privileged information. If you are dealing with attorneys from other countries, one of the matters that you need to know is what constitutes the attorney/client privilege in that country, because different countries have different obligations. For instance, what may be covered by attorney/client privilege in America may not be exactly the same as what is covered by attorney/client privilege under Japanese law. Be careful not to give information unprotected by the attorney/client privilege in that country; or, the opposite, which is not to receive information that you must provide because the information is not covered by any privileges in that country. Just be aware of the fact that every country does not have exactly the same rules governing attorney/client privilege.

1. 米国法における代理人と依頼者との秘匿特権
Attorney/Client Privilege under U.S. Law

> **Attorney/Client Privilege under U.S. Law**
>
> ❖ The attorney–client privilege is codified in Rule 501 of the Federal Rules of Evidence
>
> ❖ Its purpose is to **encourage open communication** between attorneys and their clients
>
> ❖ The privilege recognizes that sound legal advice and advocacy serve public ends and that such advice and advocacy depend upon the lawyer's being fully informed by the client
>
> ❖ The privilege exists to protect not only the **giving of professional advice** to those who can act on it but also the **giving of information** to the lawyer to enable her to give sound and informed advice

Attorney/client privilege in the U.S. in federal court is based on Rule 501 of the Federal Rules of Evidence. Its purpose is to encourage open communication. The privilege exists not only in giving professional advice, but also in giving information to the lawyer to enable them to give accurate advice. Generally speaking, it is not only what the lawyer gives to the client, but also the information the client gives to the lawyer.

2. 企業内弁護士と秘匿特権
In-house Counsel — Protecting Attorney/Client Privilege

> **In-house Counsel**
> **Protecting Attorney/Client Privilege**
>
> **Client-Attorney Relationships are Key**
>
> ❖ **Who is your client?** Corporate counsel represents the corporate entity. Do you also represent any **affiliates**? Do you also represent any **individual officers, directors, shareholders, or employees**?
>
> ❖ When you have identified who your client is, be sure to **communicate** that to your client and any others who might incorrectly believe they are also your client
>
> ❖ **Consider your title and what impact it may have on the privilege.** Many in-house lawyers have both a *legal title* and a *business title*, such as **Vice President and General Counsel**. When communicating on legal matters, consider using only the legal title

An initial consideration of the attorney/client privilege is to know who is the client. If you are in-house counsel or a law firm representing a corporation, you have to know exactly who you are representing. Do you represent the corporation? Does the corporation have affiliates or subsidiaries? Are you representing those entities? This is really important because it defines your obligations and the information that is subject to the privileges. For instance, if you send an e-mail that includes individual officers, directors, and they technically not your clients, that information might not be covered by the attorney/client privilege.

One of the concepts in common law is if I give information or have a conversation and someone is present who is not covered by the attorney/client privilege, whether it is a partner or customer, then anything that I say or any conversation is actually not privileged information. This is important especially when giving information by e-mail or on a conference call. If you include people who are not your client, you might actually jeopardize the ability to claim attorney/client privilege later on. Therefore, knowing your client is crucial.

When identifying the client, be sure to communicate that to your client and any other person who might incorrectly believe they are also your client. If you are only representing Company X, but not the shareholders and directors of Company X, you need to make sure that you write to those shareholders and directors and let them know that the client is Company X, and you are or are not included in the representation. Make sure there are no misunderstandings.

Also, especially for in-house counsel, often your title might not only be lawyer or in-house counsel or general counsel. Sometimes, in-house counsel will have legal titles and business titles. You might have the titles of vice president and general counsel. This is something you also have to be very careful about, not combining your business obligations with your legal obligations. Your legal advice is privileged. Business advice is not privileged. You cannot claim that any business advice you give is privileged under U.S. law. If you have one of these titles that is half legal and half business, you have to be careful about which title you are using when signing letters or sending out information, because if you start using the non-legal title, then there can potentially be a claim later on that this was business advice. If you or someone in the company has that type of mixed title, then when communicating on legal matters, they should consider only using their legal title in that situation to avoid problems later on.

> **In-house Counsel**
> **Protecting Attorney/Client Privilege**
>
> **Writing Emails – best policies and procedures**
> ❖ Email policies and procedures are another key consideration in protecting the attorney–client privilege. **You should consider training company employees on how to seek your advice. For example:**
>   - Words like "*I need your legal advice*" or "*request for legal advice*" will go a long way to preserving the privilege and are more effective than "<u>*I have a question*</u>."
>   - **Legal opinion requests should be addressed specifically to you or an attorney on your team rather than to a business person with just a cc to the lawyer**
> ❖ **To protect the privilege:**
>   - Avoid communications with an "**intermingled**" purposes
>   - **Do not let privileged discussions continue in a long email chain** because the topic will stray and new people may be added thereby risking the privilege protection
>   - Do not use the standard privilege language that automatically attaches to most attorneys' email if the message is not privileged
>   - **Consider who truly needs to see the email.** <u>**If an email group includes people who are not involved in a particular legal matter, assume those communications will not be privileged**</u>

When protecting privileged information, it is good practice to have a system in place, particularly regarding e-mails. If working in a company as in-house counsel, you should consider training company employees on the best way to seek your advice about maintaining privileged information. This is important because you need to make sure that they are doing it in a way that makes a clear that they are seeking legal advice. This way, you can protect any communications under the attorney/client privilege.

For instance, if someone from the engineering department in your company writes you an e-mail requesting information or requesting opinions, you should train them to use phrases like, 'I need your legal advice' and then explain the issue. Make sure the language is obvious by having the title of the e-mail as, 'Request for legal advice.' Otherwise, the advice might not be legal advice, which is not protected.

Further, legal opinion requests should be addressed specifically to you as in-house counsel, law firm counsel, or a lawyer on your team rather than having that e-mail addressed to a business person with the 'cc' to the lawyer. If their request is to some business person with the copy to the lawyer asking a question, that information might not be protected as privileged information because it is not going to the lawyer.

Also, be careful about who you copy on the communication. If it gets copied to someone who is potentially not covered by attorney/client privilege, it might be determined that you waived the privilege. For example, if someone from an affiliate or subsidiary of the company, such as a director or someone who is not the client, a court might determine later that the document or e-mail is not privileged because you shared it with someone who is not your client.

To protect the privilege, it is best to avoid communications with intermingled purposes. If giving business advice and legal advice then separate them. Write a separate e-mail regarding the legal advice, and then write another e-mail regarding any business advice you might give. Do not write one e-mail that gives business advice and legal advice because it might be determined that the communication is not privileged.

Another issue that often arises is when legal advice is offered in some long e-mail chain. Be careful not to respond to these long e-mail chains with legal advice that you want to be privileged information. Otherwise, this is a form of mixing business and legal advice that could make the communication fall outside of the privilege. Make a routine practice of separating the advice, writing separate messages, even if the issue first arose as part of an e-mail chain.

> **In-house Counsel
> Protecting Attorney/Client Privilege**
>
> **Policies, Resources and Written Communications**
> - Mark written communications as "**Confidential, Subject to the Attorney–Client Privilege**" (Note: These designations help to sort documents by the key word "privilege")
> - **Company policies can help make employees and other personnel aware of when the company expects the privilege to apply**
>   - Policies addressing **internal investigations** should include a statement that ***they are undertaken for the purpose of obtaining legal advice.*** If litigation may arise with regard to a particular transaction, all the in-house counsel's documents relating to that investigation should specifically state that they were created "*in anticipation of litigation.*"
>
> **DOES IT NEED TO BE IN WRITING? IF NOT, DON'T WRITE IT**
> - In-house counsel should use labels on written communications with corporate employees
>   - When writing a memorandum to an employee, a subject title should be included such as "**REQUEST FACTS FOR LEGAL ADVICE** "
>   - When an employee sends a memorandum to in-house counsel, it could be helpful for the memorandum to contain prominent language such as "**FOR THE PURPOSE OF RECEIVING LEGAL ADVICE**"

One of the other matters to consider is the compamy's policies for maintaining privileged communications.

Good policies will instruct employees to give clear language indicating that some privilege applies to the communication. At the top of that communication write, 'Confidential, Subject to Attorney/Client Privilege.' If you do not mark the communication, people later will argue that if you wanted it to be confidential, you should have written 'Confidential' on the document. Courts will look at the steps you took to preserve the confidential nature of the document because that will show your intent to keep the document privileged.

Company policy also can help make employees and other personnel aware of when the company expects the privilege to apply. For instance, if you have policies addressing internal investigations, the policy statement should say 'these investigations are undertaken for the purpose of obtaining legal advice.' Other good language would be, 'This information is being developed in anticipation of litigation.'

Always think about whether the communication needs to be in writing. Can you communicate the information orally? If it does not need to be in writing, then do not write it, because if you write something down, you might be compelled by a court to produce the information later.

In-house counsel should use labels on written communications with corporate employees. If you are writing a memorandum to an employee, the subject title should be, 'Request facts for legal advice.' If you are trying obtain information from employees to give advice, you would write. 'Request Facts for Legal Advice.' Likewise, if someone sends you a memo from the company, they should write in bold type, 'For the purpose of receiving legal advice.'

I. Sample E-mail

In-house Counsel Protecting Attorney/Client Privilege – Sample E-mail
Sample of E-mail with Intermingled Purposes Re: Purchase Agreement for Tokyo Inc. **Confidential – Subject to the Attorney/Client Privilege** Dear Mr. Jones,
I am writing **to gather facts to give legal advice to the Board of Directors regarding appropriate provisions for the Purchase Agreement for Tokyo Inc.**
We are currently reviewing the proposed Purchase Agreement received from counsel for Tokyo Inc. There is a question regarding whether the purchase of equipment from Tokyo Inc. accurately reflects the agreement made during final negotiations on May 23, 2017.
Can you please inform us of the final agreement reached regarding the purchase of equipment from Tokyo Inc. on May 23, 2017, including providing any notes, memos or other documents you have related to the negotiations.
Additionally, in response to your question yesterday about which equipment to purchase and a fair price, you should consider purchasing all heavy equipment for no more than $500,000.00 for all of the equipment combined. (Business Advice)
Please let us know if you have any questions.

311

Here is a sample e-mail that has mixed legal and business advice. Let's say we are talking about the purchase agreement for Tokyo Inc. 'Confidential, Subject to the Attorney/Client Privilege' is written on the top of the letter or e-mail.

In the letter, you are requesting the client to inform you of the final agreement regarding the purchase, including providing any notes, memos, other documents. Let's say in this situation, the client also asked you about the purchase of the equipment and what you think is the fair price for the equipment. 'Additionally, in response to your question yesterday about which equipment to purchase and a fair price, you should consider purchasing all heavy equipment for no more than $500,000.00 for all the equipment combined.'

This is an example where in one portion, you are receiving information to give legal advice and then another portion in which you are addressing another question that came to you about which equipment to buy and how much you think the equipment should cost. This is an example of a situation where it would be better practice to write separate e-mails on each subject or clearly separate the subjects within the letter using headings.

第3部　米国民事裁判手続における秘密情報保持の法律実務
——Law Practices for Confidential Information in U.S. Civil Litigation Cases

Now, I want to talk about law practices for confidential information in U.S. civil court cases, specifically about responses to discovery requests and privilege logs.

1. 秘密情報を守る方法－ディスカバリーへの応答と秘匿特権リスト（プリビレッジ・ログ）
Methods for Protecting Confidential Information - Discovery Reponses - Privilege Logs

> **Methods for Protecting Confidential Information**
> **Discovery Reponses - Privilege Logs**
>
> ❖ A **privilege log** describes documents or other items withheld from production in a civil lawsuit under a claim of **"privilege"** from disclosure **(Ex. attorney–client privilege, work product doctrine, joint defense doctrine, etc.)**
>
> ❖ When a party withholds information otherwise discoverable by claiming that the information is privileged or subject to protection as trial preparation material, the party must:
>
> ○ Expressly make the claim; and
>
> ○ Describe the nature of the items not produced or disclosed -- in a manner that will allow other parties to assess the claim. FRCP 26(b)(5) (1993)
>
> ❖ Common practice in Federal and State Courts

Privilege logs are a list of the documents and communications that you potentially want to claim attorney/client or attorney work product privilege. Perhaps the opposing party requests documents from you, but some of those documents, in your opinion, are covered by the one of the privileges. If you plan to withhold documents or communications on the basis of some privilege, then you are obligated under the civil procedure rules to give the opposing party a list or privilege log reasonably describing the documents and communications that you claim are subject to the privilege. The handout has a sample privilege log.

When a party withholds information that might be discoverable by claiming that the information is privileged or subject to some protection, you have to: (1) expressly make the claim, meaning I am not providing you this document because it is subject to some privilege; (2) expressly say why you are not providing that document; and (3) describe the nature of the items not produced or not being disclosed in a manner that will allow the other party to assess the privilege claim. Otherwise, if you receive a communication saying we are not going to give some document because it is subject to attorney/client privilege and they do not provide the title of the document and what the document is, you have no way of knowing whether that document is privileged. You need have a basis to at least know whether the document is privileged. This is common practice and required in federal and state courts.

2. 秘匿特権対象リスト（プリビレッジ・ログ）—どの時点で何をリスト化するのか
Privilege Logs — When and What to Log

**Privilege Logs
When and What to Log**

- Parties need to log **any time client/counsel withholds documents on privilege grounds**, except for negotiated limitations on discovery or very unusual circumstances (ex. the client itself is a privileged piece of information or if logging is truly an undue burden)
- The log should contain the following information for each entry:
    - **Type of document, i.e., memorandum, email, letter, etc.**
    - Name of the document **author**
    - Names of the document **recipients**
    - Document **date**
    - **Title or description** of the document
    - **Subject matter** of the document
    - The **privilege claimed**: "attorney work product," "attorney client communication," etc.
- Some states **(ex. New York)** allow a **categorical privilege log** (listing documents by category and not individually)
- **See Handouts for sample Privilege Log**

When and what to log? Any time a party withholds the document on the ground of privilege, except if you have a negotiated agreement with the other side as part of discovery, you have to provide a privilege log. Privilege logs should contain the following specific information: Type of document, meaning is it a memorandum, an e-mail, or a letter; the name of the document author, meaning the person who wrote that document; the name of the recipients; the date of the documents, title or description of the documents and subject matter the document, meaning you are describing the document. The privilege log also should contain the type of privilege you are claiming—attorney/client or attorney work product.

It is important to organize the document and things on the log by category, such as e-mails, memos, reports, etc. Listing documents by category, not individually helps to more easily identify documents for discovery.

For example, if you are a pharmaceutical company and the case involves a patent dispute. The other party is requesting all information and documents related to the results of the clinical trial tests for the past 10 years. There might be hundreds of thousands of documents related to those clinical trial tests. You do not want a list every document related to all the 10 years of tests that you did for that drug. You can list the categories of documents instead of each individual one.

3. 企業内弁護士と秘匿特権——英文メールの参考例
In-house Counsel Protecting Attorney/Client Privilege — Sample E-mails

In-house Counsel Protecting Attorney/Client Privilege – Sample E-mails	
Sample Letter Requesting Information from Opposing Counsel **Re: Company X Failed Purchase of Tokyo Inc.** Dear Mr. Jones, We are the law firm currently representing Tokyo Inc. with regard to potential claims they may have in relation to the failed purchase transaction with Company X in April 2017. **In this regard, we are writing to request that you provide us any and all documents Company X is in possession of related to the April 1, 2017 Purchase Agreement between the parties.** **We appreciate your anticipated cooperation in this matter.** Please let us know if you have any questions.	**Sample Letter Responding to Request for Information from Opposing Counsel** Dear Mr. Smith, We are in receipt of your letter of May 23, 2017, requesting: *"all documents Company X is in possession of related to the April 1, 2017 Purchase Agreement between the parties."* In response to your request, we have searched our files and attach to this letter the following documents: - Add bullet point list of documents provided **We have also attached a Privilege Log reflecting the documents in our possession that we believe are privileged and therefore not subject to disclosure.** The log provides sufficient information to enable you to make an informed determination about the privileges asserted. Please let us know if you have any questions.

Here, are two sample e-mails to request and respond to discovery. If you are writing a letter requesting information from opposing counsel, put the case name and number in the subject line, such as 'Re: Company X Failed Purchase of Tokyo Inc.'

According to the rules of civil procedure, you need to make the requests specific enough for the other party to identify documents and information relevant to the requests. To do so, describe the category of documents you want from them. Include a certain scope of time so that the requests seek relevant information, such as 'any and all documents between 2010 and 2017.'

The language to use when requesting documents is 'any and all' so that the request is broad enough to cover the potential documents you want to receive as part of discovery. This language is commonly used, because as the requesting party, you do not know the full scope of the documents the other side may have in their possession. The requests need to be specific to identify documents but also broad enough to cover the entire pool of potentially relevant documents.

If responding to a request for documents:

'We are in receipt of your letter of May 23rd, 2017 requesting...' Reference the date and type the communication you received. Then, quote the request. 'All documents Company X is in possession of related to the April 1, 2017 Purchase Agreement between the parties.' It is important to write exactly what was requested from you because you want to establish a record that you responded appropriately and timely to the request.

Typical language to use to respond to a discovery request: 'In response to your request, we have searched our files and attached to this letter the following documents.' Again, you want to add a bullet point of all the documents that you provided to make a record of everything that you gave them.

If there are some documents that are privileged, here is the language: 'We have also attached a Privilege Log reflecting the documents in our possession that we believe are privileged and therefore not subject to disclosure.' That is good sample language to use when you are writing to opposing counsel to make clear why you are not providing certain documents.

4. 秘密情報を守る方法—— 秘密保持命令
Methods for Protecting Confidential Information - Protective Orders

Methods for Protecting Confidential Information Protective Orders

- ❖ Protective orders prevent the disclosure of certain information
- ❖ Protective orders are mainly used to **protect proprietary information and personal information (such as medical records, etc.)**
- ❖ Federal Rule of Civil Procedure 26(c) authorizes courts to order parties ***not to disclose or publish information obtained in civil discovery.*** A party must show "**good cause,**" which requires *a clear, specific, factual demonstration that the party seeking protection will incur serious injury in the absence of protection*
- ❖ **Stipulated protective orders** are commonly used tools in complex litigation and allow the producing party to designate material as "confidential," and place restrictions on the persons or entities that can view that material
- ❖ The orders limit, or even prohibit, parties from filing any material that has been designated confidential in public court documents. **In those cases, parties either file the documents containing the information "under seal," or publicly file only redacted versions of the case documents with the court.**
- ❖ **Protective Orders differ from Non-Disclosure Agreements** because NDAs are agreements made between parties during business dealings and <u>Protective Orders are requests made to the Court during litigation to protect a party from inappropriate discovery requests</u>

Next, we will discuss protective orders in the context of discovery in the litigation process. A protective order is a court order that prevents disclosure of certain information to the other party or to the public. Protective orders are mainly used to protect business proprietary information or personal information, such as medical records. For instance, if a party is asking for certain sensitive information from your client and they do not have the right to that information, but they are still requesting it even after you said will not give it to them because the information is privileged, then you can file a motion for a protective order with the court. You request the court to determine that the requesting party does not have the right to that information. In the federal courts, such protective orders are discussed under civil procedure Rule 26(c). This authorizes the court to order parties not to disclose or publish information obtained in civil discovery.

The court will require the party requesting the protective order to show good cause as to why the order should be entered. This means that you need to show a good factual and legal basis to support the argument in favor of a protective order. You have to show specifically the way in which the client would be injured by giving the information to the other side or making the information public, such as complying with the discovery request would be unduly burdensome, expensive or disclose sensitive, private information.

You also can negotiate the terms of a protective order with the other party by making a stipulated protective order. For instance, if you are dealing with another company regarding potentially disclosing new technology that is part of the litigation dispute. Neither party wants the information to become public record. As part of the litigation process, many court filings and documents submitted to the court become a matter of public record or the court's docket. In such instances, the parties can actually enter into a stipulated agreement that the documents reflecting the patent technology will be filed under a protective order so that the information is not public record. The documents are filed under seal, which means that only the parties and the court can see the full documents. Usually the sealed court record can protect the entire document or redact the portions of the document that is protected so that those documents are a part of the public court file.

Protective orders are different from non-disclosure agreements because a they are something to request as part of litigation; whereas, non-disclosure agreements are made privately between parties during business dealings that happen outside of the court's intervention.

第4部 和解契約をめぐる交渉と文書作成
Negotiating and Drafting Settlement Agreements

Finally, I want to talk about negotiating and drafting settlement agreements. Let's say that you have negotiated a settlement for the claim that is the basis of the litigation. The contract that you create reflecting the final agreement is called a settlement agreement. It reflects the negotiated agreement between the parties to end a potential claim or ongoing litigation.

1. 和解契約　—　一般的な留意事項
Settlement Agreements - General Considerations

> **Settlement Agreements**
> **General Considerations**
>
> ❖ A settlement agreement is an agreement that reflects the *final agreement negotiated between the parties to end a potential claim or ongoing litigation*
>
> ### IN-HOUSE COUNSEL TIPS
>
> ❖ A settlement agreement is **not something to leave solely to the outside lawyers** once the "deal has been made"
>
> ❖ **In-house counsel need to be intimately involved with the documentation and execution of the deal** because huge problems can arise from "bad" settlement agreements
>
> ❑ <u>**You must ensure that a settlement agreement accurately reflects the deal you (and the CEO or Board) thought you had to end the litigation**</u>
>
> ❖ *Use Summary Judgment motions and Mediation briefs in settlement negotiations*

I want to give some tips for in-house counsel or potentially corporate counsel for dealing with settlement agreements. A settlement agreement is not something that you should leave solely to the outside lawyers. If you are in-house counsel or if you have foreign co-counsel, and there have been some agreements, do not leave the drafting of the settlement agreement to them and only take part in the final approval. You should take the obligation yourself to review that agreement as well. You should be intimately involved with preparing and reviewing the documents, because if there is a bad settlement agreement huge problems can arise. The agreement should accurately reflect the client's understanding and desire of the deal.

2. 和解交渉――あらゆる不測の事態を想定して交渉する
Settlement Negotiations - Negotiate all Contingencies into Final Agreement

I. Negotiate all Contingencies into Final Agreement

Settlement Negotiations
Negotiate all Contingencies into Final Agreement

- **Clearly explain contingencies to the settlement**
  For Example:
    - If you are receiving $400,000 from the defendant to settle the litigation, is that in a lump sum or in installments?
    - If a lump sum, how long does the defendant have to pay?
    - What happens if they don't pay?
    - What happens if the ninth and tenth installments are not paid?

- Your job (and that of outside counsel) is **think about all of the things in the settlement that need to happen so that each side gets the benefit of their bargain, especially your side**

- **For each contingency there needs to be some type of consequence if the other side fails to execute,** e.g., if they don't make a payment what happens? Does the settlement become void? Is there a pre-signed consent judgment you can file?

- Among the easiest things you can do in a settlement agreement to prevent problems is to **include time frames for things to occur** (i.e., don't leave critical steps open-ended that could leave you with no options but to wait for the other side to act).

- **Think about what you are giving up and how can that be reversed if the other side defaults. The consequences then need to be set out clearly in the agreement.**

When you are negotiating a settlement agreement, clearly explain any contingencies to the settlement. What do I mean by the contingencies to the settlement? For example, let's say you have agreed to a payment of $400,000 from the defendant to settle the claim. The question then is whether defendant will make a lump sum or installment payments. If it is one payment, how long does the other side have to make that payment? And, what happens if they do not pay? If it is installments, meaning they are going to pay you ten installments of $100,000, what if they only pay five times or stop paying? These are contingencies that the settlement agreement should reflect. Basically, you are anticipating the potential problems that could arise under the agreement. You should consider all of the issues in the settlement that needs to happen for each side to benefit.

In addition, settlement agreements should have deadlines for performance by the parties under the agreement. For instance, going back to the payment situation, the agreement would contain a payment schedule and the consequences in the event of failure to comply. Otherwise, it would be difficult to enforce payment on a schedule if the agreement does not reflect such an obligation.

II. Necessary Authority

Settlement Negotiations Necessary Authority	

The insurance company/indemnitor
❖ If an <u>insurance company</u> is paying for your defense or potentially any settlement you need to discuss the settlement with them before you finalize anything
❖ If you sought **indemnity from a third party** for the litigation costs and the claim, **you likely need to involve them in the decision to settle**
❖ If the other side has made an offer you think is fair, you must always:
   o **get the client to agree to accept the offer**
Note: For in-house counsel that's either the business unit involved in the litigation -or- the Board of Directors
   o **Always have a process in place to get the necessary input and approvals**
❖ ***Don't be afraid to ask the other side about their logistical process***
	Sample Language
	<u>Authority</u>. The Parties represent and warrant <u>that they possess full authority to enter into this Agreement and to lawfully and effectively release the opposing Party as set forth herein</u>, free of any rights of settlement, approval, subrogation, or other condition or impediment. This undertaking includes specifically, without limitation, the representation and warranty that <u>no third party has now acquired or will acquire rights to present or pursue any claims arising from or based upon the claims that have been released herein.</u>

Another issue to consider when negotiating settlement agreements is the necessary authorities to approve such an agreement. For instance, if an insurance company is involved in settling the claim, then you likely must obtain approval from the insurance company for any settlement. It is very common that an insurance company or a third party that might fund all or part of your case will pay some money. You have to be sure that you have all of the necessary authorities from people to effectuate the settlement, including obtaining approval from your company's board of directors, etc.

Then, you also should confirm the person(s) on the other side having the authority to enter into the agreement. You do not want to have a situation where you think there is an agreement, but in the end, the other party should have obtained approval from some insurance company or bank, but failed to do so. That would render the settlement invalid. It is acceptable to confirm with the other side that they, in fact, have the authority to execute the settlement.

Here is some sample language in the slide that should go into your settlement agreement regarding authority. The language should reflect that everyone signing or a party to the agreement has the authority to do so. This is the language to protect your interests to ensure that no third party has now acquired or will acquire rights or pursue any claims arising from or based upon the claims that have been released in the agreement.

III. Guard Against Accidental Agreements

Settlement Negotiations
Guard Against Accidental Agreements

"Accidental" settlement agreement
- If your response to an offer is "*Sounds like we have a deal*" vs. "*Let me think about it,*" you may have **accidently accepted a settlement offer** that you (a) really did mean to accept and (b) you did not have authority to accept
- You need to be **very careful** during settlement negotiations, especially when exchanging drafts or term sheets via email, to not somehow create a **binding** settlement agreement you did not otherwise mean to accept.

   Example: you are satisfied with the $400,000 in cash offered but you also need a dismissal with prejudice. If you end up with just the $400,000 only because you were too quick to write "agreed" without stating your conditions, you will find yourself in a very difficult position

- **Make it clear that nothing is final until you agree it's final.** Consider including the following language in communications with the other side regarding the settlement:

   "*All discussions and correspondence regarding a settlement are confidential, and are for negotiation purposes only. There is not yet any authority to enter into a final, binding agreement on behalf of [the Company]. The execution of a separate, formal agreement is a material term of any settlement and there is no settlement without one...*"

Next, we will discuss guarding against 'accidental agreements.' Be careful of what you say to the other side, because if you are not clear, you might accidentally accept an agreement that you did not mean to accept. For instance, if having back and forth negotiations with opposing counsel or outside counsel and you say, 'sounds like we have deal,' versus 'let me think about it.' 'Sounds like we have a deal' can be interpreted as giving approval of a deal. On the other hand, if you say, 'I need to get back to you' or 'I need to get authority from...,' that means you have not finalized the deal yet. Try not to use language that is too vague or leaves open the possibility of agreeing to terms that are not finalized. Some people put on the bottom of their e-mails or communications that 'all discussions and correspondence regarding settlement or confidential are for negotiation purposes only' to make clear that there is no final settlement.

3. 和解契約書 —— 一般的な規定
Settlement Agreements —Common Provisions

Settlement Agreements Common Provisions	
Scope of the release – the claims	Sample Language
❖ The core of a settlement agreement is the release of claims ❖ **Determine whether you are agreeing to a specific or a general release** ❖ A "<u>specific</u>" release will resolve only the specific claim(s) at issue in the litigation ❖ A "<u>general</u>" release is broader and is usually worded as "**any and all claims**" the plaintiff has against the defendant, whether alleged in the lawsuit or not	(Name of Party), on its behalf and on behalf its subsidiaries, divisions, affiliates and agents, <u>releases, remises, and forever discharges (last name) from all claims, suits, actions, charges, demands, judgments, costs and executions,</u>…. X. This Settlement Agreement and Mutual Release <u>shall not constitute an admission of any of the allegations against the other and shall not be considered as an admission of liability,</u>… Note: If suit is already filed, the claims can be <u>dismissed with or without "prejudice."</u> If the claims are dismissed with prejudice then they are completely extinguished and cannot be filed again by the plaintiff

Our last topic of discussion is to review the common provisions that are negotiated and included in settlement agreements. First, the scope of the release is the critical part of the agreement that defines the release of the claims in the litigation matter. The parties are determining that the claims will no longer be a disputed matter. You should determine whether the agreement is a specific release, which is a release of only that specific claim or a general release, which is much broader and usually covers any claims.

For strategic purposes, if you are making claims or are a plaintiff, you want to negotiate for a specific release of only the pending claims because that type of release gives you the ability to file future lawsuits against the opposing party. However, if you are on the other side, meaning someone has claims against you, it is best to negotiate for a general release of all future claims. A general release is much broader and this is language to use in this situation.

Also be aware that when seeking to dismiss the claims, the dismissal can be 'with prejudice' or 'without prejudice.' A claim dismissed with prejudice means that the claim can never be made again in the future. Here is the sample language: 'These claims will be dismissed with prejudice.'

If the claim is dismissed 'without prejudice' that means that the opposing party can possibly make a claim again based on similar allegations in the future. The effect is that the parties to the settlement agreement are only agreeing to dismiss the claims for now. Usually, dismissals without prejudice are in case the settlement does not happen or the deal fails. Essentially, plaintiffs are reserving their right to file the lawsuit again in case there is a problem in the future.

> **Settlement Agreements**
> **Common Provisions (2)**
>
> **Scope of the release – the parties**
>
> ❖ In the settlement agreement you must state which parties are covered by the settlement/release
> ❖ Corporations typically want to ensure that not only are they released, but also their officers, directors, employees, agents, affiliates, parent companies, etc.
>
> **Sample Language**
>
> **Effective upon timely payment as provided in Section _ below, the Parties, on behalf of themselves, and all persons or entities claiming by, through or under them, and their respective heirs, successors and assigns, hereby fully, completely and finally waive, release, remise, acquit, and forever discharge and covenant not to sue the other Parties, as well as the other Parties' respective _____ [*specify, as appropriate: officers, directors, shareholders, trustees, parent companies, sister companies, affiliates, subsidiaries, employers, attorneys, accountants, predecessors, successors, insurers, representatives, and agents*] with respect to any and all claims, …and causes of action arising out of or in any way relating to ____ [*specify, as appropriate: the Litigation or the Underlying Dispute*].**

The scope of the release also should be clear to identify the proper parties subject to the agreement. For instance, if you represent a company or multiple entities in the lawsuit, typically the language should name the various entities, but also name the categories of individuals related to the entities as well, such as the company officers, directors, employees, agents, affiliates, and parent companies, etc. You would not name only 'XYZ Corporation' without naming the officers, directors, employees, etc., because you do not want to give the other side the ability to say that the claim against XYZ Company is finished, but now they could sue the directors separately.

> **Settlement Agreement**
> **Common Provisions (3)**
>
> **Confidentiality**
>
> ➢ As you are working on the settlement, think about the terms you want to keep confidential (and be sure to bring the business into the analysis as you may miss something they are concerned about)
>
> ➢ You'll also likely need/want to to share the document with your outside attorneys, accountants, and auditors. If you're a publicly traded company, there may need to be some accommodation for you to disclose parts of the settlement in a quarterly filing.
>
> **Sample Language**
>
> **Confidentiality.** The Parties and their respective counsel represent and agree that, **except for matters of public record** as of the date of this Agreement, **they will keep the terms and contents of this Agreement confidential, and that they will not hereinafter disclose the terms of this Agreement to other persons except as compelled by applicable law or to individuals who have a need to know about this Agreement and its contents, such as Parties' legal counsel, tax advisors, or other retained professional representatives**, all of whom shall be informed and bound by this confidentiality clause.

Another important provision of a settlement agreement is the confidentiality statement. Here is the sample language, which is similar to the confidentiality language generally contained in contracts that we covered in the previous lectures.

> **Settlement Agreement
> Common Provisions (4)**
>
> **Enforcing the settlement - no waiver of rights**
>
> ❖ Always include a provision defining what to do if there is a **breach of the settlement** agreement, e.g., the other side does not make the required payments
>
> ❖ **Consider**: Do you want the same court to keep jurisdiction of any disputes around the settlement or do you want a different court to handle it?
>
> ❖ Be sure to also consider **choice of law, injunctive relief, and attorneys' fees and costs, etc.**
>
> **Sample Language**
>
> Governing Law and Jurisdiction. <u>The laws of the State of _____ [state] shall apply to and control any interpretation, construction, performance or enforcement of this Agreement.</u> The Parties agree that <u>the exclusive jurisdiction for any legal proceeding arising out of or relating to this Agreement shall be _____</u> [the court] and all Parties hereby waive any challenge to personal jurisdiction or venue in that court.
>
> No Waiver. No failure to exercise and no delay in exercising any right, power or remedy under this Agreement shall impair any right, power or remedy which any Party may have...

When drafting the agreement, always include language to enforce your rights in the event of a breach. The main provisions are choice of law or governing law and choice of forum or jurisdiction provisions. Again, these are the same considerations for contracts generally. You want to identify the jurisdiction, the law that will apply, and the mechanism to hear any disputes, such as litigation versus arbitration. Here is the sample language you can use in this situation.

> **Settlement Agreement**
> **Common Provisions (5)**
>
> **Provisions Tolling Statute of Limitations**
> - A **Statute of Limitations** is the period of time allowed under the law for a party to assert a claim or defense
> - **Counsel must protect their client's right to assert claims or defenses in the event that the Settlement Agreement is breached**
> - A provision tolling the Statute of Limitations for all claims and defenses during the period that the Settlement Agreement is effective **ensures a client's right to make these assertions later on**
>
> **Sample Language**
>
> **Statute of Limitations.** Any and all statutes of limitation applicable to any causes of action or claims that arise from or are related to the [describe claims here] ("Tolled Claims"), shall be prospectively tolled and suspended as of the Effective Date of this Agreement. The tolling and suspension of the applicable statutes of limitation for the Tolled Claims shall continue until the Termination Date of this Agreement as provided in Paragraph X below. The parties hereby waive any defense of statute of limitations for the period of time accruing from the Effective Date to the Termination Date. The time period during which this Agreement remains in effect shall not be included in determining whether the statutes of limitation ran against any Tolled Claims that may be brought by either party.

The last point is to talk about provisions tolling the statute of limitations for claims. There is a set period of time to make any type of claim. Statutes of limitations are critically important because if a party does not bring the claim within the set period, they may lose the right to bring the claim forever. For example, U.S. states generally require breach of contract claims to be made within three to fifteen years once the facts giving rise to claim becomes known. You want to make sure that the settlement agreement tolls the statute limitation, meaning whatever deadlines there are to bring the claims will be suspended until performance under the settlement is complete.

For example, if a party to the settlement stops making payments, the plaintiff bringing the claim wants to preserve their right to file the claim again. This concept is closely related to dismissing the claim 'with' or 'without' prejudice. Usually, settlement agreements will contain a tolling provision and have the claims dismissed without prejudice to refiling the claim in the event there is a breach of the settlement. Here is good sample language that you can use to protect the client's rights related to the ability to bring future claims.

Thank you for all of your attention. I have sincerely enjoyed these six lectures. I hope that they have been useful for you. Thank you very much.

あとがき

　東京弁護士会弁護士研修センター運営委員会では，専門領域における業務に対応しうる研修を目指し，平成13年度より特定の専門分野に関する連続講座を実施して参りました。平成18年度後期からは，6ヶ月間を区切りとして，受講者を固定して，特定分野に関する専門的知識や実務的知識の習得を目的とする「専門講座」を開始し，毎年好評を博しております。

　本講義録は，平成29年度前期の専門講座であり，テンプル大学ロースクールから講師をお招きし，全6回の講座として実施した内容をまとめたものです。本講座では，契約，外国法・外国法取引に関する経験的知識の体得を目的とし，基本知識から網羅的に解説しており，実に充実した内容となっています。

　ぜひ本書をお読みいただき，日々の業務遂行と適切な事件対応にお役立ていただければ幸いです。

　終わりに，この専門講座の企画，実施と本書の発行にご協力いただきました講師の方々，弁護士研修センター運営委員会担当委員各位，そして株式会社ぎょうせいの編集者の皆様に厚くお礼申し上げます。

平成31年1月

東京弁護士会弁護士研修センター運営委員会
委員長　　軽部　龍太郎

弁護士専門研修講座
国際法務をめぐる交渉・文書作成術

平成31年2月28日　第1刷発行

|編　集|東京弁護士会弁護士研修センター運営委員会|
|発　行|株式会社ぎょうせい|

〒136-8575　東京都江東区新木場1-18-11
電話　編集　03-6892-6508
　　　営業　03-6892-6666
フリーコール　0120-953-431

〈検印省略〉

URL：https://gyosei.jp

印刷　ぎょうせいデジタル㈱　　　　　©2019 Printed in Japan
※乱丁・落丁本はお取り替えいたします。

ISBN978-4-324-10411-8
(5108377-00-000)
〔略号：弁護士講座（国際法務）〕